CORRUPT RELATIONS

CORRUPT RELATIONS

DICKENS, THACKERAY, TROLLOPE, COLLINS, AND THE VICTORIAN SEXUAL SYSTEM

Richard Barickman, Susan MacDonald,
and Myra Stark

COLUMBIA UNIVERSITY PRESS
NEW YORK 1982

710019855-4.

Clothbound editions of Columbia University Press books are Smyth-sewn
and printed on permanent and durable acid-free paper.

Library of Congress Cataloging in Publication Data
Barickman, Richard.
Corrupt relations.

Bibliography: p.
Includes index.
1. English fiction—19th century—History
and criticism.   2. Women in literature.
3. Sex role in literature.   4. Feminism and
literature.   I. MacDonald, Susan (Susan Peck)
II. Stark, Myra.   III. Title.
PR878.W6B35   1982   823'.8'09352042   82-4534
ISBN 0-231-05258-8   AACR2

Columbia University Press
New York   Guildford, Surrey

CONTENTS

PREFACE

SINCE works of criticism are more often the product of individual than of collective effort, our triple authorship may need some explanation. Two seminars in successive years at MLA conventions brought it into being. We found ourselves delivering papers on Dickens, Thackeray, Trollope, and Collins that all seemed to make the same basic point in spite of the great differences among these novelists. In the easy, non-stop discussions that conventions in mid-winter cities induce, we began to see that it was not a simple coincidence that drew us to the same issue. For all their diversity, Dickens, Thackeray, Trollope, and Collins participated in a common enterprise: a complex, persistent, and radical critique of the Victorian system of sexual relationships.

This book is the working out of those long discussions. It was thought out and talked through during meetings in New York and New Haven, written, revised, and sent back and forth through the mail. This is a less lonely way to write a book than the customary one, and, we hope, a way that benefits from the exchange and reconciliation of differing perspectives.

It is also not by chance that all four of the authors whose novels deal with this theme are male. Sexual status, along with class, determined the conditions of life in Victorian England—a rigidly class- and sex-conscious society. Dickens, Collins, Thackeray, and Trollope were the beneficiaries of this cultural system simply because they were male, and all shared to some extent its patriarchal values. But all four also recognized that Victorian sexual roles and values were inflicting massive, radical damage on the individuals who composed their society. The novels they wrote embody their intuitive perceptions about Victorian England as well as their conscious allegiances. The system is thus both asserted and negated, in ways that expose its contradictions and point to the gathering crisis in Victorian sexual life. What links these writers is just this reluctant, often unwitting exposure of the persistent victimization at the heart of Victorian society—crippling in its effects on both oppressors and victims, but most devastating in its impact on women.

In this regard Dickens, Collins, Thackeray, and Trollope can be considered radical and even revolutionary novelists. On the surface their novels often follow traditional plots of courtship and marriage, or deal with crime and fraud in conventional melodramatic structures. Just below the surface, however, these novels raise issues of identity, power, freedom, and human fulfillment that ultimately call into question the whole system of sexual relationships in nineteenth-century England.

This reluctant perception of a failure in Victorian sexual relations coexists in the novels with a strenuous insistence on traditional values. The tension created between conscious intention and intuitive perception creates a persistent ambivalence that is a defining characteristic of their fiction. Their ambivalence leads to novels that work by indirection, often wrenching the fictional material into strangely revealing forms. Conflicting impulses agitate the narrative voice. The contradictions, excesses, and puzzling evasions of the narrators alert us to developments in the novels' themes that extend and frequently contradict the direct presentation of the characters' experiences. Ultimately these tensions point us to the patterns of symbolic analogy that form basic structures of meaning within these novels.

These indirect techniques account for the fact that many readers have seen only stereotypic or confused sexual values at work in this fiction. Much of the indirection undoubtedly arose from conflicts within the authors' own personal attitudes toward their material. Like so many of their characters, they repressed conscious awareness of what troubled them. But the clash between a restrictive conscious attitude and a rebellious emotional perception produced fiction that is a remarkably accurate record of the underlying sexual conflicts of the Victorian period—and a remarkably stimulating image of our own culture's confusion.

ACKNOWLEDGMENTS

AS with most collaborative works, our first word of gratitude for encouragement, sympathy, and editorial advice might go to each other. But other acknowledgments are certainly due: to the three spouses who listened, counseled, inspired, and—like Faulkner's Dilsey—endured; to the scholars who helped arouse and nourish our love of nineteenth-century literature, Jerome Buckley, William Buckler, Dwight Culler, Martin Meisel, Karl Kroeber, Martin Price, Gordon Ray, and Joseph Wiesenfarth; and to that group of feminist scholars—many listed in our bibliography—who provided new perspectives on Victorian literature that are basic to our study. We would also like to thank our editors at Columbia University Press, William Germano and Karen Mitchell, who were particularly helpful in shaping this book for publication.

An excerpt from chapter 3 has appeared under the title "The Subversive Methods of Dickens' Early Fiction: *Martin Chuzzlewit*" in *Charles Dickens: New Perspectives*, edited by Wendell Stacy Johnson (Englewood Cliffs, N. J.: © Prentice-Hall, 1982), and is reprinted here by permission of the publisher.

NOTE ON EDITIONS

WE have used the New Oxford Illustrated Dickens (London, 1947–58); the *Works of Thackeray* (Centenary Biographical Edition; London, 1910–11); and *The Works of Wilkie Collins* (New York: P. F. Collier, 1900), a thirty-volume edition also available in reprints from AMS Press. There is still no standard edition of Trollope's novels. All our quotations from Trollope except those from *John Caldigate* are taken from the Oxford World Classics edition and are referred to by chapter numbers.

CORRUPT RELATIONS

I

THE PERPLEXING ANGEL:
THE WOMAN QUESTION AND DICKENS,
THACKERAY, TROLLOPE, AND COLLINS

ALTHOUGH the ideal of the angel in the house is an icon of Victorian middle-class culture—exerting tremendous power over the behavior and attitudes of women—it is hardly a definitive image. We are now beginning to see how often the domestic sanctuary was shaken by the rebellious angel within it. Recent scholarship in women's studies, in making the study of women a respectable intellectual endeavor, has also begun to make clear the complexity of social roles that Victorian women actually performed. What has already emerged is the intensity of the century's debate about the status, the role, the very nature of women. To call it a "debate," however, is a little misleading, for there was nothing structured about it. Rather it was a set of issues, impulses, preoccupations—a pervasive social climate of questioning and change that eventually reached into every class and affected, however slowly, nearly every relationship between men and women in nineteenth-century England. No doubt most people in Victorian England remained unaware of the very existence of such issues; but the "Woman Question," as it was called, became a major preoccupation of Victorian society.

The pervasive social effects of the Woman Question were largely a result of congruence between the reforms it helped to stimulate and the major trends of the age. The reform of the English legal system, one of the century's major achievements, included the long and ultimately successful struggle to change the divorce laws, and the even more far-reaching struggle to pass the married women's property bills. The extension of the suffrage was also a major step in the democratization of England; although women's suffrage had to wait until the twentieth century, it was first introduced in Parliament in 1869, and agitation for its passage was an undercurrent throughout the era. When a series of parliamentary commissions scrutinized the lives and working conditions of the poor, they revealed the plight of women workers in mines, factories, and the needle trades. Two other movements crucial to the Woman Question were also in line with the reformist character of the age: the widening of occupational opportunities for women so that the restrictive categories of governess/domestic servant/factory worker at the beginning of the century grew by the end to include teaching, nursing, office work, shop work, and social work; and the opening of the universities to women. Far from being a fringe movement, then, the movement for widening women's rights was near the center of the social changes that characterize the Victorian period.[1]

If the term "debate" is at all accurate, it describes a ceaseless accompaniment to this social change—the questions endlessly asked and answered in magazines, in popular fiction, and in literature: What was woman's mission? What was the proper sphere for women? Was there a girl of the period? Was woman redundant? Who was the new woman? In 1869, Frances Power Cobbe, journalist and feminist, wrote:

Of all the theories current concerning women, none is more curious than the theory that it is needful to make a theory about them. That a woman is a Domestic, a Social, or a Political Creature; that she is a Goddess, or a Doll; the "Angel in the House," or a Drudge, with the suckling of fools and chronicling of small beer for her sole privileges; that she has, at all events, a "Mission," or a "Sphere," or a "Kingdom," of some sort or other, if we could but agree on what it is,—all this is taken for granted.[2]

As the multitude of titles with the word "Woman" in them attests, the social changes of the nineteenth century were accompanied by a chorus of commentary.[3]

This area of controversy influenced the Victorian novel profoundly, especially since the novel attempted to reflect the conditions of contemporary social life to a degree no other literary genre—or the novel itself before the nineteenth century—had ever attempted. Literary critics have recognized that the treatment of the Woman Question in the Victorian novel is hardly unambiguous, even in novels like *Shirley* or *Middlemarch* that address themselves explicitly to the oppressive treatment of women. Some of the most determined explorers of this new territory, like Charlotte Brontë and George Eliot, retreat from the kind of scrutiny of the whole system of sexual values that seems promised by the initial terms of their novels. Rather than appearing as a necessary consequence of the Victorian social system, their heroines' constricting circumstances are finally treated as accidents of a particular social situation, to be remedied through the standard choice of an appropriate husband.

But at least critics generally recognize that these novelists and many other women novelists of the period are deeply, if uncertainly, involved with a fundamental reconsideration of the place of women in society. Prevailing critical opinion about the major male novelists, however, is that they either did not participate in the debate at all or that their ideas about women were so reactionary that when they did approach the subject, it was only to satirize feminism.[4]

We believe that this view of four major Victorian novelists—Dickens, Collins, Thackeray, and Trollope—is simply wrong. Their novels all reflect, or perhaps more accurately, refract the changing conceptions of women's roles that characterized Victorian England. These novelists do seem to offer their readers hundreds of "pattern young ladies" (Inspector Bucket's term for Esther Summerson) and equally stereotypic shrews, rapacious spinsters, rosy coquettes, raven-haired temptresses, and so forth. And this tendency has understandably seemed to many readers merely a passive reflection of prevailing masculine attitudes. But these same novelists, in a multitude of ways, draw attention to their processes of distortion, so that we become aware of the stereotyped attitudes as well as of the stereotypes themselves. At the same time, symbolic structures opposed to the sexual values of the direct narrative gradually form and emerge, often constituting a distinct "counterplot" to the overt handling of theme and characterization. The authors' ambivalence is expressed through narrators who mingle desire, fear, and hostility toward female characters in a way that both represents and exposes Victorian sexual values.

When these novelists confronted the Woman Question personally, they often issued familiar rationalizations and evasions. Trollope's antifeminist statements are the most notorious: "the necessity of the supremacy of man [over woman] is as certain to me as the eternity of the soul," he wrote in one letter.[5] And their personal treatment of women hardly set a new standard of egalitarian sexual relations. But the limitations and excesses of their own lives provided additional impetus to create fictional forms that might allow a freer exploration of Victorian sexuality. In a curious way, the suppression of genital sexuality from the notice of the respectable Victorian reading public caused both writers and readers to be preternaturally sensitive to the nuances of sexual expression in every area of social and personal life.[6] (That a similar culture in Vienna produced Freud should be no surprise.) So a "family" novelist writing for a supposedly squeamish and sexually obtuse audience creates a number of scenes like this:

The last of the Patriarchs had been so seized by assault . . . that he had not a word to offer in reply. He appeared to be meditating some Patriarchal way out of his delicate position, when Mr. Pancks, once more suddenly applying the trigger to his hat, shot it off again with his former dexterity. . . .

Quick as lightning, Mr. Pancks, who, for some moments, had had his right hand in his coat pocket, whipped out a pair of shears, swooped upon the Patriarch behind, and snipped off short the sacred locks that flowed upon his shoulders. In a paroxysm of animosity and rapidity, Mr. Pancks then caught the broad-brimmed hat out of the astounded Patriarch's hand, cut it down into a mere stewpan, and fixed it on the Patriarch's head.

Before the frightful results of this desperate action, Mr. Pancks himself recoiled in consternation. A bare-polled, goggle-eyed, big-headed lumbering personage stood staring at him, not in the least impressive, not in the least venerable, who seemed to have started out of the earth to ask what was become of Casby.

[*Little Dorrit*, II, xxxii, 802–3]

It is not at all surprising, of course, that a major nineteenth-century issue like the Woman Question should have influenced the novels of the leading male writers of the era. What is surprising is that the forms the influence assumed should blind many readers to its presence. True, we do not find in the novels of Dickens, Trollope, and Thackeray explicit appreciation of the specific issues raised by the women's movement during the nineteenth century—widening employment opportunities for women, changing property and divorce laws for married women, the opening of universities and professions to women—nor do we find very much awareness that these issues were being raised in Victorian society. (Collins does assail certain inequities in the marriage laws and at least acknowledges the constraints on women's economic roles; but the issues he raises are often curiously peripheral to the major causes of economic and social oppression of women, and his explicit appeals for reform are directed to very localized problems.) On the rare occasions when Dickens or Trollope set out to deal with feminists, they produce satiric portraits like Miss Wisk, the woman with a "Mission" in Bleak House, or the American women's rights lecturer, Olivia Q. Fleabody, in Is He Popenjoy?, all presented as severe, unattractive, and secretly longing for marriage. This occasional derision of militant feminists seems a corollary to the more general proposition that marriage is the "proper sphere" for women.

Yet this focus on marriage does not preclude concern with the questions of woman's nature and status, her rights and her identity. There is little doubt that all these novelists reflect the attitude of most Victorians that, as one of Trollope's narrators declares, "Marriage [is] the only career open to women."[7] But in focusing on courtship and marriage, the chief concerns of most Victorian women, Dickens, Collins, Thackeray, and Trollope raise fundamental questions about their culture's sexual practices. As Martha Vicinus claims in her introduction to A Widening Sphere: "The classic works of Victorian literature cannot tell us much specifically about female suffrage, the rising number of single women, or job opportunities, but they can illuminate the emotional conflicts and resolutions of men and women concerned with women's proper place."[8]

Tony Tanner has argued in *Adultery in the Novel* that "marriage is *the* central subject for the bourgeois novel" in general:

For bourgeois society marriage is the all-subsuming, all-organizing, all-containing contract. It is the structure that maintains the Structure, or System (if we may use that word, for the moment, to cover all the models, conscious and unconscious, by which society structures all its operations and transactions). The bourgeois novelist has no choice but to engage the subject of marriage in one way or another, at no matter what extreme of celebration or contestation.

Tanner's central thesis is that adultery in the Continental novel and the adulterous woman in particular serve to expose the contradictions within bourgeois society—and in the myths the society fashions about itself.[9]

This perception that the nineteenth-century European novel is intimately, inescapably drawn toward the exposure of fundamental social contradictions is very close to our own view of these Victorian novelists. Tanner shows how the Continental novel pivots this concern (or anxiety) on the symbolic interchanges of women within a patriarchal structure and especially on an "exchange" that threatens the whole system:

the action of adultery portends the possible breakdown of all the mediations on which society itself depends, and demonstrates the latent impossibility of participating in the interrelated patterns that comprise its structure. . . . It is only when marriage is seen to be the invention of man, and is felt to be the central contract on which all others in some way depend, that adultery becomes, not an incidental deviance from the social structure, but a frontal assault on it.[10]

The four Victorian novelists we deal with never give adultery the central place that it has in so many Continental novels of the century. This is not a prudish evasion or a self-Bowdlerizing act of deference to reader's modesty, however these motives may operate in some Victorian fiction. (All four are quite explicit about adultery when it does become significant to their fiction, in *Dombey and Son, Vanity Fair, Is He Popinjoy?,* and *Woman in White,* for instance.) They are, instead, creating fiction that reflects the distinctive qualities of middle-class Victorian English society.

One of the most distinctive features is the suppression of basic contraditions, the strenuous effort to maintain the facade of a harmonious and stable system. The contractual sense of marriage that Tanner stresses becomes, in this middle-class mythology, an inviolable structure, so that when adultery does occur, it is seen not as a "gap" threatening the whole system but the offender's banishment from the system. Of course this "official" view does not—in fiction or in actual Victorian society—really avoid the anxiety of a fundamental challenge to sexual values; it suppresses or displaces that anxiety into other forms. But that is our point here. To base a novel on a heroine's resistance to assuming her role in the central institution of her society (*Bleak House, Can you Forgive Her?, No Name*) or on the slow dissolution of marriage or family through internal corruption rather than the "frontal assault" of adultery (*Martin Chuzzlewit, Phineas Finn, The Law and the Lady*) is to describe a substantially different form of bourgeois society than we find in *Madame Bovary* or *Anna Karenina*.

Courtship and marriage plots in the works of these four novelists present the primary issues of identity, freedom, and power as they actually confronted most Victorian women of the period. In *Phineas Finn* and *Phineas Redux*, for example, the hero's apprenticeship in the political world of London is paralleled in the careers of Lady Laura, Violet Effingham, and Madame Max; what politics is for men, marriage is for women. The same parallel occurs in *The Prime Minister*; Trollope draws explicit comparisons between the ministerial career of Plantagenet Palliser and his wife Glencora's attempts to find a career of her own.

The focus on courtship, marriage, and the family, then, is a means of locating the primary source of social disorder. In presenting sexual relationships as a central area of conflict, Victorian novelists were, in fact, concentrating on the most fundamental arena of crisis and change in their culture. When Mr. Osborne returns from the stock exchange savage and brutal toward his children, when Mr. Sedley returns home ruined, it may seem that the force of the economic world has overpowered the domestic world. But the exact opposite is true. *Vanity Fair* centers on the domestic world because that is both the origin and the only possible site of resolution of the conflicts that are reflected in the London economic world and even in the Napoleonic Wars. Because of the inflation of patriarchial values—and as an inevitable complement, the subservience of the wives and daughters who make up the "genteel Harem" (as Thackeray calls it)—the London merchants have carried family discord into the stock market and made it as much a reflection of the radical family disorder as the Court of Chancery in *Bleak House.*

As the nature of Victorian domestic life becomes a question more and more consciously considered (often with the implication that it is in a state of crisis) the urge to place marriage and the family at the center of fiction increases. Two tensions are distinguishable in the presentation of the family by these four novelists: on the one hand, it is honored as the origin of Victorian ideals and their best representation; on the other hand, the family appears, more and more frequently, as the breeding ground for conflicts in sexual identity and for the forces of oppression and repression which inevitably spring from these conflicts. Because of this clash in perspectives, the novels' narrators, and the novels themselves, are agitated by a profound ambivalence toward Victorian family structure and toward rituals of courtship and marriage. Women and the family were so linked in the Victorian mind that this ambivalence both complicates and intensifies the narrators' involvement with the novels' female characters.[11]

ANGELIC AND REBELLIOUS WOMEN

The Victorian novel in general shifts attention from courtship as a relation between individuals to courtship as a ritual conditioned by family life. Courtship continues to provide the main plot structures of most Victorian novels, but it often seems a framework for other, broader social concerns. (*Bleak House, Middlemarch, Wuthering Heights, Vanity Fair, The Way We Live Now, North and South,* and *The Woman in White* all exemplify this shift in emphasis.) As part of the shift from an erotic to a domestic center, the courted woman tends to be valued for her ability to sustain family life, to maintain or restore moral, emotional, and spiritual

homosexuality

integrity for the household, rather than for any distinct erotic qualities. Jane Eyre, Dorothea Brooke, Margaret Hale, and Amy Dorrit are a few among the multitude of these Victorian domestic heroines. It is only a short step from bearing the burden of a family's conscience and sensibilities to sustaining and regenerating the whole culture's values.

In the Victorian novel, then, women begin to act not against but through their ordinary social roles, not by seizing "male" roles, but by acting from within "female" ones. Where traditional Western literature tends to present women's power in the extremes of horror (Clytemnestra or Lady Macbeth), farce (Lysistrata, Dulcinea), or religious veneration (Beatrice, Una), the Victorian novel begins to document power exercised by women in their ordinary modes of social interaction. When women like Becky Sharp, Mrs. Joe, and Mrs. Proudie seize masculine powers, they do so within the limits of customary female social roles, acted on by the commonplace social realities of marriage or motherhood. When the Victorian male novelists we are considering undercut the powerful female characters they have created, their narratives reveal how threatening woman's power can be even when it is exercised covertly within existing social roles.

Far from being apologists for Victorian sexual orthodoxy, however, Dickens, Collins, Thackeray, and Trollope challenge one of its most significant creeds: that the virtuous woman has a nearly sacred social power. By placing "bad" or even criminal characters like Becky Sharp, Madeline Neroni, Lydia Gwilt, and Miss Havisham in positions of power, they imply—however circumspectly—the radical idea that the "good" woman has little real independence or power. And by presenting the "bad" woman as a victim of a cruelly oppressive sexual system, they undermine the orthodox position still further.

The Victorian ideal of the sacrificial woman that they subvert was stated memorably—or notoriously—by Ruskin. His formulation is extreme, but for that reason also extremely clear:

So far as she [woman] rules, all must be right, or nothing is. She must be enduringly, incorruptibly, good; instinctively, infallibly wise—wise, not for self-development, but for self-renunciation: wise, not that she may set herself above her husband, but that she may never fail from his side: wise, not with the narrowness of insolent and loveless pride, but with the passionate gentleness of an infinitely variable, because infinitely applicable, modesty of service. . . .

There is no suffering, no injustice, no misery, in the earth, but the guilt of it lies with you [women]. Men can bear the sight of it, but you should not be able to bear it. Men may tread it down without sympathy in their own struggle; but men are feeble in sympathy, and contracted in hope; it is you only who can feel the depths of pain, and conceive the way of its healing.[12]

Like so many male Victorian writers who reflect on the state of women, Ruskin writes not of fact but of desire. We may sympathize with this desperate need for an order, purity, and harmony that was not and could not be present in actual Victorian social relations. And we may understand the emotional force of the idealization that asked women to suffer as the new Christ for Victorian men of failing faith. But is is hardly possible now, with the welcome benefits of hindsight, to ignore the evasive and oppressive urges concealed within Ruskin's plea. His essay seeks, however unconsciously, to place on women all the burden of masculine inadequacy, timidity, and guilt for the failure of so many masculine enterprises.

In commenting on Ruskin's concept of the home, Walter Houghton emphasizes how the ideal stability was not so much a fact as a desperately felt need:

[The home] was both a shelter *from* the anxieties of modern life, a place where the desires of the heart might be realized (if not in fact, in imagination) and a shelter *for* those moral and spiritual values which the commerical spirit and the critical spirit were threatening to destroy, and therefore also a sacred place, a temple.[13]

Yet the demand that women act as repositories of a whole culture's values requires them to endure a passivity that verges on paralysis. There could be no better exemplification of Simone de Beauvoir's conclusion about the status of women in a patriarchal culture:

This, then, is the reason why woman has a double and deceptive visage: she is all that man desires and all that he does not attain. . . . He projects upon her what he desires and what he fears, what he loves and what he hates.[14]

Throughout Victorian culture—but especially through the beliefs and practices of the middle classes who provided the audience and the main subject matter for most fiction—the oppressive force of male desires intensifies even as the patriarchal system of values comes under direct attack. Like barroom bravado, rigid authoritarianism nearly always conceals massive insecurity and anxiety—however repressed. Yet the crisis in Victorian cultural values was obviously not simply the anxious response of a patriarchy whose own particular authority was challenged. Every area of life—religious, moral, aesthetic, political, economic, and, as a necessary consequence, emotional life—experienced fundamental challenges to traditional authority.

In this unsettled period, a fictional woman who finds a way to evade stereotypic sexual roles, to transform them into satisfying and creative activities, or to fashion some new sphere for female activity is seldom found. Dorothea Brooke's life falls at last into the same restrictive pattern as Esther Summerson's—subordination to her husband and his career. Both "pass through" a phase in which a fatherly figure becomes a husband or potential husband, and both finally accept joyfully the service to a younger man, to his home and family, as their proper sphere of activity. This process is as true of novels by George Eliot and Charlotte Brontë, who resolutely broke with antifeminist taboos in their own lives, as it is for the novels of Trollope, who defended those taboos in his personal life. One of the most powerful reasons for this phenomenon was the perception shared by the most discerning of Victorian novelists that the patriarchal Victorian culture was morally and spiritually debilitated, for all its outward show of confidence, and for all the devastation of its victims. As a consequence of this perception, Victorian novelists turned for a restoration of values to those in their culture who were trained to accept and inculcate values without question. Or, if women yearned for some life of independent significance—like Dorothea Brooke, Alice Vavasor, and Jane Eyre—they were urged to empathize with the suffering egos of men and, at the moment of crisis, to sacrifice themselves to save a man from despair, ruin, or bachelorhood. In this fiction, and in this society, women were asked, to a degree unexampled in Western culture, to take on not only the subjectivity of the race but the burden of regenerating its spiritual, moral, and social values.

When we see how much the careers of some of the most creative, powerful Victorian women—women like Florence Nightingale and George Eliot herself—were influenced by traditional conceptions of feminine roles, it is hardly surprising that Victorian novelists, male and female, could seldom find a real alternative. A number of Victorian women did, of course, find alternative roles, but novelists were seeking possibilities for the society at large; and there the pressures for conformity to the stereotypes were so great that exposure of the destructive consequences of stereotypic roles was achievement enough.

Because oppressive sexual roles are endemic to Victorian culture and manifest in every area of life, Victorian novelists present them as a fact of life. This can mean, and does for the four male novelists who are the subject of this study, that the novels reveal the ways in which a patriarchal system of sexual relations ravages institutions, family life, and individual personalities. But these same novels may be no more able—or bound—to present a solution to this crisis than Shakespearian tragedy can present a program for protecting society against Macbeths and Iagos.

Even writers like George Eliot and Charlotte Brontë who consciously set out to oppose oppressive stereotypes about women and sexual relations find the idea of woman as the benign, all-suffering restorer of cultural values powerfully attractive. The motif of the pure young woman who ministers to the broken faith of a ruined older man and tries to become the new source of values in his life is often associated with Dickens. But it is equally present in Brontë's Jane Eyre and Eliot's Dorothea Brooke. It is not difficult to see in this shift from a "standard" courtship relation to a daughter-father relation a yearning for the redemption of patriarchal values.[15]

Interestingly, Victorian women novelists often endorse this conservative (or regressive) resolution of sexual conflict more thoroughly than the male novelists we are considering. A rebellious urge against the injustice of a system that requires its chief victims to rescue it from self-induced disaster, at the cost of their own personal goals, does take symbolic shape in many novels written by women (as Sandra Gilbert and Susan Gubar have recently argued in *The Madwoman in the Attic*).[16] But this symbolic opposition is nearly always hermetically sealed from the main narrative values. It is not that novels like *Shirley* and *Middlemarch* fail to do what novels can seldom do with any success, endorse some program for wholesale social change. Rather, they shift almost imperceptibly from a social to a personal scale; they eventually offer a strictly personal fulfillment and tacitly abandon the idea of masculine injustices in the culture's sexual values—an idea that each novel has strenuously developed before this shift.

Thus, the child-like Ladislaw replaces the fallen patriarch Casaubon. Though he is more personable and more attuned to Dorothea's own personality, their marriage simply has no real bearing on the urge for a life of independent purpose and "wider significance" that Dorothea yearned for. A familiar pattern of courtship has replaced the inchoate but powerful sense of something fundamentally wrong that caused Dorothea first to reject marriage and then to create a fantasy of a marriage that might transcend all the usual social limitations.

In a similar way Rochester is a symbolic replacement for the tyrannical and sadistic Reverend Brocklehurst. Like Ladislaw, he offers no real alternative to the sexual system that has oppressed Jane Eyre; he becomes a chastened and tender patriarch, but he relies on feminine subordination nearly as much as Brocklehurst does. (Robert Moore of *Shirley* and Paul Emmanuel of *Villette* are similar patriarchal figures.) The resolution of the novel is once again not even a confirmation of the thematic status quo but a regression from the rebellious impulses of the novel's opening. The authors' choice to strike down Casaubon and Rochester surely is a covert assault on patriarchal oppression, but the assault remains isolated and fragmentary, never affecting the basic articulation of narrative values and perspectives. As Gilbert and Gubar argue, this authorial rebellion is deeply concealed within the novels:

"women from Jane Austen and Mary Shelley to Emily Brontë and Emily Dickinson produced literary works that are in some sense palimpsestic, works whose surface designs conceal or obscure deeper, less accessible (and less socially acceptable) levels of meaning." And even this concealed rebellion is often countered by "an obsessive interest in [the] limited options" offered to women and also by "obsessive imagery of confinement that reveals the ways in which female artists feel sickened both by suffocating alternatives and by the culture that created them."[17]

Given the overwhelming and often sadistic obsessiveness of the Victorian patriarchal system itself, these obsessions are understandable, perhaps inevitable, and certainly irreproachable. And more important for the reader of fiction, they reveal much about the insidious nature of the sexual system. But thematically as well as dramatically, the plot developments that strike down the patriarchs unfortunately also rescue the heroines from the most interesting and revealing consequences of their own moral and psychological development. Or, more simply, they evade the central sexual dilemma each novel has created as an expression of the heroine's nature and as an expression of its own primary themes. The novels thus pull back from acknowledging the systemic crisis that grips Victorian sexual relations. By contrast, when Dickens' hypocritical patriarch Casby is attacked by the raging Pancks and sheared of his hair, his hat brim, and his pretensions; when the Marquis of Steyne is left with "livid face and ghastly eyes"—impotent in his hatred of Becky and equally impotent in his desire for his latest mistress—these scenes remain in our memories as indictments of the Victorian patriarchy.

Gilbert and Gubar argue that many Victorian women novelists are forced into a kind of subterfuge, displacing both insecurity about female roles and hostility toward the masculine traditions that deny women the right to write:

this female anxiety of authorship is profoundly debilitating. Handed down not from one woman to another but from the stern literary "fathers" of patriarchy to all their "inferiorized" female descendents, it is in many ways the germ of a dis-ease or, at any rate, a disaffection, a disturbance, a distrust, that spreads like a stain throughout the style and structure of much literature by women, especially . . . by women before the twentieth century.[18]

The symbolic expressions of this largely unconscious motivation reveal primarily an authorial conflict rather than a conflict that grows from the social and psychological conflicts of the characters. The "madwoman" Bertha Mason, Rochester's wife imprisoned in the attic, thus represents Brontë's more than than Jane's rebellious urges. As we have argued, Jane Eyre and Dorothea Brooke are placed in situations that seem designed to arouse a rebellion against masculine tyranny; they are endowed by their creators with passionate, intelligent, imaginative natures that might well flush the iniquities of Victorian society into the open; but this potential development is simply never realized. The power they finally exert—giving purpose to the hero's life, reclaiming or forestalling the hero's decline—is the subservient power of the traditional female character of Western literature in a domestic Victorian guise.

This is disturbingly close to Ruskin's fervent wish for a Woman "enduringly, incorruptibly, good . . . with the passionate gentleness of an infinitely variable, because infinitely applicable modesty of service." Many Victorian novels written by women do seem to support the idea that the highest act women can aspire to is self-sacrificial, boundless empathy for the needs and sufferings of others. The thematic climax of *Middlemarch,* for instance, comes when Dorothea extends sympathy to both Lydgate and Rosamond in ways no one else has been able to. Even Farebrother, the most sensitive and compassionate male character in the novel, shies away from Lydgate, for fear that he was indeed implicated in the poisoning of Raffles. But Dorothea's self-sacrificing sympathy (she thinks Ladislaw is in love with Rosamond) is so strong that she can partially restore Lydgate to the Middlemarch community, rescue him from despair, save his marriage, and compel even the ordinarily egoistic Rosamond to emerge from her self-absorption.

Similarly, Margaret Hale of Gaskell's *North and South* prevents the rioting strikers from killing Thornton by timely use of her power as a woman ("We all feel the sanctity of our sex as a high privilege when we see danger," she says). Her marriage to Thornton seems designed to wed an otherwise ruthless male energy to a female compassion and sense of social responsibility. Yet this emphasis upon the power of female compassion and the "instinct" for self-sacrifice conceals a basic ambivalence—a mixture of wishful thinking, the perception that women do exercise considerable power covertly, and a desire to change some of the more destructive features of male power in Victorian culture. All this seems to demand that women take on, in Adrienne Rich's phrase, "the burden of carrying the subjectivity of the race."[19] Woman has been set back in the traditional symbolic ambience that includes so many of the stereotypic roles assigned to her in and out of literature.

Even *Wuthering Heights*, whose heroine is openly passionate, self-willed, and rebellious, shifts the narrative from a protest against the social system that hems Catherine in to a concern with a "spiritual" level of erotic relationship. And the novel, structurally as well as thematically, turns its attention from Catherine to Heathcliff. Although this is not so much an evasion of possibilities for exploring sexual values as a disclosure of Emily Brontë's more fundamental interests, we nonetheless see the familiar shift from female to male character, from the nature of a whole society's values to the dimensions of one special relationship.[20]

As Myra Jehlen has recently argued, novels written by women in a patriarchal culture cannot establish a separate sphere of "authentic" female values and relations; for values and relations—even those of the most creative and enlightened artists—do not exist apart from their historical context.[21] One of the clearest and simplest statements of this cultural conditioning was written by a Victorian, John Stuart Mill:

. . . I deny that any one knows, or can know, the nature of the two sexes, as long as they have only been seen in their present relation to one another. If men had ever been found in society without women, or if there had been a society of men and women in which the women were not under the control of the men, something might have been positively known about the mental and moral differences which may be inherent in the nature of each. What is now called the nature of women is an eminently artificial thing—the result of forced repression in some directions, unnatural stimulation in others. It may be asserted without scruple, that no other class of dependents have had their character so entirely distorted from its natural proportions by their relation with their masters. . . .[22]

What we should expect to see, and do see, in the greatest of Victorian novelists—women and men—is distortion, contradiction, evasion precisely where their perceptions are most radical, most critical of their culture's values. We are not attempting to determine which novelists are superior by some modern standard of sexual enlightenment (subject itself to the conditions of a particular historical moment); we are trying to distinguish the characteristic ways that male and female novelists dealt with the contradictions inherent in their material and their relations to it.

The major women novelists—Eliot, Gaskell, the Brontës—focus attention more directly, and what is equally important, more admiringly on female characters who passionately desire a life of their own and who work, initially at least, to achieve it. None of the male novelists of the period do so with such consistency or sympathy. But the women novelists also present, with apparently equal admiration, the abandonment of their heroines' desire for an independent life—Dorothea Brooke's "life of wider significance"—in a process of heroic self-sacrifice that, not accidentally, returns us to a social status quo.

The male novelists we are dealing with are less able to conceive a powerful, intelligent woman who is not somehow socially, morally, or even physically aberrant (a Becky Sharp, Miss Havisham, Lydia Gwilt, or Madeline Neroni). And they are certainly more likely to rhapsodize over women who cater to sentimentalized masculine erotic desires: the coquettes, the angels, the dimpled innocents. But they also are more likely to express conflicting sexual attitudes directly in their narratives and in the psychological and social circumstances of their characters. They keep attention focused on the system itself, on the preconditions that shape their characters' personal choices. And this is true even when their novels' resolutions seem most patly, sterotypically domestic. The more Dickens' Esther Summerson tells us how thoroughly blessed and happy she is with her husband, house, and children, the more aware we are likely to be of how unresolved the novel has left the social disorder of England's other families—from the Court of Chancery, which thrives on family disputes, to the abandoned children of London's slums.

At least part of this difference lies in the different circumstances faced by male authors. Their insecurities lie not so much in the act of writing itself or in the way that society regards their roles as authors as in the whole complex of masculine roles that are their cultural inheritance. In the major novels of the authors we are dealing with here, personal ambivalence toward women and sexual roles in general intersects with the crisis in sexual relations that manifests itself throughout their culture; and the tensions within their attitudes toward this primary material wrench the narratives into complex and revealing forms.

Contradictory attitudes are not simply embedded in symbolism that awaits the imagination of a reader already alert to contradictions in Victorian values; they agitate the narrative voice itself. They produce extreme, often grotesque variations on sexual stereotypes, plots that suggest the presence of repressed conflicts, and contradictory behavior on the part of the characters. All this manifest complexity can lead the reader to probe the patterns of symbolic analogy that form a primary structure of meaning within these novels. We are not confronted with a palimpsest (a story "written over" the author's personal "subtext") but with a continuous text whose contradictions from a coherent design. Because the male writers' ambivalence is less hermetically expressed than ambivalence often is in the works of female Victorian novelists, it generates a fuller development of the novels' own sexual material. (All four novelists wrote, by choice, in looser or more episodic forms than many of their fellow Victorian novelists preferred. This permitted a freer expansion and interrelation of symbolic material, a freer expression of intuitive and unconscious designs, than a more tightly formulated aesthetic might have allowed.)

Paradoxically, it is often the very blatancy of sexual stereotypes

in these novels that alerts us to the complex, psychologically and
socially accurate material that the novel is trying both to suppress
and to explore. Similarly, the domestic resolutions of these novels
are likely to cause us to reexamine the narrative's development
of sexual material precisely because they seem arbitrary or extreme. What makes these novels different from simply stereotyped
fiction is the presence *within the novels themselves* of the complex
psychological and social forces—the "reality"—which stereotypes
seek to deny. This fiction not only presents sharply conflicting
images of women and conflicting evaluations of their roles; it also
offers a sustained, progressive (though almost entirely implicit)
critique of its own overt sexual attitudes. The Victorian patriarchal
value system is both asserted and negated. The ambivalence toward women that is a distinctive feature of their fiction reveals
a special, fearful fascination with women's power. But this fascination also creates a special sensitivity to the way women may
exercise power covertly—the other side of the desire to impose
confining stereotypes. Becky Sharp, Mrs. Joe, Glencora Palliser
are women who represent the realities of power and status in
actual social practices.

Thus the ambivalence these four male novelists share takes a
different and perhaps more radical form than the ambivalence of
most female novelists of this period. Whereas Dorothea Brooke,
Margaret Hale, and Jane Eyre become powerful through their
goodness, the virtuous heroines of the male novelists are less powerful than the unconventional women they are paired with. Becky
Sharp has some power while Amelia has scarcely any. Eleanor
Bold of *Barchester Towers* does little more than react to others'
schemes and actions while Madeline Neroni upsets nearly everyone and by so doing helps to revitalize Barchester. Collins'
conventional good heroines—Laura Fairlie, Norah Vanstone, and
Rachel Verinder—have almost no power to influence events.
Dickens' Florence Dombey and Biddy merely wait and hope
events will turn our favorably while Edith Dombey and Miss
Havisham, despite all their self-torment and destructiveness, take
powerful action to resist their oppressors.

Becky Sharp is representative of a type of woman who appears increasingly at the center of these Victorian novels: a woman who manages to think for herself not by breaking with her assigned stereotypic role, but by exaggerating that role in order to exploit it, turning its power back on the male establishment who created it for their own psychic and social advantage. At the other extreme is the domestic angel like Esther Summerson, a seemingly unlikely sister of Becky Sharp. Yet Esther's efforts to embody so many different roles and to fulfill so many selfless ideals virtually parody the demands placed upon the wives and mothers of Victorian middle-class households. And this is not a modern reconstruction of the novel; Esther's verbal and physical tics and the novel's symbolic structures reveal the destructive pressures exerted on her by the very virtues which the narrative explicitly extols.

Esther's repression of her own sexual desires, her efforts to deny her own will and the needs of her emotional life, are an extreme version of the struggles of more ordinary wives and mothers in the Victorian era. By and large these four male novelists show the Becky Sharps to have power that the Esther Summersons do not, but the novels expose the male social system through their use of both types of women, the usurping and the submissive. Whether women try to act as the perfect domestic angel or try to subvert and transform the roles available to them, they come up against the limitations and frustrations imposed on them by the prevailing system.

A number of these novels, like *Vanity Fair* and *Bleak House*, focus directly on the conflicts between a heroine's individual personality and the social roles that constrain her life. Taken together, they tend to develop a narrative situation that reflects the special condition of women in Victorian society—given more freedom of action even as social pressure to conform to reductive stereotypes increased. As we see in the case of Esther Summerson, the clash of intensifying impulses toward self-development with intensifying pressures toward conformity to social stereotypes was likely to produce greater anxiety, obsessive behavior, and exaggerated devotion to narrow and rigid ideals of behavior. But we can also see how this very intensification of the conflict could force an acknowledgment that there is, in fact, not only a problem but a crisis.

As these novelists intimate that Victorian sexual values conceal a fundamental corruption, they also implicitly challenge their culture's growing reliance on a consciously directed moral will as the means to correct the world's evils. None of them even locates the center of fictional interest in consciousness as, say, Austen, James, Eliot, and Woolf do. Consciousness is not the source of primary conflict, nor the agent of resolution; it cannot even provide the sort of mitigating insight so important to the basic conception and basic value of characters like Isabel Archer and Lily Briscoe. Characters in the novels of Dickens, Thackeray, Trollope, and Collins realize the emotional effects of the conflicts they undergo, of course (as Esther remembers both the form and intensity of her feverish dream after recovering from smallpox); but they are just as incapable of understanding the major implications of the psychological processes they endure as Esther is of interpreting her dream. Consciousness in these novels is a partial, imperfect register of conflicts whose psychological depth and social range can only be represented through symbolic configurations of plot and character.

Events, both psychological and physical, are affected very little by conscious insights and will, even when the characters have some clear grasp of their situations (as Becky Sharp and Alice Vavasor do). The compelling forces in these worlds are primarily unconscious, even obsessive—complex sexual roles so internalized that they seem instinct with personal desire. Consciousness can be adroit in its local manipulations of the social world (in the machinations, for instance, of Becky Sharp, Glencora Palliser, and Magdalen Vanstone), but it is nearly always subordinate to the unconscious forces that largely shape the lives of individuals and the society they inhabit.

The subordination of the conscious will is more easily recognized in the novels of Dickens and Collins, which explicitly draw their characters in a secret nexus of crime and fraud and subject them to bewildering external events. But plot has the same primacy over conscious motivation in *Vanity Fair*, making the initially arch narrative metaphor of characters as puppets an accurate thematic metaphor by the end of the novel. It is true that Becky Sharp's challenge to this restrictive view of the conscious will sets and keeps in motion the main action of *Vanity Fair,* that to a large extent her plots shape the novel's plot. But it is the failure of her effort, together with the less brilliant failures of the other characters' designs, that the novel chiefly describes. Becky succumbs to the obsessive power of her own desires, which she pursues more and more feverishly as she understands or even reflects on them less and less. As in the novels of Dickens and Collins, the plot here is not at all an arbitrary contrivance and not simply a reflection of manifest social disorders. It is the concrete expression of psychological motives whose nature is unknown to the characters themselves.

Even Trollope, who seems to write in the "realist" or "mimetic" tradition, creates novels in which the conscious desires of characters are not only largely ineffectual in shaping their lives (often the case with characters in any novel) but are largely tangential to the psychological forces that actually determine their basic temperaments and careers. Trollope's character—especially heroines like Alice Vavasor (*Can You Forgive Her?*), Emily Wharton (*The Prime Minister*), and Clara Amedroz (*The Belton Estate*)—scrutinize their motives, reflect on them, agonize over them, and exchange confidences, rebukes, and advice with an articulate intelligence that compares favorably with any character of James or Eliot. The sudden shifts in resolve and emergence of new impulses that characterize heroines like Alice Vavasor make for exciting psychological drama. But the psychological processes that define Trollope's characters are often much more like the development of Collins' heroines than James's or Eliot's. Their traits are essentially givens of the narrative. Even when they alter, the alteration is recorded but not adequately accounted for in the direct narrative.

For example, Kate Vavasor (*Can You Forgive Her?*) describes her one controlling desire, the desire to bring about Alice Vavasor's marriage to George (Kate's brother and Alice's cousin)—the desire to which she sacrifices her own personal life and betrays her only friend—in this way:

"I've been often curious to consider what sort of husband would suit you, but I've had very few thoughts about a husband for myself. The truth is, I'm married to George. . . . If George ever married, I should have nothing to do in the world;—literally nothing—nothing—nothing—nothing! . . . If you became George's wife I should become nobody. I've nothing else in the world. You and he would be so all-sufficient for each other, that I should drop away like an old garment. But I'd give up all, everything, every hope I have, to see you become George's wife. I know myself not to be good. I know myself to be very bad, and yet I care nothing for myself."

[6]

It is perhaps not surprising that Kate can only confess, not account for, this totally consuming, "eccentric" devotion. But the narrator's failure to make any effort to account for it would be astonishing if it were not, by this point in the novel, so typical. Alice's own intense commitments and their sudden shifts have origins that are equally unexplored, by both character and narrator. And though she operates on the opposite principle from Kate's, subjugating her emotional urges to a stern, exacting moral sense, both act from impulse, not from conscious choice. Alice does not search the grounds of her moral convictions any more than Kate seeks to account for her ruinous devotion to her brother.

In psychological novels of the mimetic tradition, characters typically influence each other in ways that the narrator can assess even when the characters are deluded. And the plot is determined by the most important of these influences. (The narrator of *Middlemarch* makes this effect explicit: "anyone watching keenly the stealthy convergence of human lots sees a slow preparation of effects from one life on another which tells like a calculated irony. . . .") The heroines of *Can You Forgive Her?* have great, though temporary, influence over the men who are compelled to wait for them to resolve their protracted periods of romantic indecision. And they also determine, through this same struggle, the shape and substance of the novel itself. But they themselves are governed by overriding impulses that they have little power to change and even less to understand, nor can the narrator give any direct insight into his characters' deepest impulses. It is as if something powerful, disorienting, and basically alien to their conscious moral and emotional values has passed through these heroines, has worked itself out and left them to a typical subordination in marriage relations so patterned and impersonal that it might as well be preordained.

Glencora, Alice, and Kate are all consciously engaged in a struggle not to shape their own lives—they have abandoned that possibility before the novel's action begins—but to ally themselves with men whose lives have some promise of excitement, energy, and significance. Yet the novel gradually reveals that their intense, inconsistent desires and moods reflect a profound unconscious resistance to settling for a surrogate identity. (Both Glencora and Alice feel a persistent sense of unworthiness, uselessness, and despair much like Kate's.)

As outrageous as the behavior of these women seems to the more conventional characters who hem them in (Alice's fiancé, John Grey, can account for her reluctance to marry him only as a species of mental illness), they cannot realize the still more presumptuous motive that impels their behavior: the need for a personal life of some consequence in and of itself. The direct expression of this most basic of human needs would constitute a radical assault on their society's system of sexual relations. Glencora, Kate, and Alice simply have not encountered, within the narrow sexual categories of the social world they inhabit, any mode of behavior available to women which could stimulate the direct, conscious formulation of this need. So all their disruptions of the orderly working of the sexual system offer no direct challenge to its basic sanctions or basic modes.

. The only essential power they see for themselves is the power to devote themselves totally to the desires of a man. Each not only senses but describes this option as what it is—an act of self-annihilation. And each expresses repeatedly the sense of worthlessness that is their common sexual and social inheritance. The protracted, tormenting period of indecision they impose upon themselves is also a time of self-expression if not, in any lasting sense, self-exploration. It allows them to exert a temporary and provisional but direct control over their lives; it gives them an emotionally rich experience, however painful; it gives them a brief impact on other people and on a social system which will soon re-exert control over their lives. The novel's bitterest irony is the fact that they cannot realize the nature of their own intense period of self-assertion, a pitifully brief period in the context of a lifetime.

Neither the characters nor the narrator of *Can You Forgive Her?* can acknowledge the systematically oppressive conditions of the novel's sexual world. But what appeared to be a standard plot of courtship has been transformed in the course of the novel into a virtual exposé of the oppression concealed within respectable Victorian sexual practices. Implicit contradictions and anomalies have gathered such powerful consistency that they constitute a subversive counterplot. The forms of desire and power displayed in orthodox Victorian courtship and marriage have not been directly challenged. But in a way that distinguishes all four novelists, the psychological forces that sustain those forms have been exposed to a radical assault.

SEXUAL SWINDLING: FRAUD AND CRIME AS THE SOCIAL BOND

The conviction that Victorian society conceals fundamental disorders within its system of sexual relations finds more direct thematic expression in the plots created by these novelists. One of the most persistent of these is the plot based on crime or fraud—in *Bleak House, Great Expectations, Our Mutual Friend, The Woman in White, The Moonstone, Vanity Fair, The Way We Live Now, Orley Farm, The Eustace Diamonds,* and many others. Some critics have considered these plots feeble attempts to make melodrama serve the purposes that traditional ritual forms such as comedy and tragedy served in cultures that were more coherent and secure.[23] Yet the focus on crime or fraud can be as significant a fictional motif for Victorian culture as the corruption of the monarchy was for Elizabethan culture.

The central act of fraud or crime in these novels most often involves sexual roles and wrests the traditional marriage and courtship plots into distorted forms. The perpetrators of sexual fraud are among the most memorable and influential characters, and their intrigues often virtually determine the novels' plots (Becky Sharp, Lord Steyne, Pecksniff, Jonas Chuzzlewit, Steerforth,

Edith Dombey, Lady Dedlock, Mrs. Clennam, Sir Percival Glyde, Magdalen Vanstone, Captain Wragge, Lydia Gwilt, George Vasor, Felix Lopez, Lizzie Eustace, and so forth). The novels in which such characters exist suggest that sexual roles, values, and power relations in Victorian society are fraudulent in some basic way. The disorder is so widespread and yet so suppressed from individual consciousness and public acknowledgment that it can best be expressed in covert, symbolic form. Dickens' later novels—*Bleak House, Little Dorrit, Great Expectations,* and *Our Mutual Friend*—present the fullest elaboration of this theme, as they fuse all major Victorian institutions, from marriage and the family to whole systems of law, religion, and government into gigantic concatenations of fraud.

The sensational novels of Dickens and Collins, as their plots intertwine the respectable and the criminal worlds, imply that an elaborate criminal intrigue is the truest analogue to respectable social relations. Significantly, the respectable world becomes more impotent and demoralized as the power and complexity of the criminal plot emerges. In Dickens' late novels, *Bleak House, Great Expectations, Little Dorrit,* and *Our Mutual Friend,* crime and fraud seem inseparable from the whole complex of social relations that make up the novels' comprehensive versions of Victorian culture. This insistence on a correspondence between the "highest" and the "lowest" members of society, between the most hallowed of Victorian pieties and the most abhorred of Victorian vices, has often been called, disparagingly, melodramatic. But it is little different from the obsessive nature of Shakespearian tragic figures: the "mad" obsession proves true as the facade of ordinary social relations is stripped away.

As the novels of all four writers link social fraud (including pretensions to wealth and status) with actual crimes—through analogy and through direct interactions in the plot—the distinction between crime and fraud blurs and even disappears. It seems an arbitrary distinction attempted by moneyed and "respectable" characters in their own self-interest. This attempt to sever respectable fraud from crime is one of the many maneuvers of snobbery that the novels anatomize. But often it is also a troubled effort by decent characters to salvage some moral value from a world that threatens to collapse into a chaos of fraudulent scrabblings. When Dickens links Blandois, Mrs. Clennam, Arthur Clennam, and Amy Dorrit in secret conspiracy—or Miss Havisham, Jaggers, Pip, Estella, Compeyson, Orlick, and Mrs. Joe; or Esther Summerson, Lady Dedlock, "Nemo," and Joe the Crossing Sweeper—he is surely questioning the very basis of Victorian social and moral hierarchies. The sense that all social relations are fraudulent is one implication of the consuming, irrational guilt and anxiety that Pip, Esther, Arthur Clennam, and John Harmon seem to inherit as their Victorian birthright. And with the inexorable force of traditional tragedy, these characters discover at the climax of their careers a secret nexus of fraud that not only draws them into explicit deceptions of their own, but also gradually superimposes itself on the whole network of manifest social relations in each novel.

Collins links respectable characters to the "lowest" in their society in nearly all his novels. In *The Moonstone* the outcast, formerly criminal Rosanna Spearman is linked to Blake, Rachel Verinder, and Godfrey Ablewhite in a number of ways that the respectable characters themselves cannot see. In *Armadale* Lydia Gwilt is Mrs. Armadale's haunting reminder of her one youthful acquiescence in fraud. In *The New Magdalen* the reformed prostitute Mercy Merrick fraudulently impersonates Grace Roseberry and in the process exposes Grace and conventional Victorian society as guilty of hypocrisy, pettiness, and selfishness.

In a similar way, Trollope's narrator in *The Way We Live Now* allies himself with the aristocratic characters' contempt for the boorish, foreign, possibly Jewish, and definitely *nouveau riche* swindler Melmotte; but his sympathetic attitude becomes increasingly problematic as the novel reveals their avid attempts to court and exploit the character they despise. As *their* fraud (compounded by hypocrisy) becomes evident, as the novel stresses their similarity to Melmotte, the narrator's blithe snobbery is challenged by the novel's own analogical structures.

Those who live on nothing a year abound in the fiction of these four authors: Becky and Rawdon; Montague Tigg, the Lammles,

Pip and William Dorrit; Collins' Percival Glyde and Captain Wragge; Trollope's Felix Lopez and Burgo Fitzgerald. And the nothing they live on satirizes a social void that goes far beyond economic relations. Economic swindles—both niggling and grandiose—occupy such a large place in these novels because they may well be an emblem for the most basic relations that hold the culture together.

Where Dickens and Collins draw us toward the criminal world that parodies respectable society, Trollope and Thackeray focus on fraudulent relations that are the daily practice of respectable society. But they are aware also that the distinction between crime (or vice) and routine social fraud is often a question of class rather than virtue. Thus novels like *Vanity Fair* and *The Way We Live Now* show a Volpone-like descent through levels of social fraud until they reach the lurid ambience of Becky's supposed poisoning of Jos Sedley and Melmotte's suicide. This motif of a descent into corruption is counterbalanced by a persistent exposure of the same pattern of fraud, and more devious sorts of hypocrisy, in the highest levels of society, so that once again traditional hierarchies of value are called into question.

As all these novels collapse the social distinctions so dear to the snobs of birth, money, and virtue into a common pattern of social fraud, they push beyond the issue of social practices to the fundamental cultural assumptions that have created them and now struggle to sustain them. And here the most essential form of fraud is sexual. The emotional extortion both Blandois and William Dorrit attempt depends on the abuse of sexual relations, just as the gorgeous bosom of Mrs. Merdle is essential to Merdle's gargantuan swindle. Even Arthur Clennam's ruinous investment in Merdle's enterprises results indirectly from his despondency over a hopeless love for Pet Meagles. The initial theft of the moonstone is symbolically associated with Rachel's virginity, encourages Rosanna in her hopeless love for Blake, and encourages Godfrey Ablewhite to steal the gem again in order to support his mistress. The attempted sale of Marie Melmotte is likewise a necessary thematic culmination of Melmotte's fraud. And Mr. Osborne's patriarchal tyranny in *Vanity Fair* always vents itself in sexual terms: he first tries to bribe George into marrying the heiress Miss Swartz and, that failing, disinherits and banishes George for marrying the impoverished Amelia.

These novelists are implicated in the fraud they expose insofar as they share the underlying patriarchal values that generate sexual injustice and exploitation. Their ambivalence toward sexual relations is reflected in their arrangement of their fictional material and in their narrative techniques. Techniques that expose the crisis in sexual values even when (often precisely when) they seek to evade it are the subject of the next chapter; but one instance may be useful here. Dickens' last completed novel, *Our Mutual Friend*, rests all the resolutions of its complex plot on the "resurrection" of John Harmon from his apparent death and, equally important, from the kind of guilt that has nearly paralyzed previous Dickens heroes like Pip and Arthur Clennam. But this resurrection is accomplished by an elaborate fraud, a deception of Bella Wilfer in order to test her virtue, and a deception of the reader as well. However justified it may be abstractly, and however deftly the revelations are engineered, in retrospect the deception seems disturbingly close to the sort of sexual barter that the Lammles and Fledgeby are condemned for. Harmon's test of Bella involves too much unnecessary manipulation and emotional gratification on his part in contrast with her very real distress. The last part of the trial seems wholly unnecessary, a kind of gratuitous and egotistic luxuriating in her fidelity:

"And so, my good and pretty," pursued Mrs. Boffin, "you was married, and there was we hid up in the church-organ by this husband of yours; for he wouldn't let us out with it then, as was first meant. "No," he says, "she's so unselfish and contented, that I can't afford to be rich yet. I must wait a little longer." Then, when baby was expected, he says, "She is such a cheerful, glorious housewife, that I can't afford to be rich yet. I must wait a little longer." . . . Then he says, he'll only wait to triumph beyond what we ever thought possible, and to show her to us better than even we ever supposed; and he says, "She shall see me under suspicion of having murdered myself, and *you* shall see how trusting and how true she'll be."

[IV, xiii, 773–74]

This smacks too much of Magwitch's delight in his bought-up London gentleman in *Great Expectations*. Though Bella survives the test, the strain on her seems simply cruel. At the moment of revelation she beseeches Harmon, "I don't know what it means, but it is too much for me." We suspect it is also too much for most readers.

Certainly Boffin's about-face in personality has disturbed any number of readers. His evil, miserly, overbearing personality is a total narrative fraud. We are deluded into believing in Boffin's corruption by the power of money, and all the attractions of exploitation it offers to a man, precisely because it is so credible in the corrupt social world the novel depicts. Here the convincing evil is swallowed up in a dramatically and psychologically unconvincing effusion of goodness. (It is similar in this way to the attribution of all of John Harmon's convincingly neurotic behavior to the temporary effects of the drug he was given.)

Like less egregious acts of narrative fraud in the novels of Dickens, Thackeray, Trollope, and Collins, this fraud ultimately reveals its own deception and conflicts sharply with the novels' own exposures of sexual fraud. In a similar way, the stereotypic idyll that ends the romance of John Harmon and Bella Wilfer (and the "inexhaustible" baby) clashes with the more credible developments in the novel's other primary sexual relationship, the relationship between Eugene Wrayburn and Lizzie Hexam.

This sort of narrative fraud is a curious, inseparable blending of evasion and revelation. The subterfuges are by no means artful tricks of an intentionally ironic author. The fraud is unconscious, and, for that reason, sincerely practiced. Dickens—from all that we know of his intentions—wanted us to delight in Bella's fidelity and the Harmons' domestic bliss. But precisely because the intent of the stereotypically sentimental or moralistic narrators these novelists create is so fervently sincere, we are drawn into the countervailing material that undermines their assertions. This is not a systematic working out of an idea of ambivalence but a truly dramatic, absorbing expression of a culture torn by its own contradictions.

Because they participate in the conflict of sexual values that pervades their culture and to some extent share the patriarchal values they satirize, these novelists are able to present the workings of Victorian sexuality with remarkable subtlety and accuracy. And sexuality is, for them, not simply a matter of libidinal urges. It is a complex of desires, attitudes, roles, and norms that is virtually coextensive with all social life. The way an individual's sexuality is defined, by self and by others, is a critical and even a determining factor in areas of economic and political life that seem to have little directly to do with sexuality. We can realize this basically symbolic dimension of each novel only if we respond to a number of techniques for indirect presentation—techniques present in some form in many novels, but absolutely central to these.

2

THE AMBIVALENT NOVELISTS:
THE QUESTION OF FORM

T would be nearly impossible to confuse a novel—
or even a paragraph—by Trollope with one by
Dickens. And this is almost as true of the rhetorical
devices that distinguish Collins from Dickens, despite their shared interest in melodramatic plot construction and other affinities in their choice and
handling of subject. If we extend our comparative terms to include
such areas as the basic type of plot or the range of social classes
treated, then the features that distinguish these four novelists from
each other appear so numerous that it would be difficult even to
catalog them. Yet all four share a comprehensive ironic method
that directs their distinctive techniques toward a common purpose,
the exposure of a corrupt system of sexual values and its particularly oppressive impact on women.

This ironic method consists of several major techniques:

(1) An unstable narrative voice that is driven, in part, by concealed
desires and anxieties.
(2) Symbolic pairings and polarities in characterization, plot, dramatic scene, and description. Together these techniques of
indirect presentation form a major ironic structure, a counterplot to the novel's direct methods.
(3) Manipulation of stereotypic roles, attitudes, and situations in
ways that expose their inaccuracy and injustice.

AMBIVALENT AND OBTUSE NARRATORS

All these novelists create strong, obtrusive narrators with distinct
personalities and biases, who force us to notice and respond to

stereotypic masculine attitudes. Much criticism has, in fact, noted this quality in the narrators and usually attributes it to the prejudices of the authors—in other words, to a failure in aesthetic and moral control. Undoubtedly the narrator's fulsome praise of Ruth Pinch's cunning little apron and her adorable contretemps with the beefsteak pudding in *Martin Chuzzlewit* or the sarcastic references to feminists by a number of Trollope's narrators are versions of attitudes held at some time in some form by Dickens and Trollope themselves. It would be intriguing, though much more difficult than many critics and biographers assume, to assess just how far each novelist is personally implicated in this sort of commentary. But that issue is quite irrelevant to the effect of the sexually skewed commentary as a narrative strategy. For if we resist our own preconceptions and biases, we can discover that it is, in fact, only one element in a coherent pattern of narrative devices that direct attention not to the fallibility of the authors but to the fallibility of the narrators and, ultimately, to the falseness of an entire structure of sexual values in the culture the novels both exemplify and satirize.

The errors and excesses of these narrators do not obliterate the more persuasive values in these novels; instead, they help, by establishing a sharp contrast, to orient us toward the novels' primary value systems and themes. In Wayne Booth's term, they direct us toward perceiving the designs of the "implied" author: "the 'implied author' chooses, consciously or unconsciously, what we read; . . . This implied author is always distinct from the 'real man'—whatever we may take him to be—who creates a superior version of himself, a 'second self' as he creates his work."[1] In the novels of Dickens, Collins, Thackeray, and Trollope, this implied author regularly transcends the limited attitudes toward women that the narrators—and the public pronouncements of their creators—reveal.

These narrators, unlike those of truly stereotyped fiction, indirectly but insistently call attention to their own excesses. *Vanity Fair*'s narrator, for instance, typically mingles satire and sentiment (as he says) in his comments on women, and the unctuous sentiment is more insidiously antifeminist than the satiric jibes:

It is quite edifying to hear women speculate upon the worthlessness and the duration of beauty.

But though virtue is a much finer thing, and those hapless creatures who suffer under the misfortune of good looks ought to be continually put in mind of the fate which awaits them; and though, very likely, the heroic female character which ladies admire is a more glorious and beautiful object than the kind, fresh, smiling, artless, tender little domestic goddess, whom men are inclined to worship—yet the latter and inferior sort of women must have this consolation—that the men *do* admire them after all; and that, in spite of our kind friends' warnings and protests, we go on in our desperate error and folly, and shall to the end of the chapter.

[I, xii, 130]

This patronizing adoration, which actually seeks to depersonalize and incapacitate the object of its regard, has focused almost exclusively on Amelia Sedley by the middle of the novel, intensifying as she is increasingly confined, humiliated, and tormented. But the sentimental terminology also becomes steadily more grotesque, so extreme that it reveals its own ambivalence toward Amelia's devotion (as the "domestic goddess" becomes an idolatrous worshiper of the shallow fop George Osborne and, after his death, of little Georgy):

She talked constantly to him about this dead father . . . into his ears she poured her sentimental secrets unreservedly, and into his only. The very joy of this woman was a sort of grief, or so tender, at least, that its expression was tears. Her sensibilities were so weak and tremulous, that perhaps they ought not to be talked about in a book . . . wherever she went she touched and charmed everyone of the male sex, as invariably as she awakened the scorn and incredulity of her own sisterhood. I think it was her weakness which was her principal charm: —a kind of sweet submission and softness, which seemed to appeal to each man she met for his sympathy and protection.

[I, iii, 36–37]

Mockery lies coiled within this praise, the same exasperation that has caused the narrator earlier to characterize Amelia's uncritical acceptance of other people's opinions as a "fidelity much too humble-minded to think for itself." Yet this is genuine ambivalence.

The grotesque interplay of tenderness and contemptuous hostility exposes both the narrator's emotional contortions and Amelia's own grotesque fusion of selfishness and self-mortification. Through his own ambivalence the narrator reveals the stress of stereotypic responses that have deformed Amelia's character.

The novel relentlessly exposes the emotional mechanism that causes her to warp Georgy into a replica of his father, an even more extreme version of the selfish masculine arrogance that is the obverse of her own selflessness. Under the pressure of this development in plot and characterization, the narrator's irony finally breaks free into direct, unmistakable condemnation of the male-controlled sexual system:

A disposition naturally simple and demanding protection; a long course of poverty and humility, of daily privations, and hard words, of kind offices and no returns, had been her lot since womanhood almost, or since her luckless marriage with George Osborne. You who see your betters bearing up under this shame every day, meekly suffering under the slights of fortune, gentle and unpitied . . . do you ever step down from your prosperity and wash the feet of these poor wearied beggars? . . . Directly she understood it to be her duty, it was this young woman's nature . . . to sacrifice herself and to fling all that she had at the feet of the beloved object. During what long thankless nights had she worked out her fingers for little Georgy . . . what buffets, scorns, privations, poverties had she endured for father and mother! . . . O you poor women! O you poor secret martyrs and victims, whose life is a torture, who are stretched on racks in your bedrooms, and who lay your heads down on the block daily at the drawing-room table; every man who watches your pains, or peers into those dark places where the torture is administered to you, must pity you—and—thank God that he has a beard.

[LVII, 556]

This reaches a nearly hysterical condemnation of masculine sadism, sadism concealed within the same sort of protective, pitying tenderness the narrator himself has lavished on Amelia. Even in this passage he virtually canonizes her for the martyrdom of her emotional and social life. At the same time the lurid voyeurism of the sexual references is unmistakable. These attitudes cannot

easily be reconciled with each other or explained away as inconsistencies of a confused and careless novelist. The narrative imagination is ambivalent but not confused, contorted, but not careless;
it is fascinating in its obsessive self-revelation but even more significant in its revelations of the corrupt sexual system of *Vanity
Fair*.

What Wolfgang Iser has said of *Vanity Fair*'s narrative techniques
holds true for major novels of Dickens, Collins, and Trollope as
well:

the narrator deliberately leaves open the inferences that are to be drawn
from this information [about characters and situations]. Consequently,
empty spaces are bound to occur, spurring the reader's imagination to
detect the assumption which might have motivated the narrator's
attitude. . . .

    . . . such a novel is not going to offer him pictures of another world
that will make him forget the sordid nature of this one; the reader is
forced, rather, to exercise his own critical faculties in order to relieve his
distress by uncovering potential alternatives arising out of the world he
has read about. . . .

    The reader is constantly forced to think in terms of alternatives, as the
only way in which he can avoid the unambiguous and suspect position
of the characters is to visualize the possibilities which they have not
thought of. While he is working out these alternatives the scope of his
own judgment expands, and he is constantly invited to test and weigh
the insights he has arrived at as a result of the profusion of situations
offered him. The esthetic appeal of such a technique consists in the fact
that it allows a certain latitude for the individual character of the reader,
but also compels specific reactions—often unobtrusively—without ex-
pressly formulating them.[2]

    Each novelist typically uses somewhat different methods for
alerting us to ambivalence in the narrator's sexual attitudes. Thackeray's narrators usually do mingle satire and sentiment. Collins'
multiple narrators display a wide range of narrative peculiarities—
from the occasional meandering of Walter Hartright to the repeated comic misogyny of Gabriel Betteredge. But these narrators
are often notable for the conspicuous irrelevance of their commentary to the immediate dramatic situations or intents of their

narratives. Walter Hartright, whose authority as a narrator of *The Woman in White* is never directly challenged, ruminates—for little apparent reason—on the memory of his first encounter with Marian Halcombe:

The easy elegance of every movement of her limbs and body as soon as she began to advance from the far end of the room, set me in a flutter of expectation to see her face clearly. She left the window—and I said to myself, The lady is dark. She moved forward a few steps—and I said to myself, The lady is young. She approached nearer—and I said to myself (with a sense of surprise which words fail me to express), The lady is ugly!

. . . The lady's complexion was almost swarthy, and the dark down on her upper lip was almost a mustache. She had a large, firm, masculine mouth and jaw; prominent, piercing, resolute brown eyes; and thick, coal-black hair, growing unusually low down on her forehead. Her expression—bright, frank, and intelligent—appeared, while she was silent, to be altogether wanting in those feminine attractions of gentleness and pliability, without which the beauty of the handsomest woman alive is beauty incomplete. To see such a face as this set on shoulders that a sculptor would have longed to model—to be charmed by the modest graces of action through which the symmetrical limbs betrayed their beauty when they moved, and then to be almost repelled by the masculine form and masculine look of the features in which the perfectly-shaped figure ended—was to feel a sensation oddly akin to the helpless discomfort familiar to us all in sleep, when we recognize yet cannot reconcile the anomalies and contradictions of a dream.

[I, 46–47]

Nothing at all comes of this grafting of a stereotypic male face onto a stereotypic female body, in terms of the overt narrative, though Hartright lingers agog over it as though it were the most significant item in the strange mystery he is recounting. Neither Hartright's facile sexual aesthetic nor his ludicrous quandary of attraction and repulsion motivate any action. Yet the scuttling of his erotic expectations does serve as an indirect insight into his love for the traditionally feminine, passive, beautiful Laura Fairlie. It also helps explain his meek abandonment of Laura in deference to the commanding authority of Marian (presumably springing entirely from her "masculine" head). Hartright is a type of irresolute young man who appears in Collins' novels in various guises, as both a quasi-hero and a quasi-villain (Frank Clare in *No Name*, for instance). He is antithetical to viciously masculine figures like Sir Percival Glyde and Count Fosco, but he seems to have lost a firm sexual identity rather than to have gained a positive masculine role. He retains only the ludicrous mannerisms appropriate to the stereotypic masculine attitudes revealed in this passage.

This narrative maundering also alerts us to the emotional conflict within Marian, who so subordinates her conscious purposes to Laura's melodramatic plight that she seems to have no legitimate life of her own. The physical hybridization that seems to be a bad antifeminist joke (and the sort of "obstinate conceit" that Dickens said made enemies of Collins' readers) recoils on Hartright and reveals both the shallowness of his initial sexual values and the strength of Marian's unconventional character. What Hartright sees as repellently "masculine" we come to recognize as a sign of Marian's intelligence and resolute will.

The sort of narrative inconsistency that alerts us to this crucial psychological anomaly (bound up with the fragmentation and abuse of female personality that forms the substance of the novel's mystery plot) is repeated in all Collins' novels, whether the narrators are personal or impersonal. A directly allied narrative method is a kind of commentary that *is* relevant to the dramatic situation but curiously inadequate. In *No Name*, for example, Norah Vanstone cannot restrain her violent objection to the romantic relationship between Frank and her sister Magdalen; like Marian Halcombe, Norah seems deeply implicated in the erotic situation in ways she does not understand. When she forces out an apology for her outburst after Frank and Magdalen are engaged, the narrator speculates that she has been motivated by "her obstinate reliance on her own opinions." This explanation is offered despite the fact that the novel will prove her distrust correct. And the intensity of Norah's passion, which would be appropriate in a rival lover of Frank whom he had rejected, is even less adequately accounted for by this brief and otiose explanation.

Collins' narrators (and his characters) are often quite willing to offer—or perhaps obtrude is a better description—lengthy evaluations of characters' motives and personalities. But these commentaries frequently underscore, by their inadequacy, the intriguing psychological material that the novels are all the while developing through indirect, symbolic methods. The commentary thus accomplishes two major ironic objectives: it focuses attention on a crucial obtuseness in the narrator, making unconscious biases as significant as conscious intents; and it focuses attention on circumstances that the narrator cannot account for, prompting the reader to seek out implicit patterns of meaning.

Trollope's narrators usually create an impression of urbane detachment from the stories they recount, as if they were dilettantes in the arts of fiction and psychology:

I am not going to describe the Vavasors' Swiss tour. It would not be fair on my readers. 'Six weeks in the Bernese Oberland, by a party of three,' would have but very small chance of success in the literary world at present, and I should consider myself to be dishonest if I attempted to palm off such matter on the public in the pages of a novel. It is true that I have just returned from Switzerland, and should find such a course of writing very convenient. But I dismiss the temptation, strong as it is. Retro age, Satanas.

[5]

This sort of commentary calls attention to itself (and deflects attention from the immediate progress of the story) just as much as the more obviously assertive intrusions by narrators of Thackeray, Dickens, and Collins. And it gradually insinuates the same sense of an intriguing gap between the story and the narrator that separates presentation from interpretation (the exact opposite of the impression that novelists like James, Austen, and Eliot try to convey).

The way the narrator of *Can You Forgive Her?* blithely ignores a crucial psychological motive—the description of Alice Vavasor's intense resistance to marriage with John Grey as a kind of madness—illustrates the characteristic failure of Trollope's narrators to respond to the psychological implications of the stories. The dramatic encounter between the two characters is so charged and potentially so subversive of the narrator's own professed attitudes that *some* acknowledgment of its import seems necessary. When Alice writes to her fiancé asking for more time to consider whether they are temperamentally suited to each other, a startling phrase breaks through the calm demeanor of her prose: "What if I should wake some morning after six months living with you, and tell you that the quiet of your home was making me mad?" (10). John Grey calmly refuses to acknowledge the validity of Alice's fears, assuming (as she recognizes) "so great a superiority that he felt himself able to treat *any resolve of hers* as the petulance of a child" (11; our emphasis); but he also describes her reactions in his own extreme terms that clash with the "imperturbed serenity of his manner":

"I learned, love, that something had been said or done during your journey,—or perhaps only something thought, that had made you melancholy, and filled your mind for a while with those unsubstantial and indefinable regrets for the past which we are all apt to feel at certain moments of our life. There are few of us who do not encounter, now and again, some of that irrational spirit of sadness which, when overindulged, drives men to madness and self-destruction. I used to know well what it was before I knew you; but since I have had the hope of having you in my house, I have banished it utterly. In that I think I have been stronger than you."

[11]

The arrogance and formal phrasing should not disguise the import of Grey's words. He refuses, infuriatingly, to accept the truth of her emotional reaction ("Oh, but I will not," he says, "if that would be adverse to my own interests") and insists on treating it as if it were a minor physical indisposition; but he has experienced a threat of emotional derangement as profound as hers. We have no reason to doubt his confession or its disturbing implications; and it makes his dogged refusal to release Alice, or even listen to her pleas, much more credible and interesting. Alice responds with appropriate force when he recommends that she convalesce from her "malady" through that Victorian cure-all, a change of air: "You treat me as if I were partly silly, and partly insane; but it is not so. The change you speak of should be in my nature and in yours" (11).

The narrator alone seems to have no sense of the crucial issues involved. He describes this fierce struggle of wills, which forces out psychological revelations that challenge the basic values of both characters, as coolly as if it were the most commonplace courtship ritual in the respectable world. He does not evaluate, make connections, underscore ironies with Thackerian or Dickensian intensities of personal response; he simply describes, chatting on comfortably as the encounter releases its explosive material.

We do not have a transparent narrative medium, however. The narrator's casual, nonjudgmental tone is, in fact, frequently a pose that allows him to stray into sexual pronouncements sharply at odds with the actual psychological developments of his characters:

> A woman's life is important to her,—as is that of a man to him,—not chiefly in regard to that which she shall do with it. . . . if she shall have recognized the necessity of truth and honesty for the purposes of her life, I do not know that she need ask herself many questions as to what she will do with it.
>
> Alice Vavasor was ever asking herself that question, and had by degrees filled herself with a vague idea that there was a something to be done; a something over and beyond, or perhaps altogether beside that marrying and having two children;—if only she knew what it was.
>
> [11]

The narrator gently regrets Alice's preoccupation with this question ("That Alice Vavasor had thought too much about it, I feel quite sure . . . till her mind had become filled with some undefined idea of the importance to her of her own life"; 11) and it is for this that he chiefly asks us to forgive her.

The revolutionary force of Alice's question builds throughout the novel, however, not only despite but because of the narrator's refusal to take it seriously. For, as with the other novelists, our frustration at the narrator's obtuseness serves to draw us into the "counterplot" of the novel, impelling us to make the connections the narrators do not make. Their very fallibility establishes them as real personalities, convincing in their imperfections. Now this may well be a narrative method that infuriates some readers, but it can be remarkably effective in disclosing counterplots of sexual oppression, in allying us with the heroines' plight, and in arousing the reader's personal involvement with this substratum of the novel.

All the while Trollope's bland, easy-going narrator in *Can You Forgive Her?*—like narrators of Dickens, Thackeray, and Collins— is quietly establishing the "data" which will form themselves into patterns that clash with his own assumptions. He sometimes juxtaposes circumstances that reflect ironically on each other without any narrative mediation. At the very moment when Glencora is likely to elope with Burgo Fitzgerald, for instance, with Alice Vavasor's censure and the narrator's patronizing pity turned full upon her ("Poor, wretched, overburthened child, to whom the commonest lessons of life had not yet been taught"), the narrator remarks, in passing, that her severely respectable husband had once himself contemplated an adulterous affair with Lady Hartletop. He offers a multitude of direct ironic comments on sexual attitudes and practices, comments which are never gathered into the general indictment of sexual values they seem to press toward. He notes, for example, the arrogance in John Grey's treatment of Alice as an appendage: "he no more thought of giving her up than a man thinks of having his leg cut off because he strains his sinews" (10); but he persists in treating Grey as a model of masculine virtue and strength.

Dickens' narrators exhibit an extraordinary range of tones and attitudes in the course of his career, so it is more difficult to categorize the ways in which his narrators call attention to their own inadequacies. They may buttonhole us and wheedle or harangue like *Vanity Fair*'s narrator; they may veer off into sentimental rhapsodies while the action idles; they may be as neglectful or wrong-headed as the narrators of Trollope or Collins. But they also have a special, characteristic tendency to reveal ambivalence toward the psychosexual matter of their narratives through forms of displacement, in which emotional energy is transferred from character to narrator.

This excessive participation of the narrator in the characters' emotional experience is especially obvious where the emotions are erotic. During the wedding of John Harmon and Bella Wilfer in

Our Mutual Friend, the narrator can neither handle the sexual situation nor leave it alone. As the narrator repeatedly intrudes and upstages him, Harmon dwindles to little more than an enveloper of Bella, who "vanishes" in his embrace. The love between Harmon and Bella produces a coy rhetoric that arises more from the sentimental desires of the narrator than from the personalities of the characters: "So, she leaning on her husband's arm, they turned homeward by a rosy path which the gracious sun struck out for them in its setting. And oh, there are days in this life, worth life and worth death. And oh, what a bright old song it is, that oh, 'tis love, 'tis love, 'tis love, that makes the world go round!" (IV, iv, 671). The narrator here does not so much misunderstand his characters as misappropriate them; he virtually burlesques their romance through his own emotional paroxysms. As the narrator upstages his characters, though, he alerts us to the distortions and repressions within the novel's erotic situations. As we suggested in the preceding chapter, multiple forms of narrative fraud underscore the fraudulence of the whole sexual world in *Our Mutual Friend*.

The way Dickens' narrators distort the characters' emotional states is most obvious in their sentimentally erotic effusions over the heroines. But it is also true of their complementary extremes of repulsion—significantly greatest when the object is male, and especially so when he is a false lover or false patriarch.

Just as sentimentality and cynicism are equally corrupt evasions of psychological reality in *Vanity Fair,* self-corrupting sentimentality is often the origin of Dickens' fulminating moral rhetoric. Like the narrator of *Vanity Fair* in his adoration of the martyred Amelia, the narrator of *Little Dorrit* exalts Amy Dorrit for the very self-mortifying virtues that are the novel's chief example of outrageous oppression. Unable to confront this contradiction, the narrator displaces his rage onto the most contrived and inconsequential of villains, the parody son, lover, and gentleman Rigaud/Blandois: "Assuredly he did look then, though he looked his politest, as if any real philanthropist could have desired no better employment than to lash a great stone to his neck, and drop him into the water flowing beyond the dark arched gateway in which he stood" (II, vii, 511).

The novel fulfills this philanthropic urge by collapsing a house on Rigaud, and the narrator describes the execution with macabre relish: "they found the dirty heap of rubbish that had been the foreigner, before his head had been shivered to atoms, like so much glass, by the great beam that lay upon him, crushing him" (II, xxxi, 794). This intense, savage hostility, only slightly more controlled in the commentary on Merdle worship and Merdle's death, vents a rage that can find no suitable villain to blame for a corruption that is implicit in the culture's system of sexual roles.

The extremes of satire and sentiment are thus in continual conflict in Dickens' novels, as in Thackeray's, not because they are actual polarities but because they have a common origin in the narrator's ambivalence. The self-protective division of the terms reaches a nearly hermetic isolation in the divided narrative structure of *Bleak House*. In this novel there is literally no communication between the two narrators or the contradictory urges they embody. Ambivalence has achieved a paradoxical as well as an appropriate form.

Thus, all these novelists engage us in their presentations of sexual values and roles through a narrative imagination that is deeply, essentially ambivalent. The narrators' most distinctive conscious attitudes are formed, at least in part, as reactions against unrecognized fears and desires, so that they are caught in the dilemma of attempting to resist as well as disclose the significance of their stories. We encounter, in other words, an imagination that reflects the reality of the crisis in sexual values as it was actually experienced by many Victorians and as it is still commonly experienced today. We know that each of these novelists could have been, at best, only partly aware of the revolutionary implications of their novels; we know that they all resisted at least some of those implications in public and private life. But this really only testifies to their powers of intuition; it does not diminish the impact of the fictions they have created.

Once again, Iser's comment on *Vanity Fair* is illuminating for all four novelists: "it is not the slice of life, but the means of observing it that constitutes the reality." As Iser has said of the novel in general, in another context, "it actively involves the reader in the process of synthesizing an assembly of constantly shifting viewpoints, which not only modify one another, but also influence past and future syntheses in the reading process."[3] Though Dickens, Collins, Thackeray, and Trollope create such narrative structures less self-consciously and less deliberately than novelists like Sterne, Melville, Gide, Joyce, or Beckett, their narrative techniques can have as profound an impact on the reader's imagination.

SYMBOLIC ANALOGIES AND THE "COUNTERPLOT"

Once we are alerted to the presence of psychological and thematic material that the narrators cannot acknowledge directly, the motifs of this counterplot proliferate and begin to form symbolic structures. Perhaps the symbolic effect most likely to arouse the reader's awareness of unannounced complexities in these novels is behavior that expresses an individual character's unarticulated emotions. In these novels it often takes the form of sudden, unexplained shifts in mood, puzzling or even bizarre physical mannerisms, or some other impulsive/compulsive behavior that is recorded but not adequately accounted for by the narrators: Esther Summerson's bursts of extreme affection for Ada and key-jingling to suppress onslaughts of agitation; Alice Vavasor's sharp fear of potential madness; Rachel Verinder's sudden, violent dislike of Franklin Blake and Rosanna Spearman's mysterious actions after the theft of the moonstone; Magdalen Vanstone's sudden obsession with acting and her remarkable facility for mimicry of the role-bound women in her family. Of course, this sort of personal psychological symbolism is as common in literature as it is in social experience. What is unusual in these instances—and an abundance of analogous instances in the novels—is the absence of a readily apparent structure of causation to account for or "contain" the aberrant behavior.

In a contrasting instance, when Dorothea Brooke is overwhelmed by a sense of misery she cannot fathom during her wedding journey, the narrator of *Middlemarch* offers the reader a direct (if incomplete) account of its psychological sources. Or, earlier, when Dorothea impulsively abandons the horse-riding she loves, we have already encountered a number of situations, narrative analyses, and metaphoric patterns in action and description that provide a context for understanding the psychological forces that motivate her. The narrator has spoken directly of Dorothea's distrust of her "pagan sensuous" nature and has implied her tendency to seek validation of spiritual desires through suppression of physical urges. In this instance, the narrator of *Middlemarch* offers no direct interpretation, but Celia is there with a shrewdness about psychological impulses we have already come to trust: "Dorothea likes giving up." Dorothea's impulse is further elucidated by the pressures exerted upon her in this particular dramatic situation. The immediate cause of her "brusque resolution" is "annoyance that Sir James would be soliciting her attention when she wanted to give it all to Mr. Casaubon." Her reaction is thus set in the context of the romantic rivalry between the two men, unsuspected at this point by the characters but clearly established for the reader by both narrative and dramatic means. The two men represent, in a plausible social situation, Dorothea's conflicting spiritual and sensous desires. None of this reduces her mental life to a formula, but it does provide a controlling pattern which guides our exploration of the subtleties in her psychological development.

Because the novels of Dickens, Thackeray, Trollope, and Collins often lack this sort of interplay between individual behavior and directly articulated patterns of theme and action, the behavior prompted by a character's unconscious motivation may at first seem excrescent. But it can be compelling even before we discover the hidden structures that will make it intelligible. In fact, this symbolic behavior usually arouses a more immediate and more convincing sense of psychological complexity than the narrators' direct assessments.

Collins frequently draws attention directly to oddities in his characters' behavior that are never fully accounted for. *No Name*, for instance, alerts us to unusual emotional forces at work within the characters, and the narrator's inadequate explanations of them underscore their importance. The novel's credibility depends directly on its mimetic accuracy. If we are convinced, it is (initially, at least) through a rather intuitive sense that a person in that situation might well behave in just that way—with little narrative mediation to guide us to this conclusion. When Norah Vanstone blurts out her furious objections to Magdalen's romantic involvement with Frank Clare, we are as surprised as Magdalen, but not likely to attribute her bitterness, as both Magdalen and the narrator do, to some vague "obstinacy" in her character:

"Poor Frank! [Magdalen says to Norah] How you do hate him to be sure. What on earth has he done to offend you?"

Norah's self-control began to show signs of failing her. Her dark cheeks glowed, her delicate lips trembled, before she spoke again. Magdalen paid more attention to her parasol than to her sister. She tossed it high in the air, and caught it. . . . Before she could catch it for the third time, Norah seized her passionately by the arm. . . .

"You are treating me heartlessly," she said. "For shame, Magdalen—for shame!" . . .

Norah, turning paler and paler, barred the way to her. "If I hold you by main force," she said, "you shall stop and hear me. I have watched this Francis Clare; I know him better than you do. . . . He is selfish, he is ungrateful, he is ungenerous—he is only twenty, and he has the worst failings of a mean old age already. And this is the man I find you meeting in secret—the man who has taken such a place in your favour that you are deaf to the truth about him, even from *my* lips! . . .

Magdalen looked at her in unconcealed astonishment.

"You are so violent," she said, "and so unlike yourself that I hardly know you."

[I, 98–99]

Frank is certainly selfish and unattractive (and Magdalen's love for him is a puzzling emotional reaction in itself), but his behavior so far in the novel has seemed more feckless than vicious. Though he will prove to be thoroughly unreliable, he has done nothing so far to justify such violent hostility.

Yet, though the narrator, as usual, fails to probe Norah's motives, and though we know too little about her at this point to make any definitive assessments ourselves, her behavior is thoroughly convincing. Norah is the elder sister, twenty-six years old, unmarried, with certain "little formal peculiarities of manner," her face habitually "clouded by a certain quiet reserve." Her eighteen-year-old sister is exuberantly active, reckless, seductive, charming, favored by both Mr. Vanstone and the household's moral guardian Miss Garth (whose temperament ought to ally her with Norah). Magdalen has just recently mimicked Norah's mannerisms as the basis for her brilliantly successful performance of Julia in an amateur production of *The Rivals*. (The mannerisms may well suggest Norah's growing anxiety at her own prospects.) And now Magdalen has attracted the young man who may be an inadequate suitor but seems to be the only available prospect for romance and marriage. These circumstances have, without the necessity for our conscious assessment of them, prepared us to accept immediately and, it may seem, intuitively the credibility of Norah's outburst. And they have certainly made her possible motives an intriguing ground for speculation.

This scene calls upon our intuitive abilities and what might be called our symbolic memory more than it does our analytical or conceptual powers—at least in its first, critical impact and in our initial efforts to probe for meaningful patterns of motivation. In the course of novels by Dickens, Thackeray, Trollope, and Collins a multitude of similar "local" revelations gradually cohere into patterns of unconscious psychological motivation. But they are not the sole means of revealing these patterns, and they do not develop in isolation. Symbolic techniques include, for instance, analogies in situation or role rather than behavioral symbolism. Once alerted by the various techniques, we are likely to discern a multiplicity of developing symbolic relations. In this way individual mannerisms quickly gather a general metaphoric significance, as elements of symbolic patterns that interconnect individual characters in a comprehensive system of hidden forces and relationships.

Thus when Amelia mourns the apparent end of her romance with George Osborne "like a mother nursing a dead infant," we have a metaphoric incident that not only enlarges our understanding beyond her particular emotional plight at this moment but sends it working in directions that seem contrary to the designs of the surface narrative. It is interrelated with a number of other metaphoric passages, all suggesting that Amelia's love for George Osborne is tainted with fatality from the beginning: her marriage bed is described in funereal terms; her life is completely sacrificed to her idolized image of George, both before and after his death; her sacrifice is explicitly described as martyrdom; and she helps make Georgy into a replica of his dead father. This consistent pattern depends on Amelia's behavior and on the narrator's metaphors—a crucial way in which narrators of all these novels signal symbolic elements that they never directly acknowledge. And it brings her circumstances into surprising analogy with her apparent opposite—Jane Osborne.

Jane is kept celibate, socially isolated, and terrified by her tyrannical father, while Amelia is indulged and encouraged to marry the man she loves by Mr. Sedley. But the emblematic image blatantly associated with Jane's condition allies her with Amelia: the clock on the Osborne mantelpiece set in an effigy of Agamemnon's sacrifice of Iphigenia. Both Amelia and Jane are sacrificed, are conditioned to sacrifice themselves, on the altar of masculine power, whether brutally or suasively exercised by their fathers, whether they are chosen or not chosen by the male suitors who have the power to determine their futures. Both so abandon their own claims to an identity separate from the men they subserve and both submit so completely to men who rule their lives that the persistent metaphors of torture, sacrifice, and death come to seem fully appropriate. This symbolic conflation of the stereotypic roles of submissive spinster and submissive wife undermines the idea that marriage is the appropriate fulfillment of a woman's life; but it also suggests that the negative condition of simply remaining unmarried offers no greater security or freedom from oppression.

Characters are consistently linked in this way through symbolic analogy, and the analogical relationships form themselves into distinct sets which challenge the assumptions that shore up manifest sexual roles. In *Can You Forgive Her?* Alice Vavasor, Glencora Palliser, and Mrs. Greenow are all women of remarkable energy, wit, and resolute will who are constrained by male-controlled rituals of courtship and marriage. The only power that each one really has is the power to choose between two deficient men. This is a power that will be lost through its exercise (the dilemma of the traditional courtship role women play), and the alternatives are both grim at best, disastrous at worst. For all the differences among these women and their situations, they share a defining dilemma.

Glencora faces either a respectable life that would stifle her sensual, imaginative, and social desires or a life of impoverished dissipation with Burgo Fitzgerald that is likely to become just as stultifying, as dominated by the egotistic needs of the male. Alice's choice lies between the suburban placidity of John Grey and the mock-Byronic destructiveness of George Vavasor. Like Glencora's alternatives, both these marriages would be controlled by the needs of the husband, which are self-centered and regressive. Mrs. Greenow seems to have freer scope as a comic analogue to the main actions. She has played the marriage market adroitly for her own economic advantage by marrying a wealthy old man. But as a widow and as a wife she has endured a boring life that cannot provide for her rich imaginative and strong sensual nature. And she can change her situation only through marriage to a man much less imaginative, vital, and attractive than she is—the same spurious choice that Alice and Glencora face. So Mrs. Greenow derives as much second-rate pleasure as she can from pitting the two rivals, Cheeseacre and Bellfield, against each other before she capitulates to the constraints of the sexual system and chooses one for a husband.

This is also the basic effect of the more tortuous, less shrewdly conscious, more guilt-ridden actions of Alice and Glencora. They too manage to forestall or subvert the constricting roles for a while and to infuse new purpose, energy, and excitement into their lives (however agonizing the process). And they manage to infuse a lesser but similar vitality into the sterile existences of the men who are romantically involved with them.

Alice, in effect, refuses to treat her money as the male-controlled commodity it would ordinarily be (as both inheritance and dowry). Instead, she intuitively discovers a strategy that exposes the pretensions of the men who are attempting to lay claim to her.

She begins to systematically destroy her fortune by giving it to George Vavasor, to enable him to buy a seat in Parliament. She makes the brutally proud, brutally masculine George dependent on her. But more than this, Alice's grants force him to live up to his political professions, to attempt a life of some significance commensurate with his exalted notions of himself. He is thoroughly humiliated in this process: bilked repeatedly by his parliamentary agent; rebuffed by the members of his party; and frustrated in his attempts to understand and use political power. All this exposes the shoddiness and pretentiousness of the man and the system. Alice's plan also causes John Grey to use his own small fortune to try to save hers (a kind of male dowry given *before* the marriage). This plot situation verges on the farcical spirit of the Greenow subplot, as John Grey feels compelled to covertly fund his rival, a man he thoroughly despises. The opposition between them becomes a bitter sort of analogy, as both engage in economic deception of Alice. Alice even succeeds in arousing her father to care for something more substantial than ordering his dinner and drawing his unearned pay.

In the analogous action of the other main plot, Burgo Fitzgerald bungles his second attempt at elopement, after wheedling one last loan from his aunt. Plantagenet Palliser is forced to abandon the cabinet post he has been working toward all his adult life (the Chancellorship of the Exchequer) in order to save his marriage with Glencora. Or, to put it another way, he is at last compelled to pay some attention to the personality and needs of his wife. By using her barrenness to rationalize her proposed elopement with Burgo, Glencora unconsciously protests her status as a Palliser-making apparatus and forces Plantagent to recognize the thorough barrenness of their marriage relationship. Glencora's near-adultery makes direct use of her erotic powers, as Mrs. Greenow's stratagems have done; but she too has to settle finally for the least inadequate of the men who court her.

Both Glencora and Alice, despite the sense each has that she is unworthy or even degraded, use their stereotypic roles to gain a somewhat better chance for personal happiness than they had originally. And their actions constitute an implicit protest against a callous and oppressive sexual system, and a plea for more decent human relations with some freedom from the brutal force of money and political power.

In similar ways, analogical relationships that challenge the assumptions and practices of the prevailing Victorian sexual system take shape in the novels of all four authors. The most complex and intriguing structures of analogy are implicit and often covert. Episodic plot structure, various discursive narrative techniques (Dickens' elaborately euphemistic, Trollope's elaborately digressive style), and the very complexity of these novelists' array of characters and situations allow a free emergence and interplay of analogies. But just as significant in stimulating the reader to perceive the existence of these analogies are the narrowness, rigidity, and obtuseness of many of the categories the narrators offer to account for the anomalous material they present. Thus, the creative effects of inadequate narrators and the presence of implicit symbolic relationships work together to disclose and develop the primary sexual themes of these novels.

SUBVERTED STEREOTYPES

Most areas of Victorian culture are marred by a fundamental ambivalence toward women. This ambivalence works most complexly and destructively, as these novels all suggest, in women themselves. They enjoy few of the pleasures that the exercise of power, however vicious, can give to men. They not only endure but often embrace their status as victims. And if they do rebel, they are prey to a self-contempt that is even more destructive than society's opprobrium. Because male fantasies of fear, desire, and hatred are so often disguised by extreme idealizations of women (and the attendant rigid moral constraints), the literature that expresses this ambivalence often seems grotesque. But its grotesqueness can both reveal and implicitly question the contradictory forces that have produced it. This makes the literature of ambivalence, which necessarily deals in stereotypes, thoroughly different in its design and its impact from truly stereotyped literature.

Truly stereotyped literature is one-dimensional. In *Ravenshoe*

(1862) by Henry Kingsley, for instance, two stereotypically fallen women are punished for their departure from the stereotype of the pure woman. Ellen Horton, a lower-class fallen woman, redeems herself by becoming a nun and serving in the Crimean War. Even though she loves a man who loves her also, despite her past, the novel prefers the retribution of perpetual chastity and self-sacrifice. Adelaide Summers comes from a higher class but jilts the hero and runs off with a man more likely to provide her with money and a title. They marry soon after and become partners in his gambling plots. At the end he is greatly reformed, but she falls off a horse and is crippled from the waist down, never again to walk or have a sex life. Her departure from pure femininity is unequivocally—perhaps even unconsciously on Kingsley's part—punished by sexual maiming. Both Ellen and Adelaide are tools of a narrative design with no psychological dimensions beyond its stereotypic patterns; nothing in their language, thoughts, or actions reveals the kind of tensions we have seen in the female characters of Trollope, Dickens, Collins, and Thackeray.

The psychological mechanism of stereotypic fiction is certainly intriguing; but understanding its nature depends almost totally on the predisposition of the reader to perceive its biases and understand their sources in the mind and culture of the author. To put it simply, we must know more than the novel does. Furthermore, the psychological terms of a novel like *Ravenshoe* are rigid, static, extreme simplifications of the experiences they attempt to represent. They are the fictional creations of an obsessive will and are designed—though the design is probably unconscious—to avoid the very complexity and the contradictory nature of experience that the novelists we have been discussing make their primary subject.

Trollope's Signora Madeline Vesey Neroni (*Barchester Towers*), though apparently crippled, like Kingsley's Adelaide, as an authorial punishment for sexual rebellion, illustrates the difference between ambivalent and truly stereotyped literature. Madeline begins as a sexual temptress of uncertain principles, marries because she is pregnant, and is crippled in one hip and leg through her husband's cruelty. As a married woman (though she has left her husband) who is poor and crippled, she is not an eligible wife for the men who pursue her. But, as Robert Polhemus has said, "the proper men of Barset love her ostentatious sexuality"—even though they cannot manage to fulfill their desires either licitly or illicitly.[4] Her own delight in tormenting them and their frustrated attraction to her create as effective an impasse to the fulfillment of sexual desires as Adelaide's experiences in *Ravenshoe*. The difference is that Trollope makes the clash of contradictory desires evident; the inadequacy is shared by men and women; and no one bears the sole burden of pious authorial censure. More than this, he uses Madeline to satirize the values implicit in the story of his conventional heroine.

Madeline's caustic estimate of Eleanor's mourning for her husband is an excellent example of this dialectic: "She is just one of those English nonentities who would tie her head up in a bag for three months every summer, if her mother and grandmother had tied up their heads before her." And in discussing marriage in general with her sister, Madeline says:

"I hate your mawkish sentimentality, Lotte. You know as well as I do in what way husbands and wives generally live together; you know how far the warmth of conjugal affection can withstand the trial of a bad dinner, of a rainy day, or of the least privation which poverty brings with it; you know what freedom a man claims for himself, what slavery he would exact from his wife if he could! And you know also how wives generally obey. Marriage means tyranny on one side and deceit on the other."

[15]

Madeline's ridicule gives her something of Becky Sharp's status as a satiric projection of the author. Her crippling, however, is evidence of Trollope's ambivalent attitudes toward such an open challenge by a woman to the respectable system of sexual relations and toward even such a subdued expression of female sexual desire.[5]

There are, of course, plenty of female stereotypes in the novels of Dickens, Thackeray, Trollope, and Collins—angels, shrews, coquettes, man-hunting spinsters, and so forth. But the contexts in which they operate usually arouse our sense of the inadequacy of the roles to contain the characters created, and imply a more fundamental challenge to the whole system that perpetuates such stereotypes.

In *Great Expectations*, for instance, Mrs. Joe begins as a shrew and "bad mother"; but even before Orlick's brutal assault, her paralysis, and her death make these semicomic roles disturbingly inappropriate, Dickens has carefully given us information that presents Mrs. Joe as a victim as well as an abuser: her gaunt, raw-visaged appearance in a marriage market that prizes the sort of feminine beauty that Estella has; the child forced on her when she was eighteen, poor, and unmarried; the husband who is no match for her energetic intelligence.

Not every stereotypic figure in these novels (male or female) is so complexly qualified and undermined as Mrs. Joe is. Some remain instances of their author's as well as their culture's biases. But the primary characters are almost never limited to the stereotypic roles that may initially confine them.

In fact, many of the major female figures in the novels of Trollope, Dickens, Thackeray, and Collins manage to subvert the roles assigned them through their own resolute actions. In most cases, the character contrives—or the novel contrives for her—to assimilate a number of stereotypic roles, both male and female. This usually involves experimentation with a wide range of roles and psychological possibilities. It may also involve a parody of stereotypes or an effort to alter and fuse them to create new roles, more satisfying to the actual range of the character's desires and capacities.

Magdalen Vanstone, in Collins' *No Name*, is one of the clearest instances of experimentation with stereotypic roles. In an effort to regain her name and her inheritance—taken from her through a legal technicality—Magdalen rejects the limited options she sees in other women's lives. As an impoverished and technically illegitimate woman, she has even more restricted options, according to the norms of respectable society. To achieve her objectives, however, she must remain energetically engaged with the social world. The course she chooses is to impersonate women in stereotyped roles, thus eluding the constraint of any one role and making them serve her purposes rather than conforming to theirs. After losing her parents, her inheritance, and the legal right to her own name, Magdalen becomes an actress. She chooses a socially suspect role in perference to the genteel, standard, but powerless role of governess. After impersonating her sister and their former governess, Magdalen invents a character in an attempt to seduce the man who has been granted her lost inheritance into marrying her. The stock resolution the novel provides for her—marriage to a decent, honorable man—is much less important than her exploration of her own character through imaginative encounters with prevailing stereotypes.

In fact, the surface conventionality of much of this fiction ought not to obscure the radical shifts in perspective that distinguish it from much earlier literature. Most Western narrative confines the action of its female characters within a male-oriented context. The power of the female character is the power to arouse male desire and stimulate male action, whether as goddess, witch, wife, or mistress.

In order for the woman of traditional Western literature to act on her own rather than as a reflex of men—to be a Clytemnestra rather than an Iphigenia, a Portia rather than a Jessica—she has to usurp a male position of power. This action, so contrary to the daily experience of the culture, is necessarily aberrant, atypical, and short-lived. However heroic, however much power it temporarily confers on the female character, it is purchased through a kind of self-annihilation: all pretense to an independent feminine nature is abandoned. This process reveals the dominance of masculine values in the culture more clearly than traditional feminine subservience usually does (direct imitation rather than moon-like reflection); and it acknowledges more directly the culture's impoverished conceptions of distinctly feminine resources.

The divine and demonic roles assumed by female characters in much Western literature are extreme projections of the subservient and the usurping woman, and ultimately just as subject to masculine patterns of will and desire. Both are temporary transfers of a male commodity. There is no Dulcinea when Don Quixote recovers his senses; Beatrice has died so that Dante may make his magnificent journey and find his salvation; Lady Macbeth's power ebbs once Macbeth is king, and she dies a suicide rather than a heroic warrior.

To many readers and critics, Victorian novels have seemed not only to perpetuate these traditional attitudes, but also—especially in the hands of male novelists—to advocate them in an extreme, regressive form. It is a virtual commonplace that figures like Little Nell and Amelia Sedley are produced by a frenzy of sentimental idealism that seeks to avoid awareness of the reality of sexual discord, and perhaps to help forestall the growing revolt against oppressive sexual conditions. Like most commonplaces, this is part of the truth. An often neglected part of the truth, however, is that some of the male authors who perpetuated and even helped to fashion the image of the angel in the house also wrote novels that began to focus—more directly, intensely, and persistently than ever before in Western literature—on the actual social and psychological conditions of women in their society.

The four novelists do subject their heroines to extreme situations that are hardly direct, simple representations of everyday life. But these extremes still focus our attention on normal roles because they appear in the context of ordinary domestic life. (Again, most earlier Western literature has empowered its female characters through some radical disruption of ordinary social life.) Even those female characters who break with the prescribed patterns— characters like Becky Sharp, Miss Wade, Magdalen Vanstone, and Madeline Neroni—are shaped by a desire to escape the same restrictive domestic roles that the "virtuous" heroines submit to. In representing contemporary sexual life, Dickens, Collins, Thackeray, and Trollope exploited stereotypes; but—as we have shown—they also explored, exposed, and satirized the conceptions of women that have dominated Western culture.

3

DICKENS

WOMEN in Dickens' novels, however they struggle for some self-definition, are always forced into restrictive family roles. Even when they set themselves directly against the family's demands upon them, stereotypic roles reappear in disguised form to shape their lives. In *Little Dorrit*, for instance, Miss Wade attempts to live apart from all ordinary social relations because they necessarily impose the subordinate feminine roles she has found so hateful; but she is finally driven to "adopt" a young girl, Tattycoram. Miss Wade's counterpart, Mrs. Clennam, though she has banished her own son (also adopted) and her own husband, is likewise drawn toward a surrogate daughter, Amy Dorrit. The "adopted" daughters are abused and abandoned; the mothering roles are vengefully destructive. What is true for these characters holds true for all Dickens' novels: despite all resistance, social roles resolve themselves into a fundamental symbolic duality, the relations between parent and child. And those relations are almost invariably both the result and the further cause of psychological abuse.[1]

Courtship plots still figure as prominently in the outward shape of Dickens' novels as they do in the novels of Trollope, Thackeray, and Collins, yet they are invariably a displacement of the conflicts between parents and children that give the novels their real energy. Pip's encounters with Magwitch and Miss Havisham, not the illusory romantic interest in Estella, form the core of *Great Expectations*. Similarly, both Esther's secret relationship with her mother and Florence Dombey's open oppression by her father deflect attention from courtship to the more basic family relations.

In novels like *Oliver Twist* and *Martin Chuzzlewit*, the courtship plot seems vestigial even in the direct narrative.

In a similar way the relations between Dickens' husbands and wives matter primarily as they influence the child—or as they reveal the adults' own status as parents and, often, as symbolic children. Clara Copperfield and Dora Spenlow are child-brides to the end, Joe Gargery is a "larger species of child," Wemmick's Aged P. an aged child. Most often, in fact, one parent is either dead or replaced by a surrogate figure, so attention is focused even more directly on a primary relationship between parent and child. And these relations are always subjected to unusual emotional demands, displacements or reversals of supposedly normal roles, fusions of conflicting roles, and so forth. William Dorrit, Clara Copperfield and Betsey Trotwood, Bumble, Brownlow, and Fagin, the Gargerys, Pickwick, Mrs. Clennam, Jenny Wren, and Miss Havisham are the typical parents in Dickens, however aberrant they are by sociological norms.

Collins, Thackeray, and Trollope share Dickens' perception that the patriarchal social system of Victorian England is thoroughly corrupt; that it is at once immensely powerful in its abuse of individuals and impotent in its ability to bring anyone lasting security or fulfillment; and that its most dangerous effects are its most insidious: the corruption of basic sexual identities and sexual roles. But Dickens' special preoccupation, his most profound insight, concerns the multitude of ways in which corrupt patriarchal values have infiltrated basic family relations, so that their oppressive effect on parent and child alike persists throughout each individual's life. In every Dickens novel this crisis in family relations is the matrix for the major developments in plot, theme, and character.

The oppressive conditions that bind parent and child together always resolve themselves, literally or symbolically, into one corrupting force: a father's tyranny. Abusive surrogate mothers like Miss Barbary and Mrs. Joe assume the forms and emotional power of masculine despotism. And an extraordinary number of female children, in a reversal of roles that is in many ways more damaging than outright tyranny, are forced to assume a parent's responsibilities for actual or surrogate fathers (Nell, Agnes Wickfield, Esther Summerson, Amy Dorrit, Jenny Wren).[2] Though Dickens is immensely varied in characterization and incident, and often wildly funny in the grimmest contexts, the taint of patriarchal abuse spreads through virtually every relationship in his novels.

DICKENS' NOBODADDIES—THE PATRIARCH AT HOME AND AT LARGE

The pitifully few happy families that exist in Dickens' novels have exerted such influence over the imagination of some readers that he is often remembered as the supreme expositor of the Victorian domestic idyll. The magically reformed Scrooge, glowing with Christmas cheer and bursting with benevolent shillings, has apparently fathered a wish that, for some, obliterates the reality of William Dorrit, Magwitch, Dombey, Ralph Nickleby, Fagin, and all the other inadequate or oppressive patriarchs who dominate the novels. The few beleaguered enclaves of domestic harmony that do survive do not quite merit all the narrative glow that suffuses them. Quite simply, something is always wrong with them. The children are nearly imbecilic in their loving innocence (Kit Nubbles, Sloppy). Or the father is unable to settle down to work that is both profitable and satisfying (Micawber, Plornish). Or the child is afflicted with some malady (Tiny Tim, the deaf and dumb child of Caddy and Prince Turveydrop). Or the happy couple is childless (the Boffins and the Bayham Badgers). Always there is a basic deformity in the loving fellowship that the narrators—and many readers apparently—yearn to have firmly established, as a touchstone if not a norm.

After *Pickwick* and *Oliver* the happy family hangs precariously on the lower fringes of the middle classes, in no way representative of the characters or social levels that are the novels' primary concerns. This peculiarly urban version of pastoral is never integrated with the novels' overwhelming indictments of the prevailing Victorian family structure; so it seems an aberration or simply an unwarranted wish-fulfillment. The most intensely sentimental of Dickens' contemporary readers, in fact, seem to have praised the uplifting nature of the narrators' enthusiasm for the few happy families rather than the accuracy of this motif as social description.[3]

Even that blessed family, the Wardles of Dingley Dell, is disrupted by a major challenge to its happiness, and to its values, the elopement of Rachel Wardle. Despite Mr. Wardle's kindly, affectionate regard for Rachel, she cannot be satisfied with the anomalous position of unmarried sister. So she readily submits to any proposal, first Tupman's and then Jingle's. Like the breach of promise suit against Pickwick, the elopement suggests that something is awry in the domestic situations of even the most benevolent patriarchs.

Pickwick fends off the implications of this and other domestic disturbances. His self-protective consciousness insulates him, for example, from the implications of the interpolated tales he encounters. (Once he simply falls asleep during the relation of a tale.) But we should remember the tales Pickwick forgets. One deals with an alcoholic father who dies raving, with no provision for his destitute family. Another involves a man who refuses to rescue the drowning son of his father-in-law because the father-in-law stood by while the man's own wife and children died. A third describes attempted patricide. Already, the novel that Steven Marcus has called the "blest dawn" of Dickens' fictional career is shadowed by the corruption of the father-dominated family.[4]

The typical Dickens family is closer to the lurid melodrama of the interpolated tales than to Pickwick's own attempt at an ideal family (five bachelors with unlimited money and leisure and a desire to avoid anything other than a spectator's role in life). The typical family is inadequate at best, vicious at worst; and the figure who absolutely haunts his fiction is the abandoned, orphaned, or abused child. Almost no family group includes both an adequate mother and father. Potentially loving parents have died or disappeared (the mothers of Oliver Twist, Esther Summerson, Amy Dorrit; the fathers of Arthur Clennam, Lucy Manette, Cissy Jupe). Or a vicious parent frustrates the loving efforts of foster parents (Dombey, John Harmon's father). In these novels, in fact, the presumptive norm of loving father and mother is almost nonex-

istent. Even a minimally nurturing family is an ideal to be struggled for, not a given. And always the family that does succeed
in loving and protecting the child provides only a temporary refuge and almost no strength to combat the forces that assail the
child's basic sense of self. So, although David Copperfield finds
a loving family at last in Betsey Trotwood and Mr. Dick, the
weaknesses in his character have already been set by the deforming
influences of the Murdstones and, even more, by his weak, silly,
childish mother.

The abuse of children by the oppressive or absent family forms
the primary analogue to massive institutional corruption and the
most powerful stimulus to the narrators' outrage. These two
forms of abuse always dominate the novels' themes, and each
novel works to show that the abuse of the child in the home is
intimately and necessarily related to the abuse of everyone in the
society at large. Institutions like Chancery and the Marshalsea and
the criminal courts stand in loco parentis in a bitterly ironic sense,
given the wholesale dereliction of parents in each novel. This is
most obvious in *Bleak House*, where the neglect of one child draws
the apparently confused and disparate society into a pattern of
secret relationships.

Institutional corruption in Dickens' novels always cloaks itself
in some version of paternalism. The workhouse, the debtors'
prison, Chancery, the government bureau, the aristocratic social
system, the stock exchange, the school, and the factory are always
presided over by a mock-patriarch: Bumble; William Dorrit—the
"father of the Marshalsea"; the Lord High Chancellor, who sits
enthroned like Satan as a parody God, his head encircled by a
"foggy glory" that transforms light into murk; Lord Decimus
Barnacle; Sir Leicester Dedlock; Merdle; Gradgrind; and Bounderby. The claims to any real personal authority are fatuous. But
the symbolic accuracy of the patriarchal parody is deadly. All the
massive institutions satirized by the novels have been modeled on
a bloated version of the father's role in the family. Chancery,
which subsists on the failure of families to reconcile their own
differences, and the Marshalsea, which blatantly equates the family

with prison society, make more explicitly comprehensive the significance of earlier mock-patriarchies like Fagin's tribe of boys, Squeers' academy, Pecksniff's school, and Dombey's firm.

Yet because they have retreated into impersonal mechanism, these institutions evade the ordinary checks on a father's exercise of power in most families (the sort of restraints that the narrators rather gleefully document in a succession of cowed husbands like Snagsby and R. W. Wilfer). By the time Chancery and the Circumlocution Office appear in Dickens, society seems at the mercy of institutional corruption that mechanically aggrandizes patriarchal power even as the individual fathers become more helpless and bewildered. *Great Expectations* exemplifies the systemic nature of this corruption. When aspirants to patriarchal status seem to lurk behind every tombstone, preside over every dinner, dole out all the money, and spring up in female as well as male form, it is clear that the whole system, not a few vicious abusers of its power, has become the aggressor. In fact, in the late novels there is no oppressive patriarchal figure like Fagin or Pecksniff or Dombey who seems powerful enough to sustain a villain's role. Instead there are such weak, misguided, or victimized figures as Sir Leicester Dedlock, Merdle, William Dorrit, and Magwitch. Increasingly also a number of male characters take refuge in regression; Skimpole, Boythorn, Joe Gargery, the Aged P., and Frederick Dorrit all fashion some childhood role for themselves to avoid the insecurities and anomolies of the father's role in society. The end point of this process is reached, appropriately, in the last completed novel, where old Harmon's will reaches out from the grave to deform the sexual lives of the children. His heritage is filth, the dust mounds that both symbolize and create cash transactions— the most impersonal form of human interconnection in modern society.

Having malformed the family in its own image, a grotesque patriarchal system of values—beyond the control or comprehension of any individual character—has now transformed the whole society into a gigantic parody of the corrupted family. When the virtuous characters, still cherishing a belief in Victorian domestic pieties, confront this parody of a parody, it is little wonder that they are virtually paralyzed.

These characters are doubly victimized by family disorder, first through their own miserable childhoods and then through family-generated social institutions that are so massive, complicated, fraudulent, and impersonal that they cannot even be confronted directly (Arthur Clennam's experience with the Circumlocution Office). Caught in this dilemma, the heroes and heroines all seek to retreat, consciously or unconsciously, to some version of the only structure they have really ever known, the family. But even the most loving families are flawed in some basic way: hence Agnes Wickfield cannot save her alcoholic, guilt-ridden father, Joe Gargery cannot protect Pip, Amy Dorrit cannot check the degrading pretensions that work away at her father's sanity.

This wholesale dereliction of patriarchal values helps account for the alliance between the benevolent patriarchs like Jarndyce and the virtuous sons like Woodcourt to "feminize" the family. When Jarndyce imports Esther Summerson to manage all his self-created family's affairs, he consciously tries to substitute "feminine" values for the rapacious and fraudulent patriarchal values of Chancery. When David Copperfield subdues his desires to Agnes Wickfield, he is choosing a maternal figure not only to manage his domestic life but to provide him with an entirely new system of values. Neither erotic love nor masculine friendship nor work has offered enough to sustain him. Such characters—always abetted by the narrators—seek in this "feminized" family ideal an alternate source of values, essentially different from the chaotic and vicious world outside.[5]

Rapacious sons, like Quilp, Heep, and Orlick, seek to destroy the traditional family structure and subject its women totally to brutal, anarchic masculine will. Predatory fathers, like Fagin, Dombey, and Podsnap, aggrandize the father's traditional powers until they claim absolute dominion over all the family members. Yet the virtuous male characters, with the best of conscious intentions, also perpetuate the system of male domination. Their attempt to shape families to a stereotypic feminine rather than a stereotypic masculine ideal is yet another projection of sexual fantasies, more insidious than the direct assertions of power by the Jaggerses and Bounderbys. The little mothers who must assume all the moral and emotional burdens cast off by their masculine charges receive a full measure of sentimental and even religious adulation with every new imposition. But this suasive system can be as incapacitating as open abuse, which is at least felt as pain even when the abuse is unchallenged.

VICTIMS OF THE PATRIARCHY

We do not have to comb a Dickens novel to find victims of tyrannical male power. Nancy murdered by Sikes, Smike beaten by Squeers, Florence Dombey repulsed by her father's cold hostility, Jo the Crossing Sweeper hounded to his death by Tulkinghorn and Bucket—these and scores of other obvious victims are thrust before us by outraged narrators. But there are characters more subtly and disturbingly victimized, characters whose whole personalities have been shaped to the contours of warped sexual values.

Three types of psychological victim are especially significant to the novels' indictment of the sexual system: surrogate mothers who mimic the patriarchs' despotic powers; young women who are thrust prematurely into parental roles; and young men who seek refuge from brutal masculine roles by adopting stereotypically feminine emotional and moral values. Together these three types suggest how insidious and pervasive the power of patriarchal values is, how it corrupts the deepest recesses of the personality. Beyond this, it is a power so fueled by masculine insecurity and hostility that it ultimately turns against those who use it, invading and tormenting their own emotional lives as it torments their victims.

Although mothers as well as fathers abuse their children, and though the particular forms of abuse seem almost inexhaustibly ingenious, the patriarchal model prevails here also. The abusing mothers all ruthlessly suppress the traditional mannerisms of fem-

ininity. Although they escape from the standard forms of victimization in this way, they submit themselves as obsessively as any
deranged patriarch in Dickens to the stereotypic forms of masculine power. Figures of this type, such as Mrs. Joe, Miss Barbary,
Mrs. Clennam, and Jane Murdstone, reveal the same basic mannerisms: austere speech and gesture that fends off all intimacy;
intimations of barely suppressed rage; authoritarian solemnity;
somber, angular clothing that conceals even the physical signs of
their sex; and pious harangues that thrive on guilt and intimidation. Their speech alternates between iciness and fierce vitupera-
tion; it is a weapon to inflict pain or to ward off imagined challenges to their authority. They have fled all the stereotypes of
femininity that victimize so many characters but taken refuge in
the opposite extreme; mimicry of the same aggressive masculinity
that has created the stereotypes. This mode of behavior is even
more destructive than submission to stereotypes of feminine passivity, more destructive to the women themselves and to the children they abuse. Their self-torment is so intense and so violent
that it erupts into symbolic physical punishment: the strokes that
paralyze Mrs. Clennam and Miss Barbary and the murderous
assault that paralyzes Mrs. Joe.

Extreme Calvinism provides the typical model of dress and
behavior for these despotic maternal figures and also the code of
values that justifies it. The point is not just to satirize an abhorrent
religious creed; this motif also suggests the most extreme form
that patriarchal claims can take—the claim to divine sanction.
Characters like Miss Barbary have so permanently terrorized the
children consigned to them that the assumption of Godlike power
is hardly false in its psychological dimension, however it degrades
and falsifies religious values.

These maternal figures thoroughly pervert the proper responsibilities of parents, of course. The fact that their children are
godchildren, stepchildren, nieces, or adopted children underscores
the fraudulent and inadequate nature of the relationships. Yet these
"masculinized" maternal surrogates do not serve as horrible inversions of the standard maternal ideal, inversions designed to
redirect us toward admiring appreciation of the stereotype. They

are actually sexual hybrids, not inversions, grotesquely fusing traditional attributes of mothers and fathers and parodying both in the process.

Mrs. Joe, in a particularly mordant example of this fusion, wears an apron with a "square impregnable bib in front, that [is] stuck full of pins and needles" (II, 6). When she cuts bread for Pip and Joe, she jams it against her fortified bosom, emitting pins and needles into the bread and thus into the mouths of her victims. Though she is slavishly devoted to all the stereotypic external duties of a housewife and mother, she always uses them in this way as instruments of aggression—a mode of behavior that allies her with Jaggers and Orlick, not with Sarah Pocket and Biddy.

David Copperfield's variations on maternal types illustrate in a particularly clear way the function of this sort of despotic woman in relation to analogous characters. As Jane Murdstone shows the way masculine stereotypes can deform the surrogate mother's features, Clara Copperfield reveals the inadequacy of the stereotypic mother's role. She is gentle, loving, submissive to any husband it is her lot to have, however he treats her—and totally helpless to protect or nurture David. Jane abuses the child, doubling her brother's brutal character. Clara submits to the opposite role, the negative version of the same patriarchal model, a false anima who caters to the male's desires, rather than representing an opposing principle.

The foster mother who replaces both these sharply contrasting but equally inadequate mothers is a third variation on the motif of sexual hybridization. To survive and act in this world, to keep her strong personality intact, Betsey Trotwood has had to go on the defensive—a comic version of Mrs. Joe's and Miss Barbary's perpetual vigilance in *Great Expectations* and *Bleak House*. She has avoided actual marriage and, in her symbolic union with Mr. Dick, she seems to have absorbed all the energy of mind and will he has lost. As Mr. Dick's surname Babler suggests, he is both a baby and a babbler; he is Betsey's child but also a caricature of a feminine stereotype, the sort of vacuous, chattering, infantile wife that David will choose in Dora Spenlow. (Betsey repeatedly calls David's mother, the prototype of Dora, a baby.) Betsey is superficially as masculinized as the wicked stepmothers, but she uses the mannerisms to disguise her real tenderness. Betsey's deception, like so many artful dodges of Dickens' loving characters, is brilliant and heroic. But it too reveals how desperate the world is when basic urges to love, protect, and nurture a child must be so tortuously concealed. And it emphatically implies that no stereotypically soft, passive maternal figure can offer the kind of care David—and all the novel's children—need. He needs the fusion of strength and loving nurture that Betsey gives him behind the facade of stern patriarchal behavior.

David's foil, Steerforth, has had a doting mother. We might attribute Steerforth's criminally self-indulgent character, in a familiar pattern, to pampering by maternal care that is, nevertheless, admirable in moderation. But the novel pairs his weakness of character with Emily's, whose family seems a model of traditional domestic virtues. Similarly, Agnes Wickfield's loving maternal care fails to check her father's alcoholism and his almost self-willed submission to Uriah Heep. The point of these analogous circumstances seems clear. The virtues of the beatitudes, enshrined in the Victorian angel mothers, may point our way to heaven; but they have little power in the earthly life that is the only real concern of Dickens' novels.[6]

In a paradox that points up the sexual dilemmas of the whole system, only those women who seize some form of "masculine" aggression for themselves can hope to exert control over their own lives. But only the very strongest of them, only Betsey Trotwood, can avoid Jane Murdstone's condition as a replica of masculine brutality.

Like most of the characters in the novels before *Bleak House*, these maternal characters are interdependent. We must see them in constellation to understand fully the psychological forces at work in the sexual values that have formed all of them. In the later novels Dickens explores the figure of the maternal despot (as he does other recurrent character types) in more sustained and searching presentations of individual characters. Mrs. Joe is per-

haps the most impressive and the most revealing character in a
brilliant group that includes Mrs. Clennam and Miss Wade in
Little Dorrit and Miss Barbary in *Bleak House.*

Mrs. Joe has not, however, fared well with the critics; the criticism she has received is a case study of how Dickens' use of
stereotypes has misled a number of readers. Carolyn Heilbrun
claims that Dickens was "unable to understand or sympathize
with women" and could not see them as complex human beings.
Dickens denies humanity to half the race, Angus Wilson writes,
by either idealizing or depreciating his women characters. Katherine Rogers finds that Dickens so diminishes Mrs. Joe that she
becomes an "intrinsically improbable caricature."[7]

Now Dickens began, no doubt, with the stereotype of the
abusive shrew and the cruel stepmother, but what he created from
the stereotype is a credible psychological portrait of an enraged
and resentful woman, acting blindly and unconsciously in ways
that are fully consistent with her motivation. "You're a foul
shrew, Mother Gargery," Orlick shouts before he attacks her.
Like the stereotyped shrew, Mrs. Joe is angular and bony, red-
faced and unattractive, utterly different from the plump, soft ideal.
Her nature, too, is shrewish. She is "given to government," as Joe
puts it. Caustic, snappish, bad-tempered, and violent, she expresses in her behavior a conviction that she is ill-used, and therefore nags and mistreats husband and child. So foul a shrew is she,
in fact, that only a violent physical attack that permanently damages her mind can improve her temper. She is rendered speechless
and physically helpless by Orlick's attack, but for the first time,
harmless. The horrible extremity of this "cure" suggests in itself
the force of the passions that have driven her.

Mrs. Joe is as desperate and harried in her own way as Magwitch, though the causes of her desperation are hidden while the
forces that menace him are obvious. She seethes with unconcealed
animosity and finds in the most innocent occurrences intimations
of "rebellion." Her sustained passion prevents her from doing
anything calmly. She always rushes into whatever object, animate
or inanimate, seems to obtruct her spirit, throwing, stamping,
jamming, slapping, knocking, banging, or shaking it about.

Something goads her continually, so that she does indeed endure a life of "fret, and fright and worry." The "something" in Magwitch's case has an objective reality in the soldiers, the prison ship, the cruelty of the weather and landscape. Mrs. Joe demonstrates the condition not as it operates at social extremes but in daily household routine, through ordinary, hidden pressures rather than extraordinary causes.

The deadly nature of Mrs. Joe's aggressiveness, the truth of all the analogies to Magwitch, is climatically revealed in Orlick's attack, her illness, and her eventual death. The strangest part of the incident is not the scant motivation given Orlick but her attitude toward him after the attack:

> I confess that I expected to see my sister denounce him, and that I was disappointed by the different result. She manifested the greatest anxiety to be on good terms with him . . . and there was an air of humble propitiation in all she did, such as I have seen pervade the bearing of a child towards a hard master.
>
> [XVI, 116–17]

"The bearing of a child toward a hard master"—a complete and significant reversal of Mrs. Joe's role toward the child Pip. The narrator's simile suggests that her attitude compounds fear, timid respect, and an obsequious desire to placate. Her fear is understandable, but if she really believes that Orlick was her attacker (as she seems to), she could easily denounce him and drive him from the forge. Instead, she desires his daily presence, as if she derives some necessity of her altered existence from him.

The nature of her former belligerence suggests the most compelling reason for her altered behavior. For all her apparent mastery, Mrs. Joe has had to live a life of constant vigilance lest anything threaten her position. Her power, somewhere in her own mind, appears precarious, even though she has the least rebellious of subjects. Her near-hysteria of self-assertion springs from a fear of her own impotence.

We must piece together the history of thwarted expectations that have so embittered Mrs. Joe; but the brutal attack that cripples and kills her should in itself prevent us from classifying her with the comic shrews in Dickens whom she resembles in some ways. A stock comic character who is exposed to real anguish complicates our responses. We can delight in the humiliation of Pumblechook because he is so smugly impervious and emotionally shallow, but Mrs. Joe's emotions seethe up from sources that are too deep for easy delight in her discomfiture. And when discomfiture is followed by maiming, derangement, and death, then the character is no longer comic at all.

A woman so tall, bony, and raw-complexioned, and more ill-favored in temperament than in features, who must make a man marry her "by hand"—this childless woman of forty who had a young brother thrust upon her in her twenties—may well suffer from legitimate grievances that a comic "heavy" is not supposed to have. In retrospect at least, as the social forces that have helped distort her emotional life are gradually revealed, she should gain a good deal of our sympathy despite her shrewishness. Joe, who has seen so much in his own mother's life and death "of a woman drudging and slaving and breaking her honest hart and never getting no peace in her mortal days" (VII, 45), has chosen a wife who also drudges and slaves and in his kindness toward her has made a kind of atonement for his father's abuse. Mrs. Joe is not tyrannized by Pip or Joe or even by the drudgery necessary in a poor village household, but she is more subtly tyrannized by a society that offers no satisfying way of life to a poor woman with Mrs. Joe's shrewd intelligence and fierce energy (and very few options to any woman). Frustrated by this most elusive of oppressors, she may understandably—if unjustly by ordinary ethical standards—rage against a marriage virtually forced upon her and an unwanted child certainly forced upon her, against a husband who seems her inferior by all society's standards except the all-important one of sex, against the domestic conditions that constrain her life into the narrowest scope.

In the small, preindustrial, rural community of the novel, with its extended family networks, child abandonment would have been unacceptable. Nor could Mrs. Joe, controlled as she is by her view of what others think of her, ever admit such a desire into consciousness. So she deflects her anger into physical and psychological abuse of Pip, without ever admitting that she is actually enraged by the enforced maternal role. She masks the truth of her resentment by insisting on his delinquency and her goodness, how much trouble he is to raise and what a good job she is doing, when the novel clearly reveals that Pip is a cowed and fearful child and Mrs. Joe an abusive parent.

If one looks at Mrs. Joe's treatment of Joe with the same willingness to consider her possible motivation, it becomes clear that a similar emotional pattern of resentment and deflected rage is at work in that relationship as well. Indeed Pip habitually regards Joe as a "fellow-sufferer" who receives much the same treatment from Mrs. Joe as he does. The early years of the Gargery marriage are mentioned only briefly, but Pip believes "that she must have made Joe Gargery marry her by hand" (Ii, 7), and Joe's own account of that decision seems to bear out this picture of a strong and determined woman having her own way. Certainly Mrs. Joe gives no indication of feeling any love, warmth, or tenderness toward Joe. The only emotion she displays toward him besides anger is exasperation. She is, in fact, as resentful at being a wife, Joe Gargery's wife, as she is at being a mother. Just as Mrs. Joe had really no choice in accepting Pip to raise, so she had no choice about marrying. For a lower-class woman, without family or money, there was no alternative but domestic service or factory work. The plight of the "redundant woman," or the "odd woman," as she came to be called later in the century, the woman who was neither wife nor mother, was a horror tale of the day. So women like Mrs. Joe married. And a woman suddenly forced to care for an infant brother had even more reason, economic and social, to marry. Joe, meek and mild, the embodiment of values that she, snob and money worshiper as she is, cannot appreciate, is to her another troublesome child—a "larger species of child," Pip calls him.

Thus, Mrs. Joe's rages are as much a signature of her psychic life as Jaggers' handwashing or Wemmick's mechanical, post-office mouth. A strong, dominating woman, in a situation she resents, unable to express or even to admit to her anger, in an age whose conditions and beliefs offered her no alternative, she be-

compare to

comes an enraged woman. She is the Victorian angel-ideal turned
inside out: self-assertive, not self-abnegating; domineering, not
submissive; destructive, not nurturing.

When Mrs. Joe is struck down and paralyzed, her conscious
mind loses its repressive control, and her unconscious fears and
desires find a symbolic fulfillment. After a period in which a
"gloomy aberration of mind" signals a mental life completely
disoriented, a new pattern of behavior emerges. It openly worships
the standards that have operated secretly before. The only man
who has had the audacity to defy her authority becomes her master, the only man who has defined her nature: "You'd be everybody's master if you durst" (XV, 106). Aggression in Orlick
breaks through conventional restraints, so that, for Mrs. Joe, he
is a kind of heroic representative of the darkest urges in her own
nature. She offers abject homage to a symbol of sheer brutal masculine power, a power she has tried to arrogate in every feature
of her marriage (even to the extent of appropriating Joe's name).
Orlick has also released her, however brutally, from the daily
hypocrisy and torment of her life, so that she may also express
a twisted gratitude. In further satisfaction of the complex of desires
that has driven Mrs. Joe, she is now free to embrace punishment
for all the torment she has caused Pip and Joe, a punishment that
might well seem appropriate to a wretchedly guilty mind. And,
finally, Orlick's power has erotic implications for Mrs. Joe
(though this is only a secondary stress in the novel; the dominant
complex of aggressive urges wrests control over sexuality as it
does over every other human concern). She has goaded Joe and
Orlick into the fight over her honor that is the immediate motive
for Orlick's attack. Like Estella during the analogous fight between
Pip and the pale young gentleman, she has furtively watched while
two males struggled for her. And now after a marriage that seems
barren of any sexual feeling, she has found a perverse gratification
in violence. Like Miss Havisham and Estella, she can only understand sexuality as a weapon of attack or self-defense.

We are not claiming, of course, that Mrs. Joe ought to be
considered an admirable character. She is the direct cause of Pip's
guilty, anxious, irresolute nature and, quite simply, a terrible per-

son to live with. Yet, though Dickens first presents her as an outrageous tyrant, his remarkable sympathy for any form of suffering and his remarkable insight into the oppressive nature of sexual relations in his society cause him to create a method of implicit characterization that arouses a divided response to Mrs. Joe. This ability to present the nuances of individual personality, to use them to probe for underlying motivation, and to arouse our sympathies without undermining our moral judgment is the basic source of Dickens' power to move beyond the narrow categories of his culture's values.

The sexual patterns of the patriarchal system hold for Dickens' women whether they grow into vicious parents like Mrs. Joe, angelic parents like Esther, studiously oblivious parents like Mrs. Jellyby, or any of the various types of single women who throng the novels, all bizarre and all just as much under the sway of the family as if they had conformed to the standard maternal models. In terms of their own freedom to choose and act independently, it makes little difference whether these characters are urged toward the vicious or virtuous extreme. Like cursed figures of folk tales— Sleeping Beauty or Rapunzel—they are transformed by forces that lie outside any expression of conscious will. Worse still, these women have never known a condition free of the curse's effects. As Esther is told explicitly by Miss Barbary, the curse began with their births and defines the basic conditions of their lives.

The young women who, like Esther, have the will or virtue or simply the luck to avoid Mrs. Joe's tormenting existence usually find themselves thrust prematurely into adult roles that are nearly as confining. Often they respond directly to the tyranny or regression of a father or paternal surrogate. Nell, Florence Dombey, Agnes Wickfield, Esther, Biddy, Amy Dorrit, Lizzie Hexam, and Jenny Wren are only a few of the girls treated this way. Although they are often spoken of as maternal figures, these child-women really assume a more comprehensive parental role. In a strange fusion of fatherly as well as motherly functions, they act as sexually neutral figures, analogous in this way to the maternal despots. The burdens of this asexual parental role (their fathers want basic protection and nurture, not erotic gratification) clearly impoverish the personality of each one. They all must struggle even to acknowledge their own personal sexual identity; and they need the intervention of the plot to accomplish the romantic resolutions which they lack the self-confidence or self-awareness to pursue.

Nell's early death presents the ultimate tendency of this psychological pattern. Symbolically the fever that kills her is psychologically fueled, as it will be for so many of Dickens' characters who fall ill. *The Old Curiosity Shop* both precipitates and forestalls Nell's sexual maturity in a perfect expression of Dickens' ambivalence toward female characters; death is the only way out of the dilemma. The responses of Dickens' contemporaries suggest that the ambivalence was cultural, not idiosyncratic, but it is a mistake to see it, as many have done, as simply a notorious instance of suppressed sadism.[8] Already the alternative roles that might face Nell if she grew up, married, and mothered a family are so unattractive that her death is, in part at least, a genuine attempt at rescue. The experiences of the Marchioness and Mrs. Quilp and Sally Brass suggest contrasting alternatives that are hardly attractive.

The narrators imply that these child-women are exemplars of the moral regeneration needed by the whole society. But in social as well as psychological terms, they are so pathetically weak and eagerly self-effacing that an assertive character like Miss Wade or Rosa Dartle can seem admirable by contrast, despite her vengeful nature. Yet the humble child-women at the very least mark out for us the area in which regeneration of sexual roles must come. They lack the will to seek their own personal development and the emotional range even to know what they might really desire. But they also lack the willful brutality of the patriarchs and the sons who struggle for the fathers' power, or the seething hostilities of the women who have adopted the aggressive masculine forms. Though Amy, Esther, Nell, Biddy, and the others experience the threat of nonentity, they hold to some purpose that is admirable and humane. The novels expose their virtues as inseparable from their weakness. Their modes of life are so impoverished that they can seem deformed (the symbolic point of Esther's scarring smallpox, Amy's diminutive figure, Nell's premature death). Their love for others and service to others' needs always seem based upon the sacrifice of their own autonomous desires. The novels simultaneously reveal this psychological impairment and their moral strength, in a particularly important instance of narrative ambivalence.

We are urged to see virtue and victimization as precariously akin—just as the character of women like Mrs. Joe and Miss Wade causes us to question how much a victim can be held accountable for her vicious behavior. These heroines are not paragons but examples of thwarted potential. Rather than representing a solution, they underscore the need for a reformation of basic assumptions about sexual identity and sexual roles.

As Dickens presents the maternal despot, Mrs. Joe, in subtle and probing psychological detail, so he explores the nature of her antithesis, the child-woman overflowing with maternal love, in Esther Summerson. Once again, the apparent stereotypes are subverted to reveal the oppressive conditions that impel a distinctly individual, complex character to adopt them so completely.

Esther Summerson has traditionally been viewed as the angel of *Bleak House*, the center of domestic and familial value in a novel that shows the breakdown of most families. In Dickens' late novels, everything in the overt plot structure insists on such a separation of angel and rebel: Esther is placed in opposition to all the neglectful mothers of the novel, as Amy Dorrit is to the rebellious Miss Wade of *Little Dorrit*. But counterbalancing this insistence is a movement to bring these figures together, to stress their similarities, to join them in an analogical pattern. For if the late novels reveal the torment of the rebels, they also present the impoverishment of the angels, the burden of the divine in a human figure.[9] The rebels in these late novels reveal more turmoil, more psychological complexity than similar characters in Dickens' earlier novels, but so do the angels. Nor are these later angels so clearly victimized; rather they internalize the standards of society and thus participate in what is being done to them. They are, therefore, less passive than the earlier figures, and also show more capacity for growth and development.

Esther Summerson has accepted the norms of a strictly traditional morality—a secularized Christian ethic of work, humility, self-sacrifice, earnestness, and cheerfulness that distills nearly the last drop of Victorian ideals. She sees these norms as thoroughly satisfactory and thoroughly consistent. They are not, however, fully adequate even to the little system of which she is the center, and her reluctant satiric perceptions break through the smooth surface of her narrative like beads of acid (when she refers to Mrs. Pardiggle's "rapacious benevolence" or bespectacled voice, for instance). Yet the pressure to bring all into conformity with her traditional view of the world causes her to muffle satire in the idiom of the modest, gentle young lady she tries to be.

Alex Zwerdling has emphasized the psychological complexity of Esther's character—the trauma of her illegitimacy and the "long wound of her childhood," which has left her with damaged self-esteem.[10] Deprived of love, she believes herself unworthy of it. Esther's humility and need for affection are born from this early experience. She has been taught through daily experience that she is sinful and unworthy of love, that the only possibility of atonement is a life of sacrifice. "Submission, self-denial, diligent work" are the penitential standards set by Miss Barbary. Esther infuses this stern creed with affection: "I . . . would strive as I grew up to be industrious, contented, and kind-hearted, and to do some good to some one, and win some love to myself, if I could" (III, 18); but the substance of Miss Barbary's injunctions remains intact, even wrenching Esther's modest phrasing into ironic shape: "to win some love for myself." Esther begins life not as an equal among equals, but as one set apart in her unworthiness; so love must be won through unremitting effort. With this in mind, we can better understand Esther's excessive raptures over the love she does receive, her excessive protestations that she is unworthy of it, and her obsessive devotion to duty. Her self-depreciating mannerisms are both confession and appeal. Serenity and anxiety co-exist in Esther's character, though her will insistently thrusts all the impulses she cannot understand outside the narrow categories of her conscious life.

In the first paragraph of her narrative, Esther interposes one of her many revealing qualifications: "And so [the doll] used to sit propped up in a great arm-chair, with her beautiful complexion and rosy lips, staring at me—or not so much at me, I think, as at nothing." Esther has no good reason, by her standards of common sense, for the last comment. It occurs, of course, to underscore her diffidence and merges with many similar comments, all making the obvious point that Esther is too modest to recognize her own merit. But the remark also suggests that her humility grows at times toward an absolute denial of selfhood.

At Greenleaf she seems to have no self to integrate or even record the process of maturing: "Six quiet years (I find I am saying it for the second time) I had passed at Greenleaf, seeing in those around me, as it might be in a looking-glass, every stage of my own growth and change there. . . ." Dickens is so far from being redundant or verbose that even the casual remark, "I find I am saying it for the second time," suggests the unreality of the passage of time to a personality abstracted from full participation in experience. Esther does not, in this metaphor, participate in her own growth and change but only sees them mirrored in the responses of others. Already at Greenleaf she has conformed to the pattern of behavior that will distinguish her life at Bleak House: almost total dependence on others for a sense of identity.

When Esther falls asleep at the Jellybys', at the onset of another major change in her life, the sense of nonentity buried in her conscious mind once more finds expression:

At first I was painfully awake, and vainly tried to lose myself, with my eyes closed, among the scenes of the day. At length, by slow degrees, they became indistinct and mingled. I began to lose the identity of the sleeper resting on me. Now it was Ada; now, one of my old Reading friends from whom I could not believe I had so recently parted. Now, it was the little mad woman worn out with curtseying and smiling; now, some one in authority at Bleak House. Lastly, it was no one, and I was no one.

[IV, 45]

The complementary processes of multiplication and conflation in this passage mark Esther's life at Bleak House. She is christened the "little old woman" by Jarndyce, and the one new name becomes many: "This was the beginning of my being called Old Woman, and Little Old Woman, and Cobweb, and Mrs. Shipton, and Mother Hubbard, and Dame Durden, and so many names of that sort, that my own name soon became quite lost among them" (VIII, 98). The names multiply, but they all dissolve into one type of nursery-rhyme character. At times Esther is the little old woman—mother and advisor—to all the other members of the Bleak House family. At other times, she is Ada's duenna, Ada's sister, Jarndyce's daughter, Richard's sister, and finally, Jarndyce's fiancée. In the legal view of Chancery, she is Ada's companion, a dubious position somewhere between a servant and a sister. Esther's personality, like her name, gets lost among the variety of roles she is expected to play. Yet all the roles merge into one bland type: the serious, quiet, humble, almost ageless servant of all who require service.

Esther cannot follow the pattern of courtship and marriage allowed a heroine like Ada. So the one deep attachment she does feel free to express, her love for Ada, assumes many of the qualities of romantic love, a version of the role she unconsciously desires, the role she would ordinarily assume in this society, the role that could most easily and fully give her the love and sense of identity she needs. Jarndyce, Richard, Ada, and more directly, Mrs. Woodcourt refuse to allow Esther to become a romantic heroine. They treat her as everything but an attractive young lady with romantic interests of her own. Though the novel, appropriately, minimizes Esther's beauty—or rather, reveals it only indirectly—she obviously resembles the beautiful Lady Dedlock closely enough for Guppy, George Rouncewell, and Lady Dedlock herself to notice the resemblance.

Deprived of possibilities for romance and marriage, forced into premature parental responsibilities, accustomed to associate women with any sort of emotional involvement, Esther fashions Ada into a surrogate lover. All that ardor Woodcourt never sees, with its expression in kisses, caresses, and tender words, is lavished on Ada. Ada's welfare becomes Esther's chief concern, and the loss of Ada in marriage, not the supposed loss of Woodcourt as lover, brings on violent grief. Esther's "altered looks," symbolizing her relinquished hope of romance, affect her primarily as they affect

Ada: "I loved my darling so well that I was more concerned for their effect on her than on any one" (XXXVI, 516). Victorian women in general enjoyed considerable freedom to feel and display love for each other, even allowing for literary heightening and idealization. And the freedom was at least partially a response to the constraints placed on the association between respectable men and women. But Dickens penetrates through the social phenomenon to some of its causes.

Esther can love Ada freely and consciously because such love involves no presumption, no radical change in her life, and no acknowledgment of her sexuality. Love for Woodcourt, or for any young man, would imply that she was worthy of love simply because of what she is, that she is a normal young woman with normal prospects. Her affection for Ada can be all service and adulation. Love for Woodcourt would demand some corresponding devotion from him—the free gift that Esther cannot accept. It could expose her to a frightening new world just when she has become securely protected by the routine of Bleak House. For these reasons, Esther shies away from the attraction Woodcourt has for her, even before her disfigurement.

In a similar way, the plot complication Jarndyce's proposal creates does more than add melodramatic suspense. (Though it does that too, in a way that infuses stock motifs with new life and significance; the plot is so managed that the roles of blocking parent, indulgent old benefactor and, for a disturbing time, romantic hero are conflated in Jarndyce.) The primary function of this protracted episode is to reveal how satisfying marriage to a kindly, fatherly old man would be to the whole personality Esther professes, and how unsatisfying to needs that she conceals more from herself than from the reader. In this sense the "rivalry" between Jarndyce and Woodcourt reveals a real conflict within Esther.

As on so many occasions, Esther scolds herself back into line:

By-and-by I went to my old glass. My eyes were red and swollen, and I said, 'O Esther, Esther, can that be you!' I am afraid the face in the glass was going to cry again at this reproach, but I held up my finger at it, and it stopped.

'That is more like the composed look you comforted me with, my dear, when you showed me such a change!' said I, beginning to let down my hair. 'When you are mistress of Bleak House, you are to be as cheerful as a bird. In fact, you are always to be cheerful; so let us begin for once and for all.'

I went on with my hair now, quite comfortably. I sobbed a little still, but that was because I had been crying; not because I was crying then.

[XLIV, 611–12]

This passage is remarkable in several ways. The habit of absolute emotional control and the urge toward emotional release are so strong and so at odds that the face and the reflection are depicted as two distinct persons. At this point of crisis in her life, Esther must insist on her happiness as never before, but she can scarcely control her sobbing.

The confrontation with her mother, her illness, and Jarndyce's renunciation to Woodcourt permit her to move beyond this impasse. She faces in her illness a hellish vision of her life that could never have penetrated her conscious defenses. Esther's account of her illness is remarkable in its revelations of suppressed attitudes toward the life that she consciously insists is as happy as it could be. The version of her life the fever allows (and encourages) to rise to consciousness is a distorted image but one that counters Esther's own habitual conscious distortions:

I had never known before how short life really was, and into how small a space the mind could put it.

While I was very ill, the way in which these divisions of time became confused with one another, distressed my mind exceedingly. At once a child, an elder girl, and the little woman I had been so happy as, I was not only oppressed by cares and difficulties adapted to each station, but by the great perplexity of endlessly trying to reconcile them. I suppose that few . . . can quite understand what I mean, or what painful unrest arose from this source.

For the same reason I am almost afraid to hint at that time in my disorder—it seemed one long night, but I believe there were both nights and days in it—when I laboured up colossal staircases, ever striving to reach the top, and ever turned, as I have seen a worm in a garden path, by some obstruction, and labouring again. . . .

[XXXV, 488]

All those "various stages" that have seemed to lead her from misery into greater and greater happiness collapse instead into one round of "cares and difficulties." Then all remembrance of her actual responsibilities fades, and duty is transformed into endless toiling up colossal stairs. Esther confronts nakedly, for the only time in her life, the problem of identity that has marred even the happiest experience and that threatens to snarl all her conflicting roles into one condition of joyless drudgery.

Ellen Moers sees Esther Summerson as Dickens' "ideal of womanhood," a "pattern young lady," as Bucket calls her. The strongest of women in a novel filled with strong women, Esther "was to represent Right Woman," acting quietly but effectively in sharp contrast to the loud and ineffective agitating women. Surely this was Dickens' conscious intention. Moers is also correct to view *Bleak House* as conveying Dickens' "own response, a deeper and wider one than has been recognized to the fact of female energies unleashed at mid-century."[11] But to gauge accurately Dickens' response, the psychological complexity of Esther's character must be taken into account as well as the disturbing but insistent pattern of analogies among the women characters of the novel.

In the character of Esther, so central a figure, so crucial to the novel, Dickens probes almost reluctantly what underlay the ideal of Right Womanhood, of selfless duty and self-sacrifice—the terrible price such an ideal exacts, the distortions it creates in the woman who seeks to mold herself to fit it, the violent response it leads to in the woman who flees from it. Dickens develops this theme in Mrs. Turveydrop, the woman worked to death by her husband, in Caddy Jellyby who exchanges one form of domestic exploitation for another, in the women philanthropists who must condemn the ideal utterly to escape its hold, in the brutalized wives of the brickmakers. Moers finds Mrs. Bayham Badger a strong woman quite at home in this novel of strong women, a "husband devourer"; but surely Dickens means us to see her as a woman with so little sense of self that she takes on the identity of each of her husbands like an insect going through radical life changes. The loss or distortion of selfhood the stereotypic ideal leads to is everywhere reflected in the women of *Bleak House*.

In *Victorian Murderesses*, Mary S. Hartman has examined the process by which female stereotypes were internalized by women themselves in the nineteenth century. The stereotype was continuously reinforced by women who molded themselves upon it. Hartman stresses

society's ability to impose its negative stereotype on women. They accepted the stereotypes and internalized them to form their self-images. Thus, not only did men relate to them in terms of stereotypical expectations, but their own feelings and behavior patterns were determined from within by the same expectations. Celestine Doudet, the dowryless girl without marital hopes, became the sex-obsessed spinster, who detected impurity everywhere. Constance, the neglected twelve-year-old runaway lacking in "feminine delicacy" who had "wished to be independent," unwittingly set herself up for suspicion of murder and then embraced her female outcast state in what one writer has called "a spirit of pure self-immolation." Ironically, this act of confession was finely "female," just the sort of submissive, sacrificial and self-destructive act which, in lesser forms, was explicitly demanded of all respectable creatures of her sex. And they, at least, may have understood. The courtroom in Wiltshire was full of weeping women.[12]

It is just this process of internalization that Dickens depicts in Esther Summerson and in a number of other women characters like her. Writing in an era in which women believed in, accepted, and molded themselves upon stereotyped notions of femaleness, believing in those notions himself, Dickens yet manages to convey in his woman characters like Esther the process of forcing a personality to fit the Procrustean bed of stereotype and the crippling that results.

Dickens' novels always operate within the context of the Victorian middle-class idealization of the family, which is itself based on idealization of Victorian women. So however the novels challenge sexual stereotypes indirectly, their presentation of family relations is always female-centered—as it is in *Bleak House*. This does not mean that female characters receive any substantial transfer of direct social power from the male characters or from the social institutions that shelter traditional masculine prerogatives. As Esther's experiences show, the immediate effect of the new insecurities that men feel about their capacities is to confine women still more in roles that deprive them of direct social power. The more woman's role in the middle-class family, as wife, mother, daughter, or sister, is defined in terms of moral rather than physical service, the more limited and precarious her power becomes. When women's power is vested in direct contributions to the economic survival of the family, acknowledged by all family members, then there is at least a basis for asserting some autonomy (as Jenny Wren and a few other female characters do). When women's primary power shifts from direct economic contribution and the physical labor involved in rearing children and managing a household to the moral impact she supposedly has on the characters of the household males (Esther's situation), then her power is totally a dependent's. Like the courtier, she derives her status and her function from the attitude of another person. And the more idealized her role becomes, the more she is expected to enshrine the culture's beleaguered values, the more vulnerable her status becomes. Like Esther, she may find her sense of autonomous identity threatened. Increasing idealization only separates her further from the psychological forces and social values actually at work, in her own personality and in the families she serves. She becomes an icon, a symbolic creature of masculine desires, which are themselves the creatures of masculine insecurities. Like the prostitute, the unmarried woman, the hostile woman who refuses to serve as a passive value-carrier, she is incapacitated. And it makes little difference in terms of real autonomy that the system values her so highly.

The symbolic pairings of female characters in Dickens' novels— maiden and whore (Rose Maylie and Nancy), child-mother and rebellious daughter (Amy Dorrit and Tattycoram), servant and shrew (Biddy and Mrs. Joe)—suggest in themselves how close the supposed extremes of idealization and condemnation actually are, and how sensitive Dickens was, despite his conscious biases, to the forces that shaped women's experiences in his culture. Almost invariably in Dickens the female characters who are established as moral and temperamental opposites in terms of the explicit commentary are secretly allied through the system of symbolic analogies.

This analogical linking does not conflate all the moral, temperamental, and social distinctions between them; but it does insist on their common state of victimization. And it persistently questions the foundations of the respectable moral and class values that would totally sequester, for example, a Rose Maylie from a Nancy, in ordinary social life.

Thus Amy Dorrit and Mrs. Clennam are brought together by the plot of *Little Dorrit* and by Mrs. Clennam's tortuous system of personal atonement; but they are more disturbingly brought together by similarities in their psychological and social circumstances, similarities that emerge through all the manifest differences that divide them. Both have suffered a paralysis of the will through a corruption of the patriarchal social system. Amy has submitted totally to the illegitimate exactions of her father; Mrs. Clennam has wrested to herself the same sort of illegitimate masculine prerogatives, only to find that they give her even less personal independence or satisfaction than Amy has. Her paralysis, as several commentators have noted, is probably a psychosomatic condition.

All three of the male characters who figure most prominently in the lives of Amy and Mrs. Clennam fail in business, suggesting that the masculine forms have lost effective power to shape the course of the larger society even as they have gained the power to psychologically maim both those who submit to them and those who seek to exploit them. Both Amy and Mrs. Clennam have shaped their own behavior to conform to Christian precepts, and both have found that they lost a personal identity in the process, while gaining no resources or direction from a transcendent power. (When Amy is made aware of "the unreality of her own inner life" during the Dorrit's grand tour, she is moving closer to the condition Mrs. Clennam has experienced for years.) As if to seal their association, Mrs. Clennam imparts the secret of the fraudulent Clennam business dealings to Amy, to reveal or withhold from Arthur. Amy withholds the secret, as Mrs. Clennam has done, though it has been the one steady object of Arthur's activities since he returned to England. In this, as in other ways, Amy is cast in the role of mother to Arthur, replacing Mrs.

Clennam as she has earlier replaced Arthur as Mrs. Clennam's surrogate child.

Mrs. Clennam has victimized others as well as victimizing herself; she has perverted every family relation and every opportunity for humane dealings that she has had. Amy has been victimized by others but has never retaliated against those weaker than she is (the half-witted "child" of Amy, Maggy, is there to underscore the difference from Mrs. Clennam's abuse of Arthur). Amy has struggled to humanize the harsh conditions of her prison life and has brought comfort to her uncle as well as her father, to Maggy, to the Plornishes, to scores of nameless Marshalsea inmates, and finally to Arthur. *Little Dorrit* does not minimize these crucial differences between Amy and Mrs. Clennam in moral character, human relationships, and personality. But the analogies that the novel develops to draw them into symbolic relationship do suggest that they, like all the female characters in the novel, labor in a context of sexual relations that impress a common pattern of constraint on all of them. The struggle to shape an immoral system into moral purpose is admirable, as it always is for Dickens. Yet the admiration for Amy Dorrit is severely qualified—in the novel's own terms—by the sense that her efforts can do nothing to change the system of sexual relations that warps the efforts of the best as well as the worst of characters.

Now all this suggests the imprisonment of women within the fossilized or perverted forms of a masculine system of values and institutions, rather than the enhancement of their power. In the late novels like *Little Dorrit*, masculine displays of power seem themselves so much empty bluster to disguise real impotence and frustration; all the characters—male and female, virtuous and vicious, aristocrats and slum-dwellers—can seem equally victimized by a system out of everyone's control. Consider the impotence of the central male figures in this novel, for instance: Merdle, William Dorrit, Arthur Clennam, Casby, Pancks, the Barnacles, even the bombastic Punch-and-Judy villain Rigaud. The corruption of the sexual system can seem so endemic to the worlds of the novel, so deeply embedded in every social form, thought, and emotion, that all hierarchies of power and moral order are obliterated.

But the novels resist this sort of reductive, and ultimately quietist view of the world. The direct narrative's account of social behavior and conscious thought keeps us in touch with the reality of moral, social, and psychological distinctions. The more the secret world of sexual fantasies, of covert, unconscious alliances among the unlikeliest of characters, insinuates itself into commonplace behavior, the more the novel makes us aware of the absolute necessity for a new system of values if any sense of conscious control is to remain possible. It is in large part the conflict between these two orders of existence—the world of ordinary, conscious social interactions and the world of unconscious motivation—that gives Dickens' novels their power to create a persuasive account of Victorian culture.

So in each novel we can distinguish oppressors who manipulate others for their own advantage, whatever torments they unintentionally inflict on themselves in the process, or however they respond to the oppressive forces within their own psychological environment. And we can distinguish victims who struggle to make a humane and moral response to the forces that cause them so much anguish. Orlick is a nightmarish version of Pip's fears about his own emotional life, not a literal double of Pip in his secret lusts and depravities. And Pip learns to act on the essentially decent impulses of his nature—as his loving protection of the returned convict Magwitch makes abundantly clear. When we compare the relative opportunities of male and female characters, we can see that Pip has had an opportunity to play out certain fantasies, to make choices and encounter a variety of experiences, as Esther has not, simply because Pip is a male.

In terms of basic control over his own personality, however, Pip is as powerless as she is. Like most of the other heroes in Dickens' novels, Pip adopts modes of behavior and emotion that are stereotypically feminine: passivity, gentleness, humility, and retreat from all forms of self-assertion. As the domineering female characters assimilate patriarchal claims to power and status, Pip and his counterparts in other novels assimilate feminine modes in an effort to avoid the brutal conflict that seems the heritage of their sex. They are inevitably consigned to the victim's role in the process. In terms of social power, basic sexual identity, and the direct expression of erotic desires, they are as neutered as the maternal despots and the bland child-women who move directly from childhood to symbolic parenthood.

The massive, brutal exercise of patriarchal power that victimizes so many characters cannot exist without its victims. It has no object other than internecine struggles for possession of the women whom it all the while tries to reduce to appendages. There is nothing self-sustaining about the patriarchy, no satisfaction in its own resources unless they are validated in the suffering of its victims. Tulkinghorn would have no outlet for his coolly sadistic intellect and carefully regulated resentment without a Lady Dedlock to torment. Magwitch, misguided where Tulkinghorn is malicious, would have had no existence in New South Wales without the thought of his "brought-up London gentleman."

This may seem to make the pursued women in the novels truly negligible—interchangeable tokens in a savage all-male game. But for all the transports of hatred, fear, and vengeful triumph, the struggles between fathers and sons, between rival patriarchs and rival sons, are strangely illusory. The masculine opponent who consumes the psychological lives of so many of Dickens' male characters is primarily a projection of the character's own flawed sexual identity. In this way the patriarchal system falls victim to its own fantasies.

Pip's nearly hysterical fear of Magwitch thus has no substantiation in the gentle, loving, totally submissive figure who appears in his London apartment. Silas Wegg fabricates his rivalry with John Harmon. The bitter irony of Jonas Chuzzlewit's patricide is that his father never limited him in the way he has imagined. Anthony Chuzzlewit's true damage to his son was not in withholding money or thwarting Jonas' various lusts but in providing the model of masculinity that has determined Jonas' personality. In his urge to murder his father, Jonas desperately wants to eradicate his own image. The madness that begins to consume him after his father's death is the sign that he has succeeded. To drive the various ironies home, Dickens contrives the action so that the attempted murder is not the actual cause of death. The whole conflict, like every major struggle between male characters in the novels, is a fantasy that has overpowered the apparently ordinary processes of the social world.

Sikes and Fagin, and the whole criminal establishment they represent, are destroyed by the woman they corrupt, manipulate, and neglect so contemptuously. Their downfall does not come, as they suppose, because Nancy has betrayed them. Instead they are destroyed because they simply cannot understand that one degraded victim might risk her life in compassion for another victim.

It is Sikes's murder of Nancy, not Nancy's rescue of Oliver, that brings justice down upon them. Dickens' passionate reenactment of this scene during his reading tours (which drained him of strength and probably hastened his death) was not just a private obsession.[13] The scene is an emblem of the self-destructive quality of the patriarchal system. Sikes smashes the woman's face turned lovingly toward his own. It is such a reproach to everything lacking in his own emotional life that he *must* obliterate it. And yet he cannot rid himself of the image and all that it represents— the qualities of tenderness, compassion, and love that have been denied him, or that he has denied himself. His death, as much as it seems to balance the scales of justice, is a blessing. The only other likely end for him is complete madness—foreshadowed by hallucinations and fever before his death.

Male characters in Dickens may seem to use the women they contend for as Agamemnon and Achilles use Briseis, an object of male honor. But they find themselves overpowered, like Sikes and Fagin, by their own unconscious desires. In *Our Mutual Friend*, Bradley Headstone and Eugene Wrayburn both lose control over their behavior as they become involved in what Eugene calls "the chase": their rivalry over Lizzie Hexam. Although it becomes clear that this is a struggle between ideas of manhood—Eugene's indolent, patronizing gentility versus Bradley's claim to self-made manhood—the one who has the power to expose the ugliness in both conceptions of maleness is Lizzie Hexam. Eugene's desire for a mistress and Bradley's for a respectable wife come to the same thing: an assertion of the right to form Lizzie to suit their own pattern of life. They both want to "educate" her; and their wholly selfish efforts help call John Harmon's own Griselda-style education of Bella Wilfer into question.

Lizzie does not wish to exert power over either of them; she tries to flee both and the power they have conferred upon her through a retreat to a nonthreatening surrogate family (Riah and Jenny Wren) and, when that fails, to an asexual existence as a factory worker in the idyllic village on the Thames. The village is a haven of benevolent paternalism, as fragile and transient as Jarndyce's utopian family, as the Maylie's rose-covered cottage, as Dingley Dell, as the nostalgic vision of the Ghost of Christmas Past. Lizzie cannot escape the power she has, of course, for it acts independently, outside the scope of her own desires. It is free of any character's conscious control, driving with inexorable force toward the suicide of Bradley Headstone, his murder of Rogue Riderhood, and his nearly fatal attack on Eugene Wrayburn.

This recoil of tyrannical male desire in a way that traps the perpetrator in an obsessive pattern, locks any number of male rivals in these novels into a mutually destructive combat that mocks their pretensions to autonomy: Martin Chuzzlewit and his Grandfather; Pip and Orlick/Drummle; Dombey and Carker; Steerforth and Ham Peggoty; Richard Carstone and Jarndyce (or, rather, Richard and the effigy of the Lord Chancellor that he takes Jarndyce to be). Although the novel's rewards and punishments vary with the moral character of the combatant, the evil and the merely misdirected both expend their energy in a self-defeating struggle.

Even those powerful male figures like Jaggers who try to keep themselves clear of direct involvement with women are drawn into the same general pattern. Jaggers serves Miss Havisham's plot (just as Magwitch's power to make Pip a gentleman is seen by Pip as a result of Miss Havisham's patronage). His aura of power is entirely sham, as far as Pip's career is concerned. Jaggers is little more than an instrument for accomplishing the designs of the two rival patrons who attempt to make Pip in the image of their frustrated desires. And without the force of Mrs. Joe's horrible example, Magwitch himself would never be able to inspire such lasting guilt and terror in Pip.

Although we are no more urged to sympathize with the sadistic male tyrants in Dickens' novels than we are to admire Mrs. Joe's abuse of Pip, the self-destructive nature of patriarchal power becomes increasingly evident. Thus the self-victimization of the patriarchal figures—both craven imposters like William Dorrit and vicious tyrants like Bounderby—becomes as important to the novels' presentation of corruption as the self-victimization of the maternal despots and the child-women. And the novels push beyond this enlargement of our understanding. The abuse of patriarchal power is so virulent that it perplexes ordinary Victorian sentiment and morality. They too are inevitably tainted by corrupt sexual values. Typically in the late novels, the narrators become more strident in the defense of traditional moral values as the forces which threaten to confound all values grow in strength and complexity.

Although the novels' symbolic action challenges and in some ways subverts the narrators' moral and sentimental pronouncements, the result is not to scuttle morality or sentiment but to expose the limitations and distortions within the traditional system of values. Taken together, the novels press, insistently though only implicitly, for a remaking of the whole sexual system.

DESIRE IN DISGUISE: COURTSHIP IN THE PATRIARCHAL SYSTEM

Like most expressions of respectable Victorian culture, Dickens' novels deal with women in ways that circumvent physical desire. Yet the disguise, displacement, and distortion of erotic desires in Dickens' novels is not primarily a result of his own or his culture's inability to deal with sexuality directly. It is rather an expression of his response to the pressures of more basic sexual disorders. For the whole culture, in fact, the shift away from explicit eroticism often discloses more fundamental problems of identity and social role.[14] Victorian euphemisms and displacements often do seem like neurotic evasions, of course, but that judgment hardly exhausts their implications. Patmore's household angel has probably prompted more strenuous reexaminations of male and female sexual roles than Moll Flanders or, for that matter, Molly Bloom.

Most of the eroticism that is diluted into sentimental rhetoric in Dickens—his most notorious novelistic treatment of women—is the narrators' and not the characters' expression. This rhetorical excess tends to occur at two particular moments in the female characters' careers and it tends to assume two distinctive "colorations." When the female characters are most victimized (Nell at the moment of her death, Amy when she is emotionally abandoned by her father) or when they are shifting from the pattern of family victimization into the pattern of courtship (Ruth Pinch cooking dinner for John Westlock, Bella Wilfer at her secret wedding) they receive the full onslaught of sentimental adulation from the narrator. The two forms this adulation takes—impassioned outrage at the abuse of innocence and self-sacrificing devotion, or coy, twittering innuendos about the woman's shy endearments—resolve themselves into one impulse: to prevent these episodes from continuing toward their ultimate implications, which might expose directly the corruption of the system of sexual relations. With just a little more lucidity about the nature of both erotic situations—outrage and coy adulation—the narrators would be forced to recognize that the first is an effort to purge masculine guilt, the second an effort to avoid acknowledging the potential strength of sensuality.

The female characters in Dickens have a power and reality as victims that they never have as actors in their own right or as objects of direct erotic desire. (The powerfully assertive women like Nancy, Rosa Dartle, Caddy Jellyby, and Miss Wade, all justify their behavior through an assertion of their victimization.) But at the point where the victim's plight might become so extreme as to directly challenge the system of family relations that is coextensive with the system of sexual relations, the narrator invariably camouflages the challenge in traditional pieties. At the same time the novel brings into play the inevitable but arbitrary rescue. And it makes little difference, in thematic terms, whether the rescue is death or marriage. The sentimental rhetoric at these moments is so extreme that it almost invariably leads to a reaction *against* the manifest fictional designs, whether it is Jeffrey's anguished, sympathetic tears at the death of Nell, or Wilde's contemptuous sneer, "One must have a heart of stone to read the death of Little Nell without laughing."[15] Dickens' sentimental rhetoric is adroit, but there is no reason to suspect that he carefully calculated its effects. Dickens' empathy with his characters was so great, his methods of creation so spontaneous and intuitive, his own ambivalence toward sexuality so profound that he needed no conscious plan for these effects.[16]

Once Dickens' female characters begin to escape the direct imposition of family demands and begin to move toward a presumptive sexual identity, they begin invariably to lose their psychological energy and thematic significance for the reader—in other words, their fictional reality. The whole plot of courtship and marriage seems irrelevant to the major concerns of each novel. Or, more accurately, it is inadequate to the thematic demands placed on it. Its primary thematic significance is often ironic, proceeding from its failure to satisfy traditional fictional expectations. For this reason, Pip's anguished love for Estella is a farce staged by Miss Havisham; the real relationship that binds them together is their status as Magwitch's children. In a similar way, the love between Amy Dorrit and Arthur Clennam can find expression and some fulfillment only when it begins to satisfy the more basic needs of parent and child. The romance of Rose and Harry Maylie fades before the destructive sexual relations of Nancy and Bill Sikes—its direct antithesis and a horrible parody of the novel's own sentimental courtship plot.

Even in *David Copperfield*, where the courtship plots are certainly more prominent than David's shadowy novelist's career or even his process of maturing, the more standard romance of David and Dora is preempted by the relationship between Agnes and David. Alexander Welsh has demonstrated the ways in which this apparently erotic relationship, like so many others in Dickens, actually fulfills religious rather than sexual longings.[17] But it is a process of salvaging as well as a process of salvation. As the daughter of a failed, impotent father and the son of a failed, impotent mother, these two are early versions of Amy Dorrit and Arthur Clennam. Their union has primary significance as an effort to retain whatever satisfaction is left from the shambles of their childhood families. Meanwhile Steerforth (whose relationship with David is not homoerotic but a parody of a standard romance) has disrupted the one harmonious family group in the novel through his seduction of Emily. The effort of David and Agnes to find in their marriage the basic family nurture lacking in their own childhoods is the common effort of three major couples (John Harmon and Bella Wilfer, Eugene Wrayburn and Lizzie Hexam, Jenny Wren and Sloppy) in *Our Mutual Friend* alone. It is the common effort of Pip and Estella, of Louisa Gradgrind, Esther Summerson, Caddy Jellyby, Martin Chuzzlewit, and so on down the list of major characters who are involved in courtship plots. All these characters have been neglected or abused by a derelict or vicious father.

Not only are all these efforts atavistic, overwhelmingly influenced by the deforming effects of early family abuse or misfortune; they invariably derive their motivating force in the action of the novels, in addition to their psychological and thematic significance, from childhood conflicts with parents. This is quite clear in the case of Esther Summerson, who labors under the transferred guilt of her illegitimate birth, so weakened in her sense of worth that she rejects any possibility of ordinary courtship and marriage for most of the novel. The real illegitimacy, the novel intimates, was her mother's and father's abandonment of their love for each other, not the fact that Esther was born out of wedlock. But in the patriarchal sexual system the shame, as Lady Barbary admonishes Esther, is a taint "that only a woman can feel."

The will of Old Harmon is another manifest assertion of destructive patriarchal influence, this time an effort to keep the father's will alive after his own death. His malicious effort to force his son and Bella Wilfer into marriage is clearly designed to corrupt them as he has been corrupted, by money and by a marriage whose basis is mutual contempt. Harmon's will becomes, of course, the chief obstacle to their marriage. When they finally marry, Bella and John play at daughter and father, just as Bella has played the coquette with her own child-like father and made secret assignations with him. The rebellious and willful Bella Wilfer resigns herself to her surrogate father as meekly as Pansy Osmond submits to Gilbert Osmond in *Portrait of a Lady*. What John Harmon demands of Bella as his test of her fidelity is the absolute relinquishment of her will, her intelligence, her urge for an independent life (the motive which confusedly expresses itself in her earlier urge for money). This parody of a Victorian father's prerogatives certainly calls into question the marriage which the narrator presents as an idyll but which is as questionable in its psychological credibility as in its moral norms.

For similar reasons, the choice of endings for *Great Expectations* is in many ways irrelevant, for both Pip's and Estella's primary orientation all along—the site of their basic psychological conflict and development, the origin of the paralyzing forces which arrest their development and suspend each in a social and emotional limbo, and the urge behind their dreams of power and freedom— has been toward the surrogate parents who dominate their lives.

It is far too simple to squeeze all these relationships into a single, narrow matrix, to say that the heroes and heroines are all simply seeking a parent's rather than an equal's love in their romantic relationships. The forces that shape them and their own personalities are too complex and varied for this. Pip does not find a mother in Estella (he would have in Biddy), even though their relationship at the end of the novel resembles the makeshift arrangements of abused and abandoned children. And the young Pip's fascination with the beautiful, imperious Estella is credible in the explicit social and erotic terms the narrative uses, even if we ignore the special needs his adult oppressors have forced upon him.

Yet it seems fair to say that a complex of relations between parents and children dominates every major courtship in Dickens' novels,[18] whatever variations on this almost archetypal motif develop from novel to novel. This predominate motif helps account for Caddy Jellyby's marriage to a little Prince, a "feminine" man, Esther calls him. Not only can Caddy mother Prince and thus fulfill, as Esther does, the need for love and protection unfulfilled in her childhood; she can atone for the inadequacies of her own mother, as Esther also does, as Joe Gargery in *Great Expectations* does, as most of the "virtuous" characters do in some way. (This is surely one of the motives which causes David Copperfield to submit himself to Dora's silliness, a caricature of Clara Copperfield's stereotypic charms.) Jarndyce himself attempts to atone for the failures of a whole society paternalistic in its pretensions but wholly inadequate to actually care for its children. Jarndyce makes the symbolic condition of all the novel's children literal in his adoption of three orphans and his effort to reform them through a surrogate family (long after their personalities have been determined, unfortunately). Jarndyce, like the passive and subdued heroes and heroines, has also retreated from any distinct erotic desires, and the brief resurgence of individuality in his proposal to Esther quickly recapitulates the prevailing pattern of courtship. Once again courtship becomes a cover for the more fundamental need to reform the system of family relations. Jarndyce gives up his courtship in order to found a second model family, the family of Esther and Allan Woodcourt.

Thus, there is very little fulfillment of ordinary erotic desires in Dickens. By the time we arrive at the novels' endings, the ground of desire has shifted, so that the heroes do not really gain an erotic reward for the virtuous and sentimental restraints they have exercised over their passions. Instead they receive, like an arbitrary act of grace (or, from the perspective of disgruntled readers, like an arbitrary contrivance of the author) a wife who is more maternal than erotic, more a refuge from a destructive social world than a partner in regeneration, more a symbol of lost cultural values than a lover and companion. Similarly, the heroines are so quickly surrounded by their children that erotic fulfillment seems even less an issue for them than it has been during their lengthy ordeals of virtue.

MARTIN CHUZZLEWIT: AN ASSAULT ON THE PATRIARCHAL SEXUAL SYSTEM

When we read through Dickens' novels in any sequence, we soon become aware of recurrent types of characters: the benevolent but troubled patriarch; the innocent, gentle, but addled or deformed young man; the unmarried woman who seethes with hostility and bristles with "masculine" mannerisms; the angelic young woman who mothers her father or a fatherly old man. As we have argued, these are not stock literary types but recurrent figures fashioned to express Dickens' special insights into his culture. Basic patterns in character and situation persist throughout Dickens' fiction because his psychological and thematic interests remain remarkably consistent throughout his career, much more consistent than various attempts to demarcate early, middle, and late periods, comic and "dark" novels, may suggest. For all the transformations in style, characterization, theme, and symbolic method that make each novel distinctive, Pickwick in the Fleet, Micawber in debtor's prison, and William Dorrit in the Marshalsea share fundamental psychological and thematic roles.

In fact, the symbolic roles of characters rather than their manifest social roles give coherence to all Dickens' novels. This has been the source of perplexity and dissatisfaction to "realists" from Lewes to Orwell to Robert Garis.[19] Orwell puts the issue, as usual, succinctly and persuasively:

Dickens sees human beings with the most intense vividness . . . [but] as soon as he tries to bring his characters into action the melodrama begins. He cannot make the action revolve around their ordinary occupations; hence the crossword puzzle of coincidences, intrigues, murders, disguises, buried wills, long-lost brothers, etc. etc.[20]

Orwell's description is shrewd and accurate so far as it goes. But his common-sense version of the social world, where manifest social roles define the scope of the action, gives way *by design* in Dickens' novels to a world of mysterious interconnection and hidden relationships. The characters do not act as "functional members of society" if we assume that society functions as it professes to. But this assumption is the major target of Dickens' social satire from the first novel to the last. The ordinary business of society, and the expectations of many readers, are frustrated precisely as Orwell complains; but as this level of action falls to pieces, as characters seem not so much static as paralyzed in terms of their overt social roles, another dimension of the action takes shape. The intensely vivid details that seemed like a "confusion of gargoyles" to Orwell cohere in an "interior" social system whose interrelations are established largely through symbolic analogies. The melodrama of the direct narrative expresses the bizarre nature of this hidden social world far more powerfully and accurately than any action based on common-sense ideas of probability could do. Like any writer in the romance mode, Dickens challenges precisely such notions of probability, seeking to reveal them as protective illusions that disguise the real business of society: the hidden motives that shape and drive both individuals and the institutions and rituals they develop.

There is abundant evidence that Dickens did not conceive of his novels in these terms, that his conscious intentions were far more commonplace than his actual creations turned out to be. For instance, *Martin Chuzzlewit*, his first novel to assail Victorian family values directly and savagely, was designed by Dickens as an assault instead on selfishness. Once the actual process of composition began, the intuitive design, the real theme and target of the novel, had become clearer to Dickens. He planned to print on the title page the motto: "Your homes the scene, yourselves the actors, here." Though the motto was suppressed on the advice of Forster, who feared that readers would be offended, the satiric purpose was not. And Forster proved to be right. The novel caused the first real breach between Dickens and his middle-class audience, who bought fewer than one-half the numbers *Pickwick Papers* and *Nicholas Nickleby* had sold, and less than one-fifth of the highest sales of the *Old Curiosity Shop*.

Though Dickens clearly became aware of his real preoccupation in this novel, he did so only in general terms. His most intensely vivid creations—those most resistant to assimilation into models of socioeconomic causality and most central to his symbolic psychological networks—continue to result from intuitive rather than analytical perceptions. Dickens always relied on intuition, visual imagination, on all the resources of nonanalytic perception for his most brilliant effects. He had extraordinary access through these methods to the processes of his unconscious mind (and, as the compulsive devotion—or, for some, compulsive revulsion—of his contemporary readers suggests, extraordinary access to the unconscious life of his audience).

One of Dickens' most revealing references to this most powerful and basic method of his imagination appears in response to a comment by G. H. Lewes concerning a passage in *Oliver Twist*: "I scarcely know what answer I can give you," he wrote. "I thought the passage a good one *when* I wrote it, certainly, and I felt it strongly (as I do almost every word I put on paper) *while* I wrote it, but how it came I can't tell. It came like all my other ideas . . . ready made to the point of the pen and down it went." So also, in reference to Pecksniff and Sairey Gamp—two of the least "functional" characters in *Martin Chuzzlewit* in Orwell's terms, two of the most functional in Dickens' symbolic vision of social and psychological life—Dickens wrote: "as to the way in which these characters have opened out, that is one of the most surprising processes of the mind in this sort of invention. Given what one knows, what one does not know springs up; and I am as absolutely certain of its being true, as I am of the law of gravitation—if such a thing be possible, more so."[21] As with the defense of his characterization of Nancy in *Oliver Twist* and of Krook's death by spontaneous combustion in *Bleak House*, Dickens asserts the truth of the romance mode in defiance of the common-sense probabilities of a rationalist's view of the world. Although his formulations are descriptive rather than analytical, Dickens seems clearly to assert that his creative imagination shifts from conscious design and attitude ("what one knows") to intuitive perception ("what one does not know"). And the latter phrase suggests that the intuitive perception is not only surprising but contrary to the original intention.

Martin Chuzzlewit exemplifies the purposes and methods of Dickens' fiction; and it is almost a model of Dickens' critique of the patriarchal system and its corruption of the family and sexual relations. The sense that the self is dispossesed, preyed on by interior motives and external pressures that seem to have little to do with ordinary social values, inevitably comes to focus on the system of sexual relations within the family. Though the intensity and directness with which *Martin Chuzzlewit* presents the family as the source of corruption is new to Dickens' fiction, the pattern is present in all the earlier novels. And they have also dramatized, as *Martin Chuzzlewit* does, the sense that the family itself has been corrupted by a patriarchy whose bizarre manipulations are thoroughly insidious, pervasive, and uncontrollable precisely because they have broken free of conscious design and conscious recognition. Pecksniff and Old Martin Chuzzlewit are the primary false patriarchs in *Martin Chuzzlewit*. They dominate theme and action more directly than Grandfather Trent, Ralph Nickleby, and Fagin; and they are corrupt and vicious in themselves, while Pickwick and Brownlow are benevolent patriarchs. But the most general implications about the patriarchal system of values are similar for all these novels. It is corrupting in ways that supercede and even neutralize distinctions of moral character, temperament, and conscious motivation.

In one of the most profound ironies of Dickens' fiction—an irony that reflects not on Dickens, as many have assumed, but on the nature of the society he portrays—the condition of women can be approached accurately only by presenting them as objects manipulated in a continual struggle for power waged among men. The male characters in *Martin Chuzzlewit* are all compelled to act, constantly and obsessively, as son or father or some combination of the two roles. All the other distinctions of social rank and role they attempt to make cannot disengage them from these primary family roles and this primal conflict. (Here, as elsewhere, Montague Tigg and Jonas Chuzzlewit are disturbingly close to young Martin Chuzzlewit). In a similar but still more radical process, the distinctions among the female characters work in constant tension against the desire of the patriarchal system to use them as interchangeable sex objects. Distinctions among mother and daughter and wife are obliterated, as the anomalous circumstances of Mary Graham, the Pecksniff sisters, Ruth Pinch, and Mrs. Todgers all suggest at various times. Mrs. Lupin, for example, is flustered by her inability to determine Mary's relationship to Old Martin, referring to her in quick, embarrassed succession as his granddaughter, daughter, and wife. (She finally suspects that Mary is his mistress.)

Although it is one of the most digressive of Dickens' novels in direct plot, *Martin Chuzzlewit* is the most complex and systematic of the early novels in its presentation of sexual conflict. The American episodes, which seem set up so that Dickens can vent his personal reactions to America, are fully integrated with the English episodes at this symbolic level. Taken together, they reveal that the promise of freedom and regeneration the United States offered meant only a more rampant, smugly hypocritical abuse of patriarchal power. Jefferson Brick, Colonel Scadder, and scores of other jingoist bullies make the point in marvelously varied burlesques of masculine mannerisms. The diseased, starving family that Mark and Martin discover in Eden presents the ultimate consequences of this abuse. The savage parody of nurture reveals destitution more extreme than in any of the English episodes.

The novel maunders about in its direct development of the action—shunting Martin Jr. from the expected confrontation with his grandfather into the picaresque journey to America; undercutting the motif of Tom Pinch's victimization by setting him up in a mock-career provided by an unknown benefactor and a mock-marriage with his sister; concocting Old Martin's pretense of senility, whose primary result is to expose Mary Graham to Pecksniff's sexual assault. But this dereliction of the direct narrative allows the symbolic patterns of analogy and the thematic material implied in the action to emerge with greater force and clarity.

To many of Dickens' contemporaries the image of the family in the novel seemed an outrageous caricature. It is actually a parody of the grotesque psychic forces masked by habitual routines and idealized assumptions about domestic harmony. The typical comic plot of the English novel—the courtship and marriage of one or more young couples—is displaced to the periphery of *Martin Chuzzlewit*, both in action and in theme. It is supplanted by a complex of plots, all centering on the corruption spread throughout the social system by the abuse of patriarchal power. The false patriarchs Old Martin and Pecksniff control the main plot (though Pecksniff increasingly becomes both the dupe and the surrogate of Old Martin). Together they parody the benign control supposedly exercised by fathers as they actually cause most of the misery in the English episodes of the novel. Jonas Chuzzlewit parodies the son corrupted by this manipulative power; he attempts to murder his father, brutalizes the wife he has wrested from the patriarchy, and succeeds in murdering a caricature of masculine sexual prowess, Tigg Montague. Meanwhile, two other parody sons, young Martin and Mark Tapley, attempt to flee the patriarchal system (and the system of marriage which it controls) by immigrating to America. But when they finally set up house in the Eden settlement, in a masculine travesty of the first marriage relationship, they have merely arrived at the heart of the most grotesque and brutal parody in the novel—a whole nation of bragging, braying, swindling, knife-, gun-, and slogan-wielding men, sons of England in perpetual rebellion against the parent they have disowned.

Most of *Martin Chuzzlewit*'s female characters are reduced to virtually interchangeable symbols within this system. Marriage becomes a male-dominated institution for conferring, withholding, or extorting power. Jonas' marriage, for instance, is an economic transaction with Pecksniff, and he easily substitutes Mercy for Charity Pecksniff at the last moment. Pecksniff in turn gladly abandons both daughters in order to pursue his own marriage plans; his assault on Mary Graham is consciously designed to ensure his power over Old Martin. Martin allows Pecksniff to pursue her as part of his own plans to entrap Pecksniff and use him to mortify the other Chuzzlewit relations: Mary is finally transferred to young Martin, for whom she was originally intended by both Martin Chuzzlewits. Mercy Pecksniff is transferred from Jonas to Old Martin to replace Mary Graham as his surrogate daughter, wife, nurse, and lover. Meanwhile, Ruth Pinch has been shifted from her employer—another bullying patriarch—to her brother and finally to John Westlock. This charade within the novel's homeostatic system of male power relations would be simply farcical if it did not reflect, through parody, the actual treatment of women in Victorian marriage.

Courtship in this world is always a front for some ulterior purpose; and the purpose invariably has been shaped by the pressures and constraints of the sexual system. As in so many of his hypocritical dealings, the mock-patriarch Pecksniff sets the pattern for the whole society in his courtship of Mary Graham. He is both fawning and coercive, mixing unctuous endearments with blackmail. His daughter Mercy accepts Jonas Chuzzlewit's proposal, even though she considers him a repulsive fool, in order to escape her father. Jonas himself is more intent on proving his masculinity to his father and to himself than in securing any erotic pleasure. Young Martin hardly gives a thought to Mary Graham; he seems more intent on fleeing all the pressures of social life in England, including the complexities of sexual relations.

All courtships that take place are tortuous, and troubled by concealed anxieties and hostilities. Jonas tacks off at Charity Pecksniff in order to court her sister Mercy. And the real pleasure he takes in marriage is humiliating and abusing his wife as he has been humiliated by his father and by more stereotypically virile characters like Tigg Montague. Pecksniff fawns over Mary as a way of ingratiating himself with Old Martin. The mannerisms of the servile son, a kind of ur-Heep, mingle horribly with the mannerisms of the benevolent father in Pecksniff's charade.

The persistent symbolic association of marriage with death and swindling provides a thematic matrix for the individual characters' fraudulent and oppressive dealings. The one happy family in the novel literally thrives on death, the snug little "harem" of Mr. Mould, the undertaker. The only other family in the novel that has the ordinary complement of husband and wife is also the only family formed in the course of the novel, the wretched marriage of Mercy and Jonas. It is, appropriately, formed as a mutual swindle (like Jonas' partnership in the Anglo-Bengalee Life Assurance Association), and it serves as the primary emblem of what marriage and the family have become—the husband is master, the wife totally dutiful, suffering his brutal treatment and being still. The grotesque courtship ritual—Mercy's affected coquetry and torment of Jonas, and Jonas' shame-faced wheedling and bullying—is replaced by mutual hatred. The household functions as if it were a tight little island in its own right; the "virtuous" characters do not interfere even though they are quite aware that

Jonas beats Mercy. There are even a parody child and nanny, the
senile old Chuffey and Sairey Gamp. And the family's chief dealings have shifted from greedy swindling to attempted patricide
(just as the Anglo-Bengalee bases its swindles on death).

With the standard Victorian ideals of courtship exposed as thorough frauds, most of the characters are thrown into bizarre parodies of traditional sexual relations. Some characters assail traditional taboos, desperate for freedom and revenge (Jonas' attempt
to murder his father; the two Martin Chuzzlewits' struggle for
possession of Mary Graham, emotionally though not technically
incestuous). Others seem to be groping toward some substitute
relationship that is less sterile and less emotionally crippling than
erotic pairings. Young Martin and Mark Tapley, Poll Sweedlepipe
and Bailey Jr., Chevy Slyme and Tigg Montague, Jonas and Tigg,
Pecksniff and Old Martin form masculine relationships of this
sort, one of the pair invariably making the intense emotional commitment we associate with romantic love. Cherry and Merry
Pecksniff, the two sisters leagued with Mrs. Todgers, Sairey
Gamp and Betsey Prig, Sairey and Mrs. Harris are the female
counterparts.

There are any number of inversions of stereotypic sexual roles
which proceed from the corruption of traditional roles. Betsey
Prig is bearded; the preadolescent Bailey Jr. vaunts nonexistent
whiskers and suspects Mrs. Gamp of harboring a secret passion
for him. Most of the traumatized individuals in Mrs. Gamp's
chamber of childbirth horrors are expectant fathers. Mrs. Todgers
is surrogate mother to a collection of commercial bachelors, a
kind of lower-middle-class mercantile monastery. (It is curious
that a number of critics, such as Steven Marcus, have seen Todgers' as a model of humane civilization. Its harmony depends directly and obviously, like Pickwick's benevolent innocence, on
the avoidance of any form of sexuality other than rhetorical sentiment.)[22] Old Chuffey is treated as a child by Jonas and Anthony
Chuzzlewit in yet another all-male ménage; Sairey Gamp is
brought in as a surrogate mother or nanny. Ruth Pinch plays at
housekeeping for her brother; Mrs. Lupin professionalizes the
housewife's role in her inn as she waits for Mark Tapley to pro-

pose. (His "humour," the idea that marriage to Mrs. Lupin would be so pleasant that he could take no credit for his cheerfulness, is another contrivance to avoid the perils of traditional sexual roles and rituals in this society.)

In a novel full of parody figures, Sairey Gamp is the sole satirist. In a novel full of con-artists, she is the sole rival of her creator, an artist who follows, in this way, the great tradition of Falstaff and the Wife of Bath. In a novel full of female characters who have succumbed to the stereotypic roles prescribed by their society, she is the only woman who refuses to be subdued to what she works in.

Sairey Gamp is everything a Victorian wife should not be. First, she is a widow—a widow, the narrator of *Martin Chuzzlewit* reports, of "such uncommon fortitude . . . as to dispose of Mr. Gamp's remains for the benefit of science" (XIX, 314). (We can assume this was before she established her profitable connection with Mr. Mould, the undertaker.) And she was as uncommon a wife as she is a widow. The Gamps had separated long before his death "on the ground of incompatibility of temper in their drink" (XIX, 314). (We later learn that "incompatibility of temper" meant, among other things, that Gamp knocked out four of her teeth with one blow.) Unlike an Amelia Sedley, a Dorothea Brooke, or Dickens' own Clara Copperfield, she has refused to subserve her husband alive or dead. Instead she has surpassed Gamp in longevity, economic career, and both spiritual and spirituous capacities.

Second, she has no discernible children. The son she mentions in one of her anecdotes has apparently died or been fabricated. Third, she is economically independent—and in a particularly vexing way for the patriarchal social system that dominates the novel. She is a midwife, who assists women when men seem as helpless as her own Mrs. Harris' husband: ". . . Mr. Harris who was dreadful timid went and stopped his ears in a empty dog-kennel, and never took his hands away or come out once till he was showed the baby, wen bein' took with fits, the doctor collared him and laid him on his back upon the airy stones, and she was told to ease her mind, his owls was organs" (XLIX, 754). The narrator himself cannot even call "childbirth" by its name, but in a euphemism that reveals his own anxiety, calls it the "curse of Adam."

Fourth, she is emotionally independent of men. Her one flesh-and-blood friend is her apparent counterpart, Betsey Prig; but her real capacities for love and friendship are invested in the woman of her own creation, the famous Mrs. Harris. Betsey's vicious assault on the reality of Mrs. Harris threatens the independence that Sairey alone of all the female characters in the novel has wrested from a hostile social world. But Sairey, though deeply shaken, defends Mrs. Harris, repudiates Betsey, and exposes her as the prig and traitor she has been from the moment she appeared in the novel: "Mrs. Prig was the Gamp build, but not so fat; and her voice was deeper and more like a man's. She had a beard" (XXV, 411).

Fifth, and this is as telling in relation to Dickens the novelist as her other virtues are in relation to Dickens the husband and father, she is a creator who rivals her author and opposes the sexual values of his overt narrative structure—the only woman in Dickens' novels who has this double distinction.

Sairey manages all this by professionalizing the social roles to which she has been confined; by pretending to be all role, she manages to be all self and thus triumphs over some of the most restrictive marital practices devised by man. And so we come to understand that this paradoxical wife is husbandless and childless because there is no available conception of marriage that can equal her own imagination and capacities. Mrs. Gamp (as the narrator most often calls her) is, both by necessity and choice, an anti-wife.

Given the supremacy of brutal masculine power in *Martin Chuzzlewit* and the corresponding victimization of the few female characters who still have some nominal status, Sairey Gamp's social role ought to restrict her as severely as any character in the novel. As a midwife, she is already a "female functionary," doubly subordinated. But Sairey is not to be dominated, coerced, ignored, or, as she sums it up, "impoged upon." She refuses to be reduced to a parody wife, a parody midwife, a parody anything. In a novel filled with parody figures—male and female—she is the sole consistent satirist, as we have seen, and the novel's chief antagonist to the stereotypes of the Victorian wife. Her primary instrument of satire is the anecdote, which typically assails the values of the overt narrative while asserting its own shrewd alternatives. Thus, in one major example, the narrator's previous effusions over Ruth Pinch make Sairey's insidiously satiric praise of her beauty all the more piquant:

'Now, ain't we rich in beauty this here joyful arternoon, I'm sure. I knows a lady, which her name, I'll not deceive you, Mrs. Chuzzlewit, is Harris, her husband's brother bein' six foot three, and marked with a mad bull in Wellington boots upon his left arm, on account of his precious mother havin' been worrited by one into a shoemaker's shop, when in a sitiwation which blessed is the man as has his quiverful of sech, as many times I've said to Gamp when words has roge betwixt us on account of the expense—and often have I said to Mrs. Harris, "Oh, Mrs. Harris, ma'am! your countenance is quite a angel's!" which, but for Pimples, it would be. "No, Sairey Gamp," says she, "you best of hard-working and industrious creeturs as ever was underpaid at any price, which underpaid you are, quite diff'rent. Harris had it done afore marriage at ten and six," she says, "and wore it faithful next his heart 'till the colour. run, when the money was declined to be give back, and no arrangement could be come to. But he never said it was a angel's, Sairey, wotever he might have thought."

[XLVI, 704]

In this seemingly random, garbled patter, Sairey insinuates a number of the forces that work to transform the ersatz angel of courtship into the actual Victorian wife: pimples, multiple child-bearing, the fading (and even the running) of sentiment, the grim permanence of marriage contracts, the economic forces that permeate the rituals of courtship and marriage, and the impossibility, for most Victorian wives, of escaping from even the worst of marriage bargains. (Sairey's two zany images of male sexual fantasies—the mad bull in Wellington boots and the blessed man who has, by the syntax, his quiverful of pregnant women—simply defy paraphrase.)

Sairey conflates Charity, Mercy, and Ruth into one "rich" image of female beauty. And thus in one stroke she overturns all the distinctions the narrator has tried to create among them. She catches him in his own contradictions; for he has, in fact, persistently equated the good and desirable woman with a familiar fragile stereotype of feminine beauty: "pretty little figure," "delicate waist," "tiny, precious, blessed little feet." Each epithet has deprived Ruth of a little more individuality, has objectified and diminished her a little more; each reveals less about the nature of women in Victorian society and more about the nature of male fantasies. The fantasy of the childlike, angelic, desexualized maiden of courtship is obviously the inverse of the aggressive sexuality that the narrator has displaced onto Jonas Chuzzlewit.

So the narrator has foisted on the reader a portrait of the maiden as angel that is as shoddy as the miniature portrait foisted on Mr. Harris. The colors run at the touch of a little sweat, just as the confusion of erotic and spiritual desires in the image of the angel is exposed by Sairey and Mrs. Harris with the eruption of a few pimples; but the real flaw in the self-defacing portrait is the poor aesthetic material from which it was created.

It is in this same episode that Sairey casually comments on the loss of her teeth: "Gamp hisself . . . at one blow, bein' in liquor, struck out four, two single and two double, as was took by Mrs. Harris for a keepsake, and is carried in her pocket to this hour." Sairey leaves us with this marvelous comic and mordant double image: Mr. Harris with his portrait, an emblem of the masculine sentimentality that aggressively defaces the woman it supposedly enshrines; Mrs. Harris with Sairey's teeth, a relic of open brutality toward wives.

Only Sairey, of all the characters in *Martin Chuzzlewit*, can transcend this polarized image, which actually reflects two extreme projections of the same antifeminist attitudes. And, given the psychic and social conditions of the novel, she can do so only in her imagination—through the marriage of the marvelous Harrises: "For if ever a woman lived as know'd not wot it was to form a wish to pizon them as had good looks, and had no reagion give her by the best of husbands, Mrs. Harris is that ev'nly dispogician" (XLVI, 704–5). Mrs. Harris may bear no ill will; but Sairey, who directs this remark toward Ruth Pinch, does infiltrate her description of Mrs. Harris' heavenly disposition with the urge to poison the beautiful, brittle creatures of male desire. Because figures who dominate the world of *Martin Chuzzlewit*—the narrator as well as the characters—cannot even conceive of the ideal of marriage created in the very earthy heaven of Sairey's imagination, much less accept it, her doses of satiric aggression and satiric exposure are the best tonic for her imagination and for ours.

Thus *Martin Chuzzlewit* develops a theme that persists throughout Dickens' work: the crippling distortions of sexual and familial roles by the oppressive patriarchy and the extension of corrupted sexual patterns into every major institution of Victorian society. Through recurrent types of characters—the angel women, the masculinized shrews, the inadequate young men, the oppressive patriarchs—Dickens expresses his vision of a world that represses, thwarts, and distorts human energies. The Dickens women, like the Dickens children, are prime indictments of this system of values. In Esther Summerson as well as Mrs. Joe, in Amy Dorrit as well as Sairey Gamp, Dickens linked Victorian stereotypes about women with the corrupt system of values that produced them. Thus the Dickens women express a criticism of patriarchal values as searching as any produced in the nineteenth century.

4

COLLINS

OF these four novelists, Dickens makes the most comprehensive assault on the total structure of Victorian society. But he explores the situations of women caught in traditional roles and avoids a direct challenge to the prevailing sexual orthodoxies. In fact, as we have shown, his radical critique of Victorian sexual values can be (and certainly has been) totally overlooked if readers are not attentive to the implications of his fiction's symbolic structures. In contrast, Collins is the most directly concerned with issues of women's rights and the most openly irreverent toward Victorian sexual conventions. For example, in a novel designed to assail what Collins called "claptrap morality," the narrator remarks "anything is welcome to the women which offers them any sort of harmless refuge from the established tyranny of the principle that all human happiness begins and ends at home" (*Armadale*, 504). Yet what most distinguishes Collins among this group is the prominence he gives in his fiction to unconventional women—often distinctly criminal or immoral by the standards of respectable Victorianism—and to conventional women in unconventional situations.[1]

Collins' novels are more obviously concerned than the other four novelists' with legal reforms affecting women. Many of his plots are structured around legal issues—wills, inheritance laws, marriage laws, and property rights.[2] In most cases it is women who are depicted as the victims of inequities in the law: Laura Fairlie and Anne Catherick of *The Woman in White*, Magdalen and Norah Vanstone of *No Name*, Anne Silvester and Hester Dethridge of *Man and Wife*.

Yet with few exceptions Collins does not focus directly on the question of reform. A novel like *No Name* begins with criticism of the divorce and inheritance laws but turns increasingly into a Bildungsroman of a very unconventional young woman and finally into a traditional courtship tale. Similarly, the focus of *The Woman in White* is more on the mystery and courtship strains of the novel than on the issue of property rights. Collins often chooses peripheral legal issues, such as the Scottish and Irish marriage laws in *Man and Wife*, rather than attack the major legal abuses directly.

It is typical of the ambivalence shown by all four authors that Collins' methods are circuitous. He subverts the principles of a sexually biased legal system only through implication as he executes a direct and in some ways diversionary attack on the tangled fringes of the law. And it is especially typical of Collins' distinctive methods of inversion and parody that he approaches his central preoccupation with women's identities through characters who consciously impersonate others and unconsciously mimic them. His almost obsessive interest in crime and bizarrely melodramatic complexities—the qualities of the sensation novel for which he is most famous—are focused on the abuse of sexual relations in nearly all his novels, usually with women as the primary victims.[3] Like Dickens, Trollope, and Thackeray, Collins can be most ambivalent when he is most relentlessly in pursuit of the sexual corruption at the heart of Victorian life. And thus, again like the others, his most incisive critiques develop through strategies of indirection.

The "appropriate form" for Collins had to be a form that released his unconscious perceptions as well as giving expression to his conscious intentions and thus drew him on toward implications that even his unconventional mind was not ready to ratify consciously. The mystery structure provided that form; twists of plot, disguises, tortuous legal complexities, and, at times, the near loss of a narrator's control through plot complications allowed Collins to enter the labyrinth of Victorian sexual relations. The labyrinth holds both the mystery and the method for disclosing it, but it also offers concealment for the pursuer. This is true for Collins' impersonators like Magdalen Vanstone and Lydia Gwilt, and for his detectives like Walter Hartright; but is is also true for the chief impersonator and detective, the novelist himself. While Collins' methods concealed some of his most radical perspectives from his uneasy or censorious readers, they also, we think, concealed them from Collins' own conscious recognition.

Collins explores issues of women's identity in Victorian culture by assailing his central female characters with bizarre plot conditions that gradually reveal themselves as parodies of conventional sexual alignments. In *The Woman in White* an illegitimate daughter confined to an insane asylum becomes the means for attacking the identity and the sanity of her double, who has been forced into marriage by her father (his authority surviving his own death). The two "women in white" are ultimately used to expose the absurd cruelty of a more conventional notion of women in white: pure, virginal, passive, emptied of all vitality, and utterly interchangeable. In a similar way the atypical plight of the disinherited Magdalen Vanstone (legally illegitimate like Anne Catherick) becomes a means of implying that most Victorian women have no firm identity, "no name," as they remain under paternal authority or pass from a father's authority to a husband's (exchanging, of course, one man's name for another's).

As Collins develops his symbolic plots that undermine, implicitly, Victorian claims to decency and order, he exploits particularly revealing extremes of sexual stereotyping. As with all of the male novelists we are discussing, the novelistic conventions here are projections of concealed social conventions. His "good" women can become passive to the point of ludicrousness—drugged, insane, surrendering their will to one man after another (like Laura Fairlie submitting to a benevolent, but deluded father, then to an evil husband, and finally to a "good" husband, with hardly a murmur of protest). The bustling Esther Summerson, with her aggressive humility, seems self-reliant and remarkably energetic in contrast to Laura, Norah Vanstone, or Anne Silvester, Collins' "good" women whose extreme lassitude of will parodies the Victorian ideal.

More obviously, Collins develops that always potentially sub-

versive stereotype of the "bad" woman far beyond the limits of
the standard Victorian melodrama, which typically uses the bad
woman as a kind of allopathic cure for endangered virtue.[4] Collins'
"bad" women in No Name and Armadale become true outlaws
who challenge pious norms with the vigor and sanity of their
deviance. He can so fuse the outlaw and the heroine as to deeply
trouble his middle-class reading public with this vivid image of
their own ambivalent desires about women (those readers, for
instance, who wanted the errant Magdalen of No Name more
severely punished for her supposed sins and certainly not given
the standard reward for a Victorian heroine—marriage to a good,
respectable, moneyed man).

Collins' variations on extreme stereotypes are diverse and depend for their full effect on the precise circumstances of his maze-
like novels. They become most significant, like their counterparts
in the novels of Dickens, through the interplay between extremes
of sexual role and behavior.

The symbolic interrelations between Laura Fairlie and Marian
Halcombe, the main female characters in The Woman in White, are
so significant that they have been described as split halves of one
personality.[5] But Collins has not simply polarized them into the
good/fair/passive and bad/dark/active extremes that appear in
much fictional stereotyping of women. Marian is dark-haired and
active but she is hardly an exemplar of wickedness. In fact, she
is so intelligent, resolute, and imaginative as the chief agent of
Laura's rescue that a number of Collins' readers have considered
her the true heroine of the novel.[6] Laura is certainly fair and
passive, but she is so passive, so acquiescent to the various men
who rule her life, and so incapable of assisting in her own rescue
that she seems a parody.

Collins has made his transformation of stereotypes still more
complex by grafting a supposedly "masculine" head onto Marian's
typically beautiful feminine body and by making this extraordi-
narily capable woman bitterly disparage her own sex. This is not,
finally, a splitting of one whole personality into two extremes but
a revelation of two women's personalities made extreme and mis-
shapen by the sexual attitudes of their society. Collins' ambiva-

lence toward his own creation here is shown in the mixed admiration and mockery that characterizes the novel's presentation of both Marian and Laura.

The plot of *The Woman in White* centers on the gradual undermining of Laura's identity through her relationship to men—as a daughter, lover, wife, and mother. In each relationship, her role, her sense of self, and her sense of failure or accomplishment is determined by the men who control her. In this regard there is no real distinction between the cruel husband who tries to commit her to an asylum and the kind husband provided by the novel's traditional conclusion, or between either husband and her father.

As a daughter, she is the victim of a father empowered by a patriarchal authority that defines women as appendages, "relative creatures" who gain identity through their relationships with men. Her father arranges a marriage with a man she does not love, and he arranges the terms of her inheritance to suit himself. Because he has left an illegitimate daughter, Anne Catherick, who physically resembles Laura, even Laura's identity as a legitimate daughter can be taken from her. More significant, the redoubling of the stereotypic "woman in white"—pure *because* she is passive—in Anne and Laura suggests how fragile and manipulable feminine identity is in this culture. The parody image of the "good" daughter and wife that Anne Catherick embodies implies that such treatment is a form of mental confinement.

As lover and wife, Laura's identity is similarly vulnerable. The lack of self-assertion apparent when she accepts her father's choice of a husband against her own desires also characterizes her courtship and marriage. She will not withdraw from her engagement to Sir Percival, allows him to set the date for their wedding, and blindly gives him a weapon to use against her when she loves someone else. Although she hopes for a release from the engagement, she does not stoop (as she would see it) to try to manipulate Percival into ending the engagement. So, for Laura the roles of daughter and wife dictate absolute suppression of self.

Her passivity makes Laura helpless before Fosco's schemes. Since she keeps no records, she is unable to prove when she left for London. As a result, she cannot prove that she is Laura Fairlie

rather than the mad Anne Catherick. Similarly, she will not eaves-
drop or spy as Marian does; she never even attempts to find Marian
when the latter has been confined in an unused part of the house.
And when she tries to follow Marian to London, she does not ask
why Marian has apparently left. As a nurse to Marian, Laura has,
moreover, been "so dreadfully alarmed and distressed that she
was quite useless" (I, 543). In her innocent rectitude and passivity,
her refusal to violate her narrow sense of feminine honor by calculated, wily, or defensive actions, Laura loses control of her own
identity so far as society is concerned and even acquieses in the
process.

After Laura's health, her legal identity, and her fundamental
sense of self have been undermined by Percival and Fosco, Hartright reenters the novel as a benevolent lover and husband. But
he is still a controlling male to whom she surrenders her will. She
needs Hartright's help both to feel emotionally secure and to gain
legal recognition. At this period of her life, she is described as
pale, thin, slow, and childlike, and her sketches are "poor little
dim [and] faint" (II, 93; II, 107). She is a psychological parasite,
dependent upon others' nurturing rather than upon her own efforts for her restoration to health. As this becomes abundantly
clear, the novel undermines its own efforts to cast the males who
control Laura into distinct roles as villains and heroes. The damage
to Laura has not been caused by one man's villainy, and it cannot
be repaired through one man's virtue; it is a disease endemic to
the system.

Laura has been made "utterly incapable of assisting the assertion
of her own case" (II, 284). So the resolution of her torment is in
perfect keeping with its origins. The question of Laura's identity
is finally decided by men—by Hartright, Percival, Fosco, Laura's
uncle, her lawyer, Pesca, even the owner of the livery stables, and
the driver who picked her up at the train station on her arrival in
London.

In fact, Laura never does gain an independent identity. Before
the last struggle with Fosco, Hartright has married her, and so
she is never restored to being either Laura Fairlie or Lady Glyde.
She merely takes on yet another predetermined role as Mrs. Hart-

right. Even when Laura does finally inherit the Limmeridge estate, she immediately transfers this portion of her identity to another male, her son, whom she calls the "Heir of Limmeridge" (II, 387).

In Laura Fairlie's plight Collins has assailed the masculine powers and prerogatives that drain women of will and identity. But the novel's ending seems to ratify the very passivity the novel has previously deplored. This ambivalence is even clearer in the portrayal of Marian Halcombe. Marian is everything Laura is not: intelligent, self-assertive, resolute, and effective. She controverts through her personal resources and behavior the very stereotypes of femininity that Laura seems to represent. And yet Collins, his narrator Walter Hartright, and Marian herself cannot fully accept these admirable qualities as legitimately feminine. The novel's two most important narrators—Hartright and Marian—constantly employ conventional stereotypes to evaluate Marian. Hartright first sees her as beautiful and sexually attractive, but when she turns around the impression is destroyed for him because her face does not fit the stereotype:

. . . The lady is ugly!

Never was the old conventional maxim, that Nature cannot err, more flatly contradicted—never was the fair promise of a lovely figure more strangely and startlingly belied by the face and head that crowned it. The lady's complexion was almost swarthy, and the dark down on her upper lip was almost a mustache. She had a large, firm, masculine mouth and jaw; prominent, piercing, resolute brown eyes; and thick, coal-black hair, growing unusually low down on her forehead. Her expression— bright, frank, and intelligent—appeared, while she was silent, to be altogether wanting in those feminine attractions of gentleness and pliability, without which the beauty of the handsomest woman alive is beauty incomplete.

[I, 46–47]

The disconcerted Hartright retreats from this shock to his conventional erotic expectations into smug "aesthetic" judgments that are equally conventional.[7] The judgments are so patently based on his own comic quandary that they are undercut immediately. What is grotesque in this scene is the characterization, not the character—Hartright's inability to harmonize the unconventional features with his own preconceptions about feminine beauty. But the novel's departure from Hartright's standards becomes much more significant when we realize that Marian's supposedly masculine traits are her greatest strengths and the traits that help Laura through crises Laura herself is incompetent to deal with. Marian's "masculine" traits are significantly chosen—the mouth with which she speaks, the eyes with which she sees, and the intelligent look that shows her understanding. These qualities are the ones denied Laura.

More problematic is Marian's own attitude toward herself and toward ideas of femininity. She abounds in self-depreciating antifeminist slurs from her first appearance in the novel, comments that are directly contradicted by her own resolute, even authoritarian behavior:

How can you expect four women to dine together alone every day, and not quarrel? We are such fools, we can't entertain each other at table. You see I don't think much of my own sex, Mr. Hartright—which will you have, tea or coffee?—no woman does think much of her own sex, although few of them confess it as freely as I do. Dear me, you look puzzled . . . are you surprised at my careless way of talking? . . . I will give you some tea to compose your spirits, and do all a woman can (which is very little, by the by) to hold my tongue.

[I, 48–49]

More significant still, Marian never openly questions Laura's resolve to submit to a hated prearranged marriage; in fact, she forms and supports that resolve as much as Laura does and banishes the strongest obstacle to its fulfillment, Walter himself. Yet Marian rages over Glyde's high-handed arrangement of the wedding date, an almost certain displacement of a bitter, spirited resentment toward the system of male domination that she thoroughly abets in word and action. Finally this utterly contradictory but plausible psychological conflict erupts into direct statement:

The question of time [the decision about the wedding date] is *our* question—and trust me, Laura, to take a woman's full advantage of it. . . . Are you to break your heart to set his mind at ease? No man under

heaven deserves these sacrifices from us women. Men! They are the
enemies of our innocence and our peace—they drag us away from our
parents' love and our sisters' friendship—they take us, body and soul,
to themselves, and fasten our helpless lives to theirs as they chain up a
dog to his kennel. And what does the best of them give us in return?
Let me go, Laura—I'm mad when I think of it.

[I, 271–72]

In his complex interplay of refashioned stereotypes Collins has
created two women whose opposed temperaments are plausible
psychological responses to the prevailing sexual system and, at
the same time, form a symbolic relationship in which they are like
split halves of a full person. At the end of the novel Marian remains
almost a third partner to the marriage of Hartright and Laura (like
the role Esther Summerson seek for herself with Richard and
Ada). She has no secure, separate identity. "After all that we three
have suffered together," she says to Walter, "there can be no
parting between us, till the last parting of all. My heart and my
happiness, Walter, are with Laura and you. Wait a little till there
are children's voices at your fireside. I will teach them to speak
for me, in *their* language; and the first lesson they say to their
father and mother shall be—we can't spare our aunt!" (II, 378–79).
Laura is the sexual entity who attracts Hartright, marries, and
bears a child, while her half-sister Marian performs other wifely
functions: writing letters, conversing with Hartright, and teaching
the children. The novel ends with Marian—not Laura—intro-
ducing the new "heir of Limmeridge" to his father.

And so Marian's identity is really no more her own than Laura's
is, for all her personal strengths and virtues. This "dark lady" is
not as thorough an antithesis to the women in white—Laura and
Anne Catherick—as she first seems to be. Throughout the novel
Marian's life is subordinated to Laura's needs, and those—as we
have shown—are totally subordinated to the various men who
rule Laura's life. Marian is forced to live a vicarious existence in
which she shares only a shadowy version of traditional feminine
"rewards" and in which her most distinctive traits are labelled
"masculine" and used only to serve others' needs.

Yet whatever anomalous circumstances and attitudes hamper

Marian from self-realization, she establishes a value system in the
novel that helps expose the shallowness of the orthodoxies seemingly ratified by the novel's ending, by Hartright's conventional
sexual values, and by Marian's own disparagement of women.
Until the end, she struggles against Percival and Fosco far more
effectively than Hartright and Laura's other male protectors. The
weapons she uses are traditional masculine resources: personal
courage, resolution, wiliness, and the written word.[8] When
Marian eavesdrops and intrigues, she feels that she has violated
principles of womanly decorum; but the novel makes it clear that
to do otherwise would risk the status, the identities, the very lives
of both the novel's heroines. No self-depreciation can detract from
Marian's real virtues and accomplishments, and thus through her
the novel's action contravenes the stereotypic implications of the
overt narrative. To call Marian's qualities "masculine" is simply
to expose the fact that male characters in the novel lay exclusive
claim to strengths and virtues that are preminently embodied in
a female character. The terms "masculine" and "feminine" have
become evasions rather than descriptions.

In *No Name* (1862) Collins again explores the constricting nature
of the roles prescribed for Victorian women. But instead of putting
a suffering, victimized woman in the foreground as he did in *The
Woman in White*, he puts an unconventional woman at the center.
Magdalen Vanstone has all the wit and will of Marian Halcombe
but few of Marian's socialized scruples. She is rebellious, self-
assertive, cunning, ready to use devices to gain her ends that
Marian would never consider. And she is not hampered by an
idea that these traits make her a sexual hybrid, a freakish combination of masculine and feminine features. Magdalen acts for
herself, not for a surrogate self, using men for her advantage rather
than subordinating herself to them. Though her conscious goal
is to regain the name and inheritance unjustly taken from her, she
is more profoundly rebelling against the fragility and emptiness
of conventional feminine identity. .

For all this, *No Name* is not a feminist manifesto but an ambivalent representation of a complex and contradictory social

world. The narrator and the "good" characters regard Magdalen's conduct as deviant or criminal, however sympathetic they are to its motives. Magdalen herself ultimately acquiesces in this judgment and returns to the norm of virtuous wife. Though less blatantly than Trollope, Collins seems to ask of his readers, "Can you forgive her?", yet he rewards Magdalen with a conventional happy ending—to the consternation of some of his contemporary readers. To further complicate our responses to the novel, the "reward" of a conventional marriage has been even more thoroughly challenged than in *The Woman in White.*

Once again Collins pits intriguingly varied stereotypes of women against each other to explore and expose the nature of Victorian attitudes toward women. Magdalen's sister Norah is the passive, pallid, good girl who accepts disinheritance and disgrace as submissively as she accepted the idle security of middle-class respectability. Even before the bizarre disclosure that typically energizes a Collins plot, Magdalen reveals her sharply unconventional temperament by mimicking Norah's mannerisms in an amateur production of *The Rivals* (a significant title for two sisters of such opposed temperaments).

Once Magdalen learns that she is illegitimate, the rebelliousness and gift for mimicry find a more significant expression. Most simply, Magdalen seeks to determine her own identity by controlling her name rather than having it controlled by men or by a legal system careless of the rights of wives and children. Magdalen's story contains two stages: first, her observations of other women and the lessons she draws from them about women's options, and second, her own parodic repetition of their roles. These are acted out self-consciously and with revolutionary intent. She sees that neither her mother, her governess, her "aunt," her maid, nor her sister has found a way to achieve happiness or independence. Magdalen mimics these roles, designedly and dishonestly, in order to gain power not otherwise available through acceptance or compliance.

Her mother has lived disinterestedly for love and has been victimized by this choice. She has agreed to live with Andrew Vanstone when he cannot free himself from his profligate wife, despite social disapproval and the inequality of their sacrifices: "Having once resolved to sacrifice her life to the man she loved; having quieted her conscience by persuading herself that his marriage was a legal mockery," (I, 187), Mrs. Vanstone runs all the risks of social disapproval while her husband runs virtually none. He feels he has been saved by her and responds "so gratefully" (I, 186) when his real wife dies that he marries Magdalen's mother, but his "gratitude" is voluntary while Mrs. Vanstone's suffering is not: she would be the one to suffer the stigma of adultery if the truth were known. When Vanstone dies before changing his will, her children are left destitute. Suddenly they are declared illegitimate, with no name and no inheritance. Mrs. Vanstone, at the age of forty-four, dies in childbirth after receiving news of her husband's death.

Magdalen's sister Norah, though she does not suffer for traditional feminine virtues so obviously as her mother has, suggests in her uncomplaining passivity a more chilling kind of suffering: existence as a virtual nonentity. It is thus not simply an authorial choice but a psychological revelation that her personality is scantily portrayed. After learning that she will lose her inheritance and name, she says to Miss Garth, "Try not to grieve over what you have heard about us this morning. Does it matter who we are, or what we keep or lose? What loss is there for us after the loss of our father and mother?" (I, 208). Later, after Norah quits her post as governess—a traditional female occupation—when her employer quarrels with her about Magdalen, she writes to the latter: "Don't suppose I am discouraged by this first check. There are many kind people in the world; and some of them may employ me the next time. The way to happiness is often very hard to find; harder, I almost think, for women than for men. But if we only try patiently, and try long enough, we reach it at last—in heaven, if not on earth" (I, 446).

This is a familiar piety, though Norah almost realizes its special Victorian application to women. But the novel is concerned with earthly misery and happiness, and Norah's only "way to happiness" turns out to be a passive waiting for rescue—by Collins— through the agency of a virtuous husband.

When Magdalen "descends" from the stifling routines of an affluent, respectable young women, she finds a world that is more dangerous but also more exciting, less stable but therefore more malleable, more fraudulent in traditional terms but also, in some ways, more candid. Her association with the swindler, Captain Wragge, for instance, exposes her to a marriage that is openly brutal and unjust in its power relations—a parody of the radical injustice that was concealed within the relative comfort and decency of her parents' marriage.

Mrs. Wragge's first role, as a waitress, is appropriate preparation for her marriage to Wragge. She is reduced to a harried servant of crude masculine desires. This is her account of Wragge's courtship:

"He was the hungriest and the loudest to wait upon of the lot of 'em. I made more mistakes with him than I did with all the rest of them put together. He used to swear—oh, didn't he use to swear! When he left off swearing at me he married me. . . . I had my trifle of money, and I had my pick, and I picked the captain—I did. He was the smartest and the shortest of them all."

[I, 295–96]

After they are married, Wragge sees his husbandly role as keeping his wife in line and exacting service from her. When Mrs. Wragge and Magdalen go to London together, Wragge writes to the latter:

"How is my unfortunate wife? I am afraid you find it impossible to keep her up at heel, or to mold her personal appearance into harmony with the eternal laws of symmetry and order. Does she attempt to be too familiar with you? I have always been accustomed to check her in this respect. She has never been permitted to call me anything but Captain. . . ."

[I, 444]

Liberated from the Captain's surveillance, Mrs. Wragge becomes exuberant in London about her release from the domestic responsibilities that usually cause a buzzing in her head: "'No cookery-book!' cried Mrs. Wragge. 'No Buzzing in my head! No captain to shave to-morrow! I'm all down at heel; my cap's on one side; and nobody bawls at me. My heart alive, here *is* a holiday

and no mistake!'" (I, 374). Her interests have become restricted
to shopping and clothes; her greatest joys come from a sort of
vegetable existence in which she neglects all that her energetic
husband demands of her—namely, personal orderliness and attention to his needs for food, cleanliness, and order.

Mrs. Wragge's failings are not presented only as abnormalities,
but as symptoms of two problems posed by conventional ideals
for her sex. First, she is troubled by the discrepancy between ideals
of femininity and ideals of wifely duty. She equates femininity
with such things as small, soft, white hands and pretty bonnets.
Collins' conventional heroines—Norah Vanstone or Laura Fairlie—show that passivity is part of the same ideal, soft hands sig-
nifying a ladylike abstention from work. But wifely duty, as Mrs.
Wragge discovers, can involve vigorous activity on behalf of one's
husband.

Mrs. Wragge's "crude," simpleminded candor discovers what
the refined decorum of Norah Vanstone never does recognize:
Victorian ideals of femininity have little regard for the reality of
individual personality. Mrs. Wragge's abnormal size is only one
of the ways in which she does not fit the ideal of the little wife
(such as Bella Wilfer or Amelia Sedley). Collins makes his point
when Wragge orders an omelette for his breakfast and his wife
cannot understand how to make one. During the whole time that
Wragge explains cheerfully to Magdalen his devices for swindling
and manipulating people, his wife sits "lost in contemplation of
one of her own thumbs," trying to discover how to make an
omelette requiring butter "the size of your thumb" when her
individual thumb is obviously too large to measure by (I, 303).
Even the cookbook assumes women all fit the same mold. Meanwhile Mrs. Wragge hears nothing her husband says because, as
Magdalen theorizes, she is "self-isolated from her husband's del-
uge of words" (I, 307). The buzzing in her head began as protective
static when, as a waitress, she tried to satisfy all the gentlemen's
demands. During marriage to Wragge she has disintegrated altogether under demands which suit him without any reference to
whether they suit her. Her self-isolation, passivity, and withdrawal from willed activity are the results.

Mrs. Wragge enters the novel as a minor comic character. She develops into a parody of the condition of all the dutiful women in the novel and a figure of pathos. Her life is spent trying to respond to demands men make of her and constantly failing. In trying to satisfy all her male customers at the restaurant without confusing their orders, she often forgot her own name (I, 294). After marrying, Mrs. Wragge is frequently called upon by her husband to adopt new names to fit his swindling schemes. The scene in which she becomes "Mrs. Bygrave" is full of echoes of the problem of a woman's identity:

"Stand straight, and listen to me," he began. . . . "Do you know whose skin you are in at this moment? Do you know that you are dead and buried in London, and that you have risen like a phoenix from the ashes of Mrs. Wragge? No! you evidently don't know it. This is perfectly disgraceful. What is your name?"

"Matilda," answered Mrs. Wragge, in a state of the densest bewilderment.

"How dare you tell me your name's Matilda? Your name is Julia. Who am I? . . . You don't know?" repeated the captain, sternly confronting his wife. . . . Don't let me have a woman who doesn't know who I am to operate on my beard tomorrow morning. Look at me! More to the left—more still—that will do. What am I? I'm Mr. Bygrave—Christian name, Thomas. Who are you? You're Mrs. Bygrave—Christian name, Julia."

[I, 469–70]

This operation, which Wragge has performed repeatedly, he calls "hammering"—a parodic inculcation of a wife's duties. Mrs. Wragge's name is whatever he decides it to be—a general condition, of course, of all married women in Victorian society. And Captain Wragge blatantly declares that the only identity that matters is his: a truth about masculine legal prerogatives the Vanstones have also discovered.

Magdalen's search for her name and her inheritance, then, involves initially rejecting the options—or lack of options—she sees in other women's lives; but she is also involved in a more active testing of these options by impersonating other women. The

theme of acting is thus very closely related to the theme of willing
or choosing, as opposed to submitting and accepting.

Magdalen first throws off her girlhood and the passivity it en-
tails when she begins to act. Until she takes a part in *The Rivals*
she seems to be merely a high-spirited, thoughtless young girl,
but when she starts to act out a personality not her own, maturity
and a seriousness about her own life suddenly come to her. Her
first role as the maid Lucy in *The Rivals* foreshadows her last role
as the maid Lucy at Admiral Bartram's house. Between her first
and last roles, she parodies almost every role lived by the other
women in the novel.

In the private theatricals she quickly assumes a second role,
foreshadowing, perhaps, the multiplicity of roles she will later
play. Julia in the play is a sentimentally faithful young girl in love
with Falkland (played by Frank Clare); her situation is close
enough to Magdalen's own (since Magdalen thinks she loves
Frank) that for Magdalen to play Julia could simply involve her
in projecting herself into the role of Julia. This she does not do.
Instead she portrays Julia as a sort of Norah by imitating Norah's
voice and mannerisms. This is only the first of a series of impersonations in which Magdalen departs from her given social role
because being herself (in the way that Norah and Miss Garth are
always themselves) involves a submissiveness that Magdalen is
trying to reject. By playing Julia as Norah, she asserts that she
can choose who she is to be, instead of being trapped in her own
destiny. And, as Norah's bitterly angry response to the impersonation suggests, Magdalen has also begun to mock the traditional feminine roles she mimics. Play-acting for Magdalen becomes a symbol of choosing, acting, and manipulating rather than
merely accepting the hardships shared by all the women of the
novel.

After losing her parents, her inheritance, and the right to her
name, Magdalen sets out in earnest to become an actress, rejecting
the genteel but impoverished life of a governess to which she and
Norah seem destined. She still hopes to marry Frank if he prospers
in China, but the life for which she once seemed logically headed
(girlhood, courtship, then marriage) has been disrupted, and in-

stead of pledging herself in marriage to Frank, she pledges herself
to a kind of mockery of marriage, a partnership with Captain
Wragge. The scene in which she makes her pact with Wragge
parodies the wedding vow. Wragge says:

"Place your departure from York, your dramatic career, and your
private inquiries under my care. Here I am, unreservedly at your disposal.
Say the word—do you take me?
    Her heart beat fast; her lips turned dry—but she said the word.
"I do."

[I, 324–25]

Magdalen's girlish attachment to Frank occurred unexpectedly
and impulsively. In allying herself with Wragge, however, she
has to plan ahead, to consider what she wants and how best to
achieve it. Had she married Frank, they would have lived on Mr.
Vanstone's (unearned) money; in committing herself to Wragge,
she hopes to support herself and Wragge by their joint exertions.
The pact with Wragge, then, is one of Magdalen's first chances
to act rather than be acted upon. That the pact is sealed in a parody
of marriage serves to emphasize the contrast between the role she
might have lived and the role she chooses.

Magdalen next impersonates her former governess, Miss Garth,
both on the stage and in calling on her cousin Noel Vanstone in
London. Her playing "Miss Garth" seems to be a rejection first
of Miss Garth's conventionally respectable protection and, second,
of the job of governess that Norah has had to take. When Magdalen goes disguised as a governess to observe Norah, she sees
Norah bullied by her young charges and their grandmother. Thus
she realizes that the respectable position of governess is no protection against coercion and that the real Miss Garth's protection
of Norah cannot guarantee Norah's happiness. Still Magdalen goes
as "Miss Garth" to Noel to see whether Miss Garth's moral authority will have any power to sway Noel, who has inherited the
money that Magdalen's and Norah's father had intended for them.
When Noel is unmoved, she knows that she will need a different,
more potent weapon.

Magdalen therefore impersonates a young, innocent, marriageable girl, the role she has rejected as a possible or even desirable option. The false and self-pitying letter she receives from Frank, though it crushes her, leaves her without illusions to cling to and frees her from many of her scruples about using her sexuality to conquer Noel. As long as Magdalen still loved Frank, she could not play at love with another man. When Frank fails her, she is ready to act with calculated control the young charmer she once unconsciously was.

After she has married Noel, Magdalen feels she has prostituted herself, as of course she has. So the next role she plays, when Noel dies, reflects her self-degradation; she adopts the name and credentials of her maid, Louisa. Although Louisa has not, like Magdalen, used sex to gain money, she is still a fallen woman in the eyes of her society and has suffered emotionally, physically, and economically for it. In contrast, Magdalen has, as she says to Miss Garth, "made the general sense of propriety [her] accomplice" (II, 276). And yet, remembering "her own loveless marriage" when she hears Louisa's story, Magdalen says, "For God's sake, don't kneel to *me*! . . . If there is a degraded woman in this room, I am the woman—not you!" (II, 297). So Magdalen switches roles with Louisa and learns to be a parlormaid while Louisa acts as her mistress so that Magdalen can get the position at Admiral Bartram's.

By acting out a declining moral and social status, Magdalen expresses her growing sense of self-degradation. As she has incorporated more and more of her society's squalid sexual morality into her routines, Magdalen has reacted with an increasing personal shame. Though this indicates a sense of personal responsibility and integrity that actually distinguish Magdalen from the blind or callous manipulators and the helpless victims who throng through the novel's world, it draws her back toward the respectable attitudes that are so cruelly out of keeping with the sexual realities she has witnessed in her "deviant" career.

This absolute contradiction between pious social claims and actual social practice is finely expressed in Magdalen's last attempt at deception. She intends, in her role as servant, to betray her employer to regain the Vanstone inheritance for herself. This "betrayal," of course, is an effort to redress the wrong done to her by the unjust legal system. At this moment of moral impasse, Magdalen is discovered with a letter she has stolen and is dismissed as a thief. Her role-playing is over—and with it the chance to discover an identity based on genuine choice and clear insight into the realities of sexual power in her society.

The ending of *No Name* contains an ambivalence characteristic of Collins. Magdalen goes through a period of severe illness and poverty, but then is restored to health, wealth, and a happy marriage. The modern reader is likely to suspect that the conventional happy ending is a retreat from the radical stance Magdalen has maintained throughout the novel. The ending seems to pass a negative judgment upon Magdalen's earlier attempts to define her identity actively; she sinks into disgrace, poverty, and sickness through her own exertions, but she is rescued from her troubles by a man. Captain Kirke (whose name even suggests conventional morality and whose former ship was the *Deliverance*) rescues and then marries her. He also seems more father than lover, as if he were designed to redeem the wrong originally done to Magdalen by her father (or the whole patriarchal legal system). In this way, passively, Magdalen gains her final, legitimate name, much as Laura Fairlie received her names and identities from men. And Magdalen finally regains the money she had so long sought, not through her role-playing but through her conventional sister Norah, who all along had been content to suffer quietly the injustice done to them. For all these reasons, the ending can be read as a negative judgment upon Magdalen, putting her in her place and renouncing her brand of rebellion against the Victorian women's condition.[9]

On the other hand, the ending can be read as a vindication of Magdalen. Contemporary reviewers often interpreted it this way, pointing out that the ending was not very punitive. One reviewer, H.F. Chorley, called the ending "a punishment gentle in proportion to the unscrupulous selfishness of her character," and Mrs. Oliphant wrote of Magdalen's "career of vulgar and aimless trickery and wickedness, with which it is impossible to have a shadow of sympathy, but from all the pollutions of which [Collins] intends us to believe that she emerges, at the cheap cost of a fever, as pure, as high-minded, and as spotless as the most dazzling white of heroines."[10] The final settling of the Vanstone money may also seem to reward Magdalen. The money is legally Magdalen's, but in repentance she tears up the secret trust Norah has finally discovered. All this means, however, is that the money goes instead to Norah's husband, George Bartram, and through him to Norah, from whom some of it will pass to Magdalen. The reviewers were quite right in thinking that Magdalen's repentance cost her very little.

But money has not been the real issue—as the title of the novel makes clear. Identity, power over one's own life, a wished-for restoration of faith in social justice—these have been Magdalen's underlying goals, even when she scarcely knew what her purpose was. As Magdalen's career of impersonation has suggested, symbolic action is often the most potent reality in a world whose social practices are so often hypocritical deceptions. So her destruction of the secret trust is, at least in part, a symbolic renunciation of the crude battles over money to which the action finally degenerates. It is also a final assertion of Magdalen's own will before she is subsumed in the role of wife and surrogate daughter.

The lingering symbolic import of this final twist of the plot is bitterer than this, however. Once again power rests with the husband, not the wife, with George Bartram. Neither the Vanstone name nor the inheritance has been restored to the daughters. When the Vanstone money passes to Norah, not Magdalen, and does so only because of Norah's marriage, *No Name* completes the pattern we have already seen in *The Woman in White*. The passive heroines' identity, name, and socioeconomic standing are determined by men. The active sisters either sacrifice part of their identity as women and are relegated to the social periphery like Marian Halcombe and Magdalen (before Kirke finds her), or else they must be tamed into passive heroines and married to men who will provide for them as Magdalen is provided for at the end. Clearly, Collins sees no way as a Victorian writer of making his active heroines triumph as whole women. Whether he is inwardly torn by his own ambiguous view, whether he sees no way of portraying such success within the novelistic conventions of his time, or whether he simply sees no models in Victorian "real" life for his heroines to imitate, Collins offers no middle ground between the passivity that causes disintegration and the activity punished by social ostracism.

Collins pursues issues of identity through a still more radical attack on Victorian sexual conventions in *Armadale* (1866). His assault on what he terms (in the novel's preface) "claptrap morality" shocked a number of his readers, who could find no positive ideals in his portrayal of the social system—though the preface defends the book as a return to Christian standards: "Judged by the Christian morality which is of all time, it is only a book that is daring enough to speak the truth" (I, 3).

It may be that the directness of Collins' exposure of a corrupt patriarchal system of power relations and his virtual mockery of the traditional courtship plot were most disturbing to his readers. For in *Armadale* vicious, murderous male rivalry is the initial focus of the plot, and the courtship plot is almost entirely a parody of the ways that conventional society uses courtship to mask brutal competition for money and power. Courtship does not lead characters in *Armadale* to maturity, virtue, or personal happiness as it does in most Victorian novels.

Male rivalry in *Armadale* is brutal almost to absurdity. The entire novel is engendered by one initial male rivalry over a woman and money. The original patriarch, Allan Armadale, in disowning his son Allan and making another Allan his heir, creates a murderous rivalry: the disowned Allan steals the other's intended wife as revenge for his own loss and as a way of recouping his fortune. From his point of view, the woman and the money seem to be interchangeable symbols of power. But the women are at the same time only pawns in the male competition. The new heir, though secure in his money, is devastated by losing the battle over the woman and ends up killing his rival out of bitterness.

Unlike *The Woman in White* and *No Name*, *Armadale* focuses on the damage the patriarchal system does to male identity. The name "Armadale," arbitrarily denied the biological son and granted to a son created only by the father's will, does carry power, prestige, and money that may well arouse murderous desire. The arrogant tyranny of the patriarch's claim is nakedly revealed in Collins' plot; and the absurdity of the rivalry engendered in the "sons" is shown by the proliferation of five Allan Armadales in the novel. The "dark" Allan Armadale who takes the name Ozias Midwinter is as dispossessed of legitimate identity as Anne Catherick or Magdalen Vanstone. What Collins suggests here is that the lust for power the system arouses in its sons can be as destructive to true identity as the helpless passivity it inculcates in its daughters.

This legacy of rivalry produces a frenzy of disinheritances— again, melodramatic parody. The blond Allan's paternal grand- father disowned his father; his uncles have disowned his mother; his maternal grandfather is dead; and his own father has been murdered. The dark Allan's father dies when his son is a baby; and Allan's stepfather is an extremely rigid and brutal man, who joins Allan's mother in abusing him as a way of separating them- selves from Allan's connection with a murderer. "There was I," Allan declares, "an ill-conditioned brat, with my mother's negro blood in my face, and my murdering father's passions in my heart, inheritor of their secret in spite of them! I don't wonder at the horsewhip now, or the shabby old clothes, or the bread and water in the lumber-room. . . . the child was beginning to pay already for the father's sin" (I, 145).[11] Respectable society tries to disavow its dark inheritance through licensed brutality. It is an outlaw— "a half-bred gypsy . . . a drunkard, a ruffian, and a thief"—who realizes the need for a total break with this corrupt system and offers Allan "a new father, a new family, and a new name"— Ozias Midwinter (I, 147).

In *Armadale* Collins uses the outlaw, the supposedly deviant individual, to develop his harshest critique of conventional social practice and conventional morality. In *The Woman In White* the exile was a helpless victim. In *No Name* the enforced role of outcast is refashioned into a series of willed impersonations; fraud and crime gradually become Magdalen's chief means to power. Lydia Gwilt, who begins as a villainess and ends as the heroine of *Ar- madale*, carries this motif still further. She consciously manipulates others, consciously deceives through impersonations, consciously uses legal dodges and secrets, and consciously uses her sexuality—all for personal gain. Through her character, Collins presents the outsider, the outlaw, the deviant as the only sane role in a totally corrupt sexual system.

Until the characteristically ambivalent ending of *Armadale*, Lydia Gwilt is probably Collins' most radical heroine. By contrast, her forerunners, Becky Sharp or Trollope's Madeline Neroni, are socially conventional women with a strong streak of unconventional wickedness; but Lydia begins as a social outcast and pursues a criminal career with much less concession to propriety than Becky or Madeline.

The events of the plot are propelled by Lydia's attempt to secure a place in the world by marrying well. Backed by the woman she calls "Mother"—a Mrs. Oldershaw—Lydia attempts to marry the respectable and well-to-do blond, young Allan Armadale, but instead finds herself drawn to Armadale's friend Ozias Midwinter, the "dark" Allan. So stated, the plot sounds like scores of other courtship plots; but Collins uses the courtship format in this enormously complex (and rather unfairly neglected) novel to attack the sexual values of his culture.[12] Lydia herself is a temptress like Becky Sharp, with an unsavory past. She has been a forger, a blackmailer, and a decoy for swindlers. She has brought destruction to a number of men—a man who shot himself for love of her, a husband she poisoned, and a man who dies after trying to save her from committing suicide by drowning. In the course of the novel she continues her criminal activities—using false references, scheming to marry Armadale for his money, tempting and ruining the old man Bashwood, lying about her past, trying three times to kill Armadale, and instead almost killing Ozias Midwinter, whom she has married in order to further her plot against Allan. In the end she kills herself. Throughout, her power resides in sexual attractiveness and her own casual and unscrupulous use of it.

Little wonder, then, that Victorian critics found her disturbing. The *Spectator* critic called her "a woman fouler than the refuse of the streets," and H. F. Chorley wrote that "the interest of

[Collins'] tale centers upon one of the most hardened female villains whose devices and desires have ever blackened fiction—a forger, a convicted adulteress, murderess, and thief. . . . While discussing this story as a work of art, it must be pointed out that every character is arranged so as to be subordinate to this horrible creature."[13]

What seemed most to bother critics was not the existence of such a creature but their perception that Collins had placed her at the center of the novel in such a way as to invite or even compel the reader's sympathy, and, in so doing, to challenge social convention. A Lydia Gwilt who lived through forgery, murder, and bigamy and then was suitably punished might legitimize Victorian morality, but Collins' heroine uses her sexuality casually, for the most part, without the guilty torments expected of the fallen woman. By creating a heroine who is unashamedly sexual, over thirty, worldly, actively scheming rather than passively in pursuit of a husband, and decidedly interested in money, Collins created a dialectic between conformity and deviance: "good" society creates deviants who then prey upon "good" society. Initially, Lydia Gwilt's role in the novel is to cheat Allan of his money, but symbolically she threatens Allan with a knowledge of their pasts (Allan's, Midwinter's, and Lydia's) and a recognition of the deviance that lies beneath, and is often produced by, their society's restrictive definitions of what is normal.

Lydia begins as antagonist, but as the novel progresses Collins' shifting narrative focus takes us further and further into Lydia's point of view. One device for shifting this focus is the interpolated story of Lydia's past—a sensational but not sentimental catalog of the perils threatening a woman on the fringes of society. Throughout her early life Lydia appears in the dual character of the victim (the social outcast, the economically threatened) who (like Becky Sharp or Heathcliff) becomes the victimizer by exploiting the system that has threatened her. An abandoned child, she was used by the underworld characters, the Oldershaws, to lure customers into buying their cosmetics. She was next taken up by a Miss Blanchard (later to become the blond Allan's mother) whose romantically sentimental view of the waif Lydia was the polar opposite of the Oldershaws'. After being used by the second generation Allan Armadale and Miss Blanchard to forge letters so that Mr. Blanchard would approve his daughter's marriage, Lydia turns victimizer again, ready to blackmail the Blanchards. At school in France she victimizes a music master, who tries to kill himself for love of her, and then becomes the victim of a priest who "worked on her feelings" (II, 317). Her next role is to tantalize men and lure them into gambling with swindlers. One of her conquests, Mr. Waldron, then turns the tables on her by exposing the swindlers so that she will have to accept his "protection" or be ruined (II, 322). By holding out, Lydia gains the security of marriage, but Waldron's willingness to blackmail the swindlers shows an underlying kinship between the conventional social world and the criminal underworld.

After Lydia becomes Mrs. Waldron, she learns the perils of respectable marriage. Victim of a stern, jealous, bad-tempered husband, she again turns victimizer when she poisons him. But she is also the victim of her would-be lover, Captain Manuel who, to gain her money, instigates the poisoning and who, after her imprisonment for two years, marries her, spends her money, and deserts her. Trying next to drown herself in grief, Lydia manages only to cause the death of her would-be rescuer, the man from whom Allan inherits his property. Her repeated alternation between victim and victimizer shows how respectable society and criminal society prey upon each other. And, like Defoe in *Moll Flanders*, Collins gradually legitimizes his heroine's criminal career by showing how much its psychological and material modes resemble the conventional world of sexual commerce.

Lydia Gwilt's scorn for conventional Victorian sexual roles and moral values is reinforced as Collins directs our sympathy away from the "light" moral characters, the blond Allan and Miss Milroy, who live on the surface quite conventionally, and toward the dark characters—chiefly Lydia and Midwinter—who are forced to live outside society. This shift occurs primarily through Lydia's diary, as the reader gradually realizes that the judgments on the light characters advanced in Lydia's diary are accurate. The dark characters are far more sensitive than the light ones.

Though all—Midwinter, Bashwood, Mrs. Milroy, and Lydia—
are psychically damaged victims, their social alienation makes
them especially responsive to other dark characters' secrets. Bashwood and Midwinter, for instance, are "drawn invisibly one to
the other . . . by those magnetic similarities of temperament which
overleap all difference of age or station, and defy all apparent
incongruities of mind and character" (I, 392). Because he is the
victim of his wife's and son's betrayal, Bashwood is as alienated
from Victorian society as Midwinter. Lydia too has a similarly
intuitive understanding about Midwinter; she says, "Having secrets to keep about my own past life . . .I suppose I am all the
readier to suspect other people when I find something mysterious
about them" (II, 135). Though Midwinter is not equally prescient
about Lydia, he has the same kind of fatal attraction to her that
Bashwood has because both he and Bashwood are responsive to
one element of her dark nature—her dangerous sexuality.

Because they are at odds with themselves or their society, the
dark characters have a great range of feelings and a special sensitivity to what is behind the surface of others' lives, but the light
characters are deficient in both areas. Linked by the childishness
and sentimentality they share, Allan and Miss Milroy readily fall
in love with each other, and Allan, despite his brief attraction to
Lydia, escapes Lydia's spell quickly and painlessly as soon as he
learns of her shady association with Mrs. Oldershaw.

When we begin, later on, to see Allan and Miss Milroy through
Lydia's eyes, we are encouraged to acknowledge the wit and just-
ness of her caustic view of her rival. Lydia writes, "[Miss Milroy]
gave [Allan] a look which finished the sentence plainly: 'I'm quite
heart-broken, Mr. Armadale, now we are friendly again, at going
away from *you!*' For downright brazen impudence, which a grown
woman would be ashamed of, give me the young girls whose
'modesty' is so pertinaciously insisted on by the nauseous domestic
sentimentalists of the present day! Even Armadale, booby as he
is, understood her" (II, 154). When Armadale then proposes and
Miss Milroy reacts with "virtuous indignation," Lydia continues,
"Any man with brains in his head would have known what all
this rodomontade really meant" (II, 155). In this way Collins

makes it possible for his readers to see that a properly conventional young woman can act just as aggressively as a woman like Lydia, and perhaps no more honestly. The courtship patterns of his society, when they do not produce the hypocrisy of a Mrs. Oldershaw, produce a similar version of it in a respectable young woman. Both are intent on peddling their wares.

Similarly, when Lydia directs her cynicism against Allan, she reveals the boorishness of one conventional type of masculinity. Lydia refers to Allan as "the hateful Armadale, so loud and red and clumsy" (II, 253). She criticizes his lack of sensitivity: "To say that he was like a child is a libel on all children who are not born idiots" (II, 266). Of his letter from Miss Milroy, Lydia says, "I had to wade through plenty of vulgar sentiment and lamentation, and to lose time and patience over maudlin outbursts of affection, and nauseous kisses enclosed in circles of ink" (II, 266). Lydia shows us that Allan's masculinity and Miss Milroy's femininity are vulgar complements of each other.

The narrator later expresses a cynicism like Lydia's about domesticity; when Dr. Downward invites visitors to his "Sanatorium" the women invited turn out in large numbers to escape their homes: "In the miserable monotony of the lives led by a large section of the middle classes of England, anything is welcome to the women which offers them any sort of harmless refuge from the established tyranny of the principle that all human happiness begins and ends at home. . . . [T]he women, poor souls . . . had seized the golden opportunity of a plunge into public life" (II, 504–5). Apparently, then, the conventional middle-class woman is not much happier with the restrictive definitions of a woman's role than Lydia herself; but she finds only weak, temporary, and in this case thoroughly fraudulent escapes from domestic drudgery, while Lydia has discarded the pretenses of the whole system.

However, while conventional, "light" characters like Allan and Miss Milroy seem boorish compared to the sensitive Midwinter or the perceptive Lydia, there are unconventional characters portrayed as truly evil, against whom Lydia is contrasted. This contrast is another method for deepening readers' sympathy with Lydia. Foremost among the evil characters is Mrs. Oldershaw.

She parodies the conventional matchmaking mother—like Mrs. Bennet in *Pride and Prejudice*. (She is even called "Mother Oldershaw" in the novel.)

Mrs. Oldershaw is one of Collins' few criminal characters devoid of any redeeming qualities to claim our sympathy; she is motivated (like the only other unredeemed characters of *Armadale*, the abortionist Dr. Downward and young James Bashwood) not by passion, but by a desire for money, and never forgets herself or commits self-destructive acts as do the sensitive sufferers and suffering sinners of the novel—Lydia, Midwinter, Mrs. Milroy, and Bashwood. Her interest in Lydia began when the latter, as a beautiful orphan, was useful to Mrs. Oldershaw in luring customers to buy cosmetics. Mrs. Oldershaw's example suggests that the matchmaking mother is an outright bawd—another indictment of the courtship system.

As S. M. Ellis has pointed out, Mrs. Oldershaw was modeled upon a contemporary of Collins', Madame Sarah Rachel Leverson, the notorious subject, years after *Armadale*, of a trial for blackmail and extortion.[14] She owned the nineteenth-century version of a beauty shop and sold cosmetics to women who were not ashamed to use them—presumably, then, to aging respectable women who wanted to regain their youth and to disreputable women as well. But she had several other ways of preying on women and using Victorian sexual practices to make money. She was a blackmailer, a procuress, and a con artist of considerable imagination. Yet when Collins wrote *Armadale* Madame Leverson's trials for blackmail were still some years distant, so that his portrayal of Mrs. Oldershaw shows his understanding of, and probably fascination with, her kind of crime well before it became highly publicized.

Like Madame Leverson, Mrs. Oldershaw runs a "Ladies' Toilette Repository" in which she sells cosmetics and beauty treatments to older women, but she has also been engaged in more criminal activities. She has helped blackmail Allan's mother, and she gives Lydia the idea of marrying Allan for his money so that once Lydia is rich Mrs. Oldershaw can take a portion of her gains. Her house in Pimlico has a bad enough reputation to shock Pedgift Jr. and to disillusion Allan thoroughly about Lydia's character (an implication that Mrs. Oldershaw deals with prostitutes).

Typical of Collins' use of polarized characters—each an extreme or transformed stereotype—there is a "good" mother to counterbalance Mother Oldershaw, the blond Allan's mother. She is a victim rather than an oppressor, punished—apparently with the narrator's approval—for a rather minor deception of her father. (She passively consented first to a letter of her father's not being mailed and then to an answer being forged so that her father would not discover that his intended son-in-law was the wrong Allan Armadale.) Though her husband's active chicanery in pursuit of her money and another man's fiancée ought to overshadow her passive disobedience, the novel stresses her betrayal of an ideal of feminine purity. She lives in seclusion and sacrifices all personal desires to keep Allan innocent of the guilty circumstances surrounding her marriage. After her death this burden is passed on like a sacred charge to Mr. Brock and Midwinter. In the last chapter, Midwinter still shields Allan not from knowledge of the murder but from knowledge of his mother's "impurity": "In those words, [Midwinter] kept the secret of the two names; and left the memory of Allan's mother . . . a sacred memory in the heart of her son" (II, 572).

Apparently the woman's crime against her father (and thereby against the patriarchal power to approve a daughter's marriage) is more horrible than the man's crime of cheating another man—even when the latter leads to murder. Here we see Collins' own ambivalence reappearing even in this most radical of his novels. We recognize the life-destroying injustice of this sexual system *despite* the narrative endorsement of Mrs. Armadale's sacrifice, because Collins has so brilliantly mocked the same system through Lydia and Mrs. Oldershaw. This ambivalence built into the novel's juxtaposition of characters also allows us to see that the fair Allan's innocence is based on ignorance—ignorance, most significantly, of what Lydia and Midwinter know, that Victorian society's oppressive and hypocritical sexual system *produces* the deviants whom it then piously condemns. It is also an innocence that has fed, however unknowingly, on his mother's total self-sacrifice.

A key element in the shift of Lydia from villainess to heroine and the consequent criticism of conventionally moral society is her sexuality. The concept of surrender that is still often associated with love (especially feminine love) is here shown to involve the woman in extreme danger. When Lydia gives in to a passion such as her love for Manuel, she falls into trouble. She becomes Manuel's victim, carrying out *his* desires (poisoning Waldron) for his ends (money) at her own expense (she goes to prison, not he). Similarly, when she falls in love with Midwinter, she jeopardizes her plan to gain Armadale's money. But even beyond that, she fears love as a form of self-abandonment, the abandoning of her will and emotions to another person. Her experience in this society has taught her that other people are largely predators. At one point when she finds herself thinking lovingly of Midwinter, she draws back in "terror" and "panic," thinking, "Am I mad enough to be thinking of him in *that* way?" (II, 82). Another time, after he has given way to "a passion of sobs and tears," she writes, "Horrible recollections came back to me of other times, and made me shudder as I touched him. And yet I did it. What fools women are!" (II, 132). Once when her lies to him suddenly disgust her, she says she "was within a hair-breadth of turning traitor to myself" (II, 259). Clearly she sees a conflict between what is good for her and the sexual feeling that almost overpowers her. Within *Armadale* Collins presents no third option for women; they either control others at the expense of passion or they are controlled. But the novel condemns this unresolved dilemma as the product of a corrupt and hypocritical system.

Lydia's end exemplifies this conflict between feeling and control and, in the process, encourages readers to view her more sympathetically and less as the cardboard villainess she was when the novel began. Though Lydia surrenders to her love for Midwinter and almost abandons her plot against Allan, other forces (her past, Midwinter's commitment to Allan, her dislike of Allan) intrude on her feeling for Midwinter, forcing her again to choose between self-preservation and love. In Naples when Manuel forces her to choose between being exposed and betraying Allan, Lydia decides to protect herself and once again feels "like herself": "The sense that I was making the villain an instrument in my hands, and forcing him to help my purpose blindly, while he was helping his own, roused my spirits, and made me feel myself again" (II, 393). Once committed to her plot against Allan, then, she must leave her husband to return to England and claim the money belonging to "Mrs. Armadale." When Midwinter confronts her in London, she is torn by the conflict between her love and her plot: "One moment more of inaction might have been the salvation of her. But the fatal force of her character triumphed at the crisis of her destiny, and his. White and still, and haggard and old, she met the dreadful emergency with a dreadful courage, and spoke the irrevocable words which renounced him to his fate" (II, 489).

In the end, though, Midwinter, intending to protect Allan by sacrificing himself, takes the asylum room meant for Allan and so becomes the near victim of Lydia's poisoning attempt. When she realizes that it is Midwinter she has almost killed, she sacrifices herself to save Midwinter: "She silently bent over him and kissed his forehead. When she looked up again, the hard despair had melted from her face. There was something softly radiant in her eyes, which lit her whole countenance as with an inner light, and made her womanly and lovely once more" (II, 558).

Collins' ambivalence toward women such as Lydia is as evident in this plot resolution as in No Name, where he also disposes of his rebellious heroine by turning her into a conventional woman in love. The heroine, however unconventional, must face a conventional ending; the novel is as ambivalent about Lydia's redemption and death as No Name was about Magdalen's rescue into conventional marriage to Captain Kirke. The narrator seems unable to commit himself, unwilling to accept those qualities in Lydia he so clearly admires, and unwilling to persist in his indictment of the society that has given his heroine no real option. That "womanly and lovely" submission to love for a man would have destroyed her several times over in the environment she has known—as it destroys her now.

Along with Dickens, Thackeray, and Trollope, Collins shares narrative strategies of indirection: he attacks issues peripherally; his narrator sometimes voices conventional—and inappropriate—sentiments that his characters and plots undermine; and his melodramatic complexities, like Dickens', must be probed by the reader before they reveal their full implications. But more than Dickens, Thackeray, or Trollope, Collins uses radical narrative techniques to acknowledge the indirection of our knowledge and the role of the reader/interpreter in discovering the meaning of events.

The mystery structure is central to Collins' narrative mode, despite differences in its form from one novel to another. *The Moonstone* and *The Woman in White* are, of course, well known for their suspense, their multiple narrators, and their mystery plots, but even those Collins novels that lack the multiple narrators or the detective elements still depend upon secrets. His plots usually involve a major secret fact or relationship that produces a sense of entrapment.

Most important, Collins' motif of secret entrapment usually involves sex roles. The secrets propel the plots, create the suspense, and mirror the crime and fraud rooted in the patriarchal social structure of Victorian society. Secrecy and sexual roles are linked in early novels like *Basil*, *The Dead Secret*, or *Hide and Seek*. In *The Woman in White* secrets are used to rob Laura, to usurp a place that would not legally belong to an illegitimate son (Glyde), and to keep Laura and Marian subservient in their home. The images of confinement for women proliferate in the locked rooms, the secretly used wing, and the feeling at Blackwater Park of being "suffocated" by trees. These images of confinement reappear in Anne Catherick's imprisonment in asylum and grave as well as in Laura's consequent imprisonment at Mrs. Rubelle's, in the asylum, and in the secret lodgings they all resort to until Laura's identity is restored.

In *No Name* the unjust divorce and inheritance laws initially generate the secrecy. Then Magdalen's rebellion against conventional sex roles leads her to impersonation, and finally she seeks and fails to find the "secret trust" which determines how the Vanstone money is to be inherited.

In *Armadale* the entire plot is generated by secrets having their source in patriarchal anger and sexual rivalry. Midwinter's secret link with Allan Armadale derives from his father's crime. Allan's mother's desire to keep her own secret derives from guilt at having departed from her ideal of female purity. And Lydia Gwilt's secret plots against Allan and his mother involve her use of sex to gain money.

In *The Moonstone* sex is, once again, at the heart of the novel's secrets. Franklin Blake's unconscious theft of the diamond may represent a symbolic theft of Rachel's virginity, while her keeping his secret may represent a guilty desire to lose her virginity to him.[15] Rosanna Spearman keeps secret her love for Blake and her knowledge that he was the thief. And Godfrey Ablewhite's secret—the mystery of who has the diamond—involves Victorian sexual roles at their worst; he hypocritically becomes a champion of charitable ladies while he is keeping a mistress, embezzling another man's money, and preying upon Rachel in order to gain control of her money. Rachel is saved from marrying him only after Godfrey secretly finds out that Rachel's personal income is all that would be at his disposal after marriage and would not be enough to pay his debts.

In *Man and Wife* the plot is propelled by the secret sexual relationship between Anne Silvester and Geoffrey Delamain, Anne's secret pregnancy, her innocent but secretly compromised position with Arnold Brinkworth (the result of the Scottish marriage laws), and eventually by the secretly kept "proof" of her Scottish marriage to Geoffrey. Anne's entrapment, like Laura Fairlie's, is mirrored in actual confinements—in the inn where she must pretend to be married, in her pregnancy, and in the locked rooms and walled gardens her husband uses to keep her a prisoner. In an essential minor character, Hester Dethridge, Collins also carries out the motifs of secrecy and sexually related entrapment. Hester is a woman with a secret, pretending to be mute in order to punish herself for having killed her husband. Hester's husband had repeatedly stolen all her belongings, but the law could do nothing for her. When Geoffrey discovers Hester's secret, he tries to blackmail her into killing Anne Silvester by the same method, but Hester in the end kills Geoffrey himself.

In all these instances the secrets produce the mystery plot, and the mystery plot hinges on sexual relationships. Thus although Collins' narrative emphasis on the mystery sets him somewhat apart from Dickens and even more so from Trollope and Thackeray, he still presents his analysis of Victorian sexual relationships indirectly. Where Trollope and Thackeray create ambivalence through an intrusive narrator, Collins creates it by fracturing his narration, sometimes dividing it among a number of unreliable characters and sometimes slipping from narrator to letters to documents and back to a narrator again. But whether he uses a first person narrator, an impersonal narrator, or a multitude of narrators, no *one* speaks with such authority or knowledge as to prevent the reader from having to piece together both information and interpretation.[16] As with each of the three other male novelists, the interpretation must be created through careful attention to analogical relationships, symbolic plot structures, and narrative anomalies.

Perhaps the most extreme Collins novel in this regard is *The Law and the Lady*. It contains most of Collins' major concerns—the law, mystery and entrapment, the piecing together of information and emphasis upon documents, outrageously unconventional characters, power struggles in marriage, and the suffering of women in marriage. Its central secret is that Sarah Macallan committed suicide because of her husband's coldness to her. *The Law and the Lady* allows us to see the intricate connections between Collins' use of plots that depend on secrecy, his experiments with narrative form, and his interest in Victorian sexual conventions.

The Law and the Lady begins with a secret discovered, proceeds to the unraveling of the secret behind that secret, and ends with a secret undisclosed. Like *The Woman in White* with its mystery about identities, *The Law and the Lady* begins with secrets about its two major characters; the newly married heroine and narrator Valeria Woodville discovers that her husband's name is Eustace Macallan, not Woodville, and then discovers that he has been tried for murdering his first wife and, under Scottish law, has received the halfway verdict of "not proven." Since he objects to her discovery of his secret (feeling that it will make their marriage impossible), he orders her not to proceed further in trying to understand why he goes by a false name. When she disobeys, he leaves her. Valeria feels she must solve the mystery (which to her means proving his innocence); if she is to rescue their marriage, she must enter the labyrinth of secrets about him. Her initial entrapment is paradigmatic of the situation of all Collins' heroes and heroines—whether it is Basil's involuntary love for Margaret Sherwin, Laura's physical entrapment in *The Woman in White*, Anne Silvester's physical entrapment in her husband's home in *Man and Wife*, or Mercy Merrick's entrapment in her own past as a prostitute and the deceit she has used to try to evade her situation in *The New Magdalen*.

The secret in *The Law and the Lady* is both explored and revealed through documents. Valeria is ignorant of why her husband goes by a false name until she finds the written record of the trial. During the trial itself Eustace Macallan's journal is used as evidence against him because in it he has written of his secret dislike of his marriage and his secret love of another woman. In his defense, however, his mother claims that his journal is not reliable evidence:

"The extracts from my son's Diary are a libel on his character. . . . And not the less a libel because they happen to be written by himself. Speaking from a mother's experience of him, I know that he must have written the passages produced in moments of uncontrollable depression and despair. No just person judges hastily of a man by the rash words which may escape him in his moody and miserable moments. Is my son to be so judged because he happens to have written *his* rash words, instead of speaking them? His pen has been his most deadly enemy, in this case—it has presented him at his very worst."

[224–25]

Record-keeping is essential, but, paradoxically, records are not to be trusted. Because of their importance, records are the likely targets of fraud—and, in Collins' vision, particularly sexual fraud. Inheritance, paternity, legitimacy are the issues that involve money and power in his society and thus provide the inducements to fraud. In the case of *The Law and the Lady* Sarah Macallan commits suicide because she has read her husband's diary—the very document his mother claims to be unreliable—and then her suicide letter is stolen by a man who wants to see Eustace punished. The compounding of untrustworthy documents accords with Collins' decision elsewhere to compound his narrators so that through a multiplicity of distorted perceptions we may piece together the truth. And the truth—if it *is* truth—in *The Law and the Lady* is literally pieced together from fragments of Sarah's lost suicide letter thrown into the Macallan rubbish heap. The physical document becomes a jigsaw puzzle to symbolize the difficulty of knowing the truth about others' lives as well as to symbolize Collins' narrative method and Valeria's detective method.

The Law and the Lady also contains perhaps Collins' most outrageously unconventional character, Miserrimus Dexter, a legless man confined (usually) to a wheelchair. He dresses in pink shirts and bracelets (in some of his moods) and has the audacity first to love Sarah Macallan and later to make sexual advances to Valeria at a time when she is pregnant. Wheeling his chair at breakneck speed across his room shouting, "I am Napoleon, at the sunrise of Austerlitz!" (276) or "walking" on his hands at night to spy on others, he is a figure inconceivable in Trollope or Thackeray and as outrageous as Dickens' Quilp. It is a sign of Collins' more radical disregard for Victorian propriety that he could first create a pregnant female detective married to an accused wife-murderer and then subject her to a legless, sexually threatening man who has propositioned his friend's first wife (Sarah), shown her Eustace's journal, and then destroyed her suicide note so that Eustace would be tried for murder.

But bizarre as *The Law and the Lady* is by comparison, for instance, with Trollope's novels, its central thematic concern finally is very Trollopian—the power struggle within marriage and woman's role in that struggle. Valeria becomes increasingly independent; she disobeys her husband's command not to seek to know more (knowledge is typically associated with power—particularly male power—in Collins). She lives without him after he leaves her, pursues her investigations, and dares to confront the dangerous and unpredictable Miserrimus Dexter. In the end she discovers the paradoxical truth that her husband is innocent of murdering his wife (since she killed herself) and yet guilty because of his neglect, his obvious interest in another woman, and his harsh comments about her in his diary.

At the end, when she keeps the secret of Sarah's suicide, she puts herself in a superior position to her husband; *he* had wanted to keep secrets from her and treated her like a child.[17] Now she keeps the secret she has fought to understand, and her husband accepts her judgment.

Sarah Macallan's death offers us a glimpse into ordinary married life that is rather rare in Collins. Despite her husband's kind intentions, she has been made miserable by his neglect, his physical repulsion, her consciousness of being ugly, and his interest in another woman. In *The Woman in White* we have seen how a tyrannical husband can torment his wife, but here in *The Law and the Lady* the honorable and well-meaning husband creates at least as much suffering. Sarah Macallan's home has scarcely been the refuge, the walled garden, of Victorian fantasy.

In the novels we have discussed in detail—and to a greater or lesser degree in all his novels—Collins turns away from the domestic setting of most Victorian fiction. Even his courtship plots are transformed into bizarre stories of fraud, crime, prostitution, murder, impersonation, and madness. In this he is even less an advocate of Victorian marriage and family life than Dickens, who also interfuses courtship with crime in order to assail the whole system of sexual values. Dickens manages to tuck a cheery family group or two into his grimmest novels. Though absolutely atypical and always maimed in some way, these domestic enclaves at least express a kind of residual hope in Victorian family values.

Collins thoroughly parodies the values and practices of the Victorian middle-class family in characters like "Mother" Oldershaw and the Wragges. He focuses on those who are outcasts of the family-centered system, who have broken with it openly, who manipulate it for their secret advantage, or who are victims of it. All this suggests that the family is—for Collins as for the other novelists of this study—an inescapable matrix, the pattern that determines in some way all variations, even those that struggle to escape its influence or to destroy. It is the implied center of crisis in Collins as it is the directly acknowledged center in a novel like *Bleak House.*

In this context, what is especially distinctive in Collins is his ability to show how the family-centered sexual system (for the patriarchy is nothing without a family to rule over) replicates itself in the unlikeliest circumstances and personalities in the society at large—the asylum, brothel, and prison, for instance. The family influence is fragmented, twisted, absorbed into individual character, social role, legal and illegal institutions. As its influence spreads outward into society at large, it loses nearly all its treasured Victorian power as a refuge, and so the domestic resolutions of Collins' novels seem especially artificial.

Collins' interest in arcane legal controversies and in bizarrely transformed circumstances of family life and courtship come together in his recognition that both primary institutions of English life, the law and the family, are adversarial systems that thrive on bitter controversy while claiming to inculcate virtue, happiness, and harmony. More than this, he sees the force of the legal system as most significantly expressed in laws that regulate marriage and inheritance. Courtship and marriage—the very functioning of family life itself, as *No Name*, *Man and Wife*, and *The Woman in White* all suggest—are harried to the point of destruction by legal controversies. This is not Collins' quirkiness, as a number of critics have suggested, but his sharp insight into his culture's workings: the law *is* an instrument of patriarchal will and inevitably turns its power on the institutions of primary concern to a patriarchal system, courtship, marriage, and the family.

In Collins' novels the whole legal system is fraudulent in its relation to sexual matters. Daughters and sons are disinherited in his melodramatic plots because he sees a massive deprivation of secure, satisfying identity in the entire culture's sexual practices. In a more bitter sense, daughters and sons are deprived of their inheritance because the patriarchal culture has little to bequeath in terms of sexual roles but shame, violence, oppression, and starved, denatured personalities.

Yet Collins stops short of explicitly confronting the patriarchal view of marriage embodied in the law that defined a wife as the property of her husband, a being without any legal identity. In this stance, Collins reveals the ambivalence he shares with Dickens, Trollope, and Thackeray. On the one hand, he creates characters, situations, and symbolic structures that implicitly indict a society that oppresses women. On the other hand, through his ambivalent depictions of those characters and situations, he stops short of acknowledging the basic premises of Victorian society. Just as in so many Dickens and Trollope novels, the actual themes and symbolic structures created within the novel are more radical than the author seems willing to admit. Thus many Collins novels, like many Dickens and Trollope novels, end by insisting on redemption through marriage, though the novels themselves have undermined that solution.

Yet there is a truth in this ambivalence that few direct, radical assaults on Victorian culture were able to perceive. Collins' direct attention to minor legal abuses in laws regulating sexuality and inheritance so clashes with his wholesale, though implicit, mockery of the Victorian sexual system that we are led to question the whole idea of legal or social meliorism. His novels, taken together, demand a thorough change in the sexual foundations of Victorian values.

5

THACKERAY

I T should be clear by now that the conflicts in narration and action in Dickens' and Collins' novels resemble Blakean contraries rather than confusion or flat contradiction. Their own ambivalent attitudes toward Victorian sexuality undoubtedly influenced their handling of fictional material; but each discovered techniques to transform potentially limiting personal attitudes into a way of disclosing the tensions within all Victorian sexual life. Thus their major novels all stress the victimization of women as a central—often the central—motif because they came to see how persistently this social and psychic abuse underlies every major area of Victorian life, its struggles for moral order and emotional expression as well as its injustices, evasions, and hypocrisies.

The interaction of contraries is a genuine dialectic in this fiction, even though much of it occurs through implicit rather than explicit juxtapositions and even though it never reaches a full thematic resolution. Because these novelists are taking on so profound a crisis in cultural values that direct acknowledgment could shake and possibly shatter the foundations of virtually every social institution, they can hardly be expected to offer a solution. To give so penetrating an account of what the crisis was, to show how pervasive, how subtle, how manifold its particular expressions even in implicit ways is remarkable enough.

The danger of subtle implications in fiction is, of course, that they may not be perceived. But even those readers who find Dickens, Trollope, and Collins pat, obtuse, bland, muddled, or virtually foundering in stereotypes also generally find them provoking, sometimes even infuriating. They are responding, we think, to a sense that something energetic and disturbing is at work in this fiction, to the agitation of the narrative medium that even implicitly ambivalent attitudes cause.

With Thackeray the unsettling effect on readers has become a commonplace of criticism. Trollope can seem bland, Collins can seem absurdly melodramatic, Dickens can seem mawkishly sentimental if we are not alert to the complexities of their fictional construction. But Thackeray's narrative presence is so aggressive and so protean that the *fact* of problematic complexity must be acknowledged. Nearly two decades ago Lionel Stevenson declared, "the status of Thackeray is perhaps more equivocal than that of any other major Victorian novelist." And more recent assessments continue to grapple with the effort to define the very nature of his fiction—its subject, its narrative methods, its appeal to readers, so that he still seems to critics such as Winslow Rogers "the most problematical of the Victorian novelists."[1]

Examples of flatly contradictory assessments of Thackeray abound. Where A. E. Dyson finds brilliant complexity ("He is one of the most sophisticated of our ironists . . . nearly every effect is very exactly and maturely contrived"), Mark Spilka sees only muddle ("Thackeray's indirection was rooted in his own confusion"). Thackeray himself declared, in reference to *Vanity Fair*: "I want to leave everybody dissatisfied and unhappy at the end of the story—we ought all to be with our own and all other stories." Yet Walter Pater, in ranking *Henry Esmond* with *Lycidas* and *The Idea of a University* as a perfect piece of literature, called it "a sort of cloistral refuge from a certain vulgarity in the actual world," offering its readers "something of the uses of a religious retreat."[2]

These few instances of sharply clashing views of Thackeray hardly represent the range of perspectives that have been offered in more than 125 years of commentary. But they do call attention to several defining features of Thackeray's fiction that may redirect us from controversies of critics to the substance of the fiction. Disagreements about just what his novelistic techniques are and how they affect the reader grow from disagreements about the subject of his fiction. Spilka's damning judgment on Thackeray's indirection is obviously related to his sense of specious substance; he argues, for instance, that Amelia Sedley is a "dramatic fraud" foisted on the reader. Dyson's argument for the brilliant success of this same technique similarly depends on his estimate of the power, subtlety, and accuracy of Thackeray's social and psychological themes in *Vanity Fair*. Whether we find in his fiction a retreat from the world's vulgarity or a bitter, even savage exposure of that same vulgarity, a spectacle that urges us to "return to our own homes and be miserable in private" (as the narrator in *Vanity Fair* says) depends on what we see enacted at the dramatic center, what all the convolutions of technique are directing us toward.

At this point, the disparity between Pater's estimate of Thackeray's design and Thackeray's own account can illuminate rather than, as it seems to, muddle the issue. It might be, of course, that Thackeray was simply confused about what he was trying to do. Or it might be that Pater foisted his own views of what literature (and life) should be on Thackeray, obdurately resisting the palpable design to make him miserable, to drag him from the cloister into the streets. But it is telling that Thackeray's comment was made in reference to *Vanity Fair*, Pater's in reference to *Henry Esmond*. From Pater and Henry James to Gordon Ray and John Loofborouw, those critics who take Thackeray's most persistent subject as the subtle unfolding of a single character's consciousness, a semiautobiographical character set apart from "the world" in a kind of noble melancholy, find *Henry Esmond* his supreme achievement. Critics like Dyson, Arnold Kettle, and Kathleen Tillotson, who see Thackeray's subject as a society "rotten in some fundamental sense," have *Vanity Fair* in mind.[3] It seems clear that, in terms of his fiction, there are two Thackerays, the Thackeray of *Vanity Fair* and the Thackeray of *Esmond, Pendennis*, and *The Newcomes*. Though it makes biographical issues even more perplexing, this realization may help sort out the perplexities that have impeded efforts to understand his fiction.[4]

The ambivalence that seems a defining quality for all four novelists thus reaches an extreme point in Thackeray, causing him to write two substantially different kinds of fiction—different in theme, plotting, technique, and in what is centrally conveyed by all these: the vision of his culture. We can easily see Pickwick persisting in Noddy Boffin, and characters like Plantagenet Palliser and Glencora literally persist from novel to novel. But Henry Esmond and Dobbin, Beatrix and Becky, are creatures born of essentially different imaginations, despite similarities in their fictional situations.

This is not a bizarre instance of literary schizophrenia but a particularly clear expression of the ambivalent attitudes toward sexuality that characterize all the Victorian novelists we have discussed. Dyson is right, we think, in his contention that *Vanity Fair* shows something fundamentally rotten about Victorian culture. And Pater was right—though he hardly meant it in this sense—that *Esmond* and other late novels offer a cloistral retreat from this disturbing perception. Yet the novels are all the creation of one imagination, however divided in perception and in expression; the underlying, unifying matrix for both the exposure and the evasion of corruption is the crisis in Victorian sexual relations, a crisis that is necessarily focused, as in Dickens, Trollope, and Collins, on the abuse of women.

The fiction most characteristic of Thackeray, in terms of sheer output, does find its best expression in *Henry Esmond*. It caters to the critics' emphasis on form and neglect of subject matter, unfortunately the dominant tradition in the study of Thackeray.[5] Part of the reason is that Thackeray's perplexities are still in many ways the perplexities of our own culture. It is thus especially tempting for a consideration of aesthetic matters to neglect the substance that is the only justification for an aesthetics of the novel, as the Victorians practiced the form. But *Vanity Fair's* formal complexity disturbs our complacencies, disrupts aesthetic detachment, provokes a confrontation with fundamental contradictions in modern culture, as the novel's most persuasive critics have argued.[6]

The basic reason that *Esmond, Pendennis,* and *The Newcomes* prompt the formalist evasion is that they are evasive themselves. This kind of fiction centers on a single sentimental male consciousness—a consciousness whose basic modes and values are shared by the narrator and the hero. The sadder, presumably wiser, and certainly more complacent narrator notes the folly as well as the exuberance and tender sentiments of the character he describes, understanding all—having been there, he says repeatedly—and forgiving all. The impulse is commiseration mingled frequently with nostalgic admiration. Not only censure but psychological exploration and even accurate portrayal often give way to this desire for emotional commingling. As the old Esmond surveys his past, as the unnamed but hardly impersonal narrator of *Pendennis* tenderly reflects on the gentlemanly doings of Pen, the narrative consciousness gradually supplants the development of the hero as the center of interest, suspending potentially exciting psychological and social material in a self-indulgent and increasingly otiose narrative.

When Pen, for example, has failed to earn his degree and has neglected his mother and Laura, with a genteel carelessness worthy of George Osborne, Helen's excuses for her son are quickly followed by the narrator's own:

Perhaps Helen no more believed in these excuses than her adopted daughter did; but she tried to believe that she believed them, and comforted herself with the maternal infatuation. And that is a point whereon I suppose many a gentleman has reflected, that, do what we will, we are pretty sure of the woman's love that once has been ours; and that that untiring tenderness and forgiveness never fail us.

[I, xxi, 257]

If we set beside this a comparable passage from *Vanity Fair*, the sharp difference in tone and in the attitude toward the prevailing sexual system which that tone conveys is immediately apparent:

Her heart tried to persist in asserting that George Osborne was worthy and faithful to her, though she knew otherwise. . . . She did not dare to own that the man she loved was her inferior; or to feel that she had given her heart away too soon. Given once, the pure bashful maiden was too modest, too tender, too trustful, too weak, too much woman to recall it. We are Turks with the affections of our women; and have made them subscribe to our doctrine too. We let their bodies go abroad liberally enough, with smiles and ringlets and pink bonnets to disguise them instead of veils and yakmaks. But their souls must be seen by only one

man, and they obey not unwillingly, and consent to remain at home as
our slaves—ministering to us and doing drudgery for us.

[I, xviii, 210]

Both passages draw back from the characters and action to
reflect on them and generalize in a way typical of Thackeray's
narrators. They both describe a woman's devotion to an unworthy
man, stress her self-deception, and characterize this sort of infatuation as a female trait that men can rely on, at least when the
woman is pure and tender and the man is a gentleman. But there
the similarity ends. The narrator of *Pendennis* has it both ways.
He patronizes Helen, calling her devotion a maternal infatuation;
but once he shifts from the particular mother to all women and
from the errant son to all gentlemen (including himself with a
casual "we"), infatuation is transformed into "untiring tenderness
and forgiveness." Although there is a mild acknowledgment, not
strong enough even to be called rueful, that men do not deserve
this devotion, the clear implication is that "we" may, in fact, "do
what we will" if we happen to have the good fortune to be
gentlemen.

The passage from *Vanity Fair* also draws the conclusion that the
genteel sexual system incorporates a basic inequity, but the attitude
it prompts is hardly complacent. Even the apparent similarity in
tone between the two passages, the easy, casual, chatty tone of
a shrewd but sentimental gentleman, is deceptive. *Vanity Fair's*
narrator bluntly asserts that George is Amelia's inferior, though
George treats her as his slave. Although the stereotype of tireless
feminine devotion is invoked in both passages, and though the
narrator again immediately allies himself with the men who profit
from it, the origin of the stereotype is clearly and emphatically
identified: it is a male doctrine that women have been made to
subscribe to, as imperious and extreme as a seraglio's prohibitions.
The narrator deals in stereotypes to reveal their arbitrary and
tyrannous power; he allies himself with his male readers in order
to show them the barbarousness of the gentleman's easy assurance.
If Amelia is "too much woman" to falter in her mindless devotion
to George, the feminine trait is not presented as an instinct, not

even as an admirable ideal fostered by a civilized system of sexual relations; it is an insidious imposition of male control.

The stereotypic feminine smiles are as much the product of a particular sexual fashion as ringlets, pink bonnets, and yashmaks, and as much a veil for the psychological realities of exploitation. The narrator's rhetoric here is as bitterly precise as it usually is in *Vanity Fair*, as candid as the rhetoric of the *Pendennis* passage is evasive. The fundamental purpose, the bedrock claim of the genteel masculine tyrants is not over the bodies of women but over their souls.[7] If that claim can be so insinuated within the minds of women and men that it seems an inalienable masculine prerogative, an innate feminine urge, then the power over the body will follow as a matter of course. The Turks have the idea but have inverted their priorities; the genteel indirection of the English system is not only more insidious, less vulnerable to challenge on humanitarian grounds; it also works much better.

This narrator still praises Amelia's "tender little heart," still lovingly lingers over the modest, innocent, tremulous sensibilities of the pure maiden; we are left with his mixed impulses and insights. The impulse to condemn the system that warps the emotions and intellects of the women it supposedly treasures struggles against the impulse to adore the deceptive charms of a woman so fashioned. The insight into the origins of the stereotype uneasily coexists with the perception that it does in fact appear to describe accurately the prevailing social reality. But in leaving us with this compelling enactment of ambivalence, the narrator urges us to acknowledge the crisis in sexual relations, not, as the narrator of *Pendennis* does, to evade it.

The kind of social satire that is the primary mode in *Vanity Fair*, exposing above all hypocrisy and corruption in sexual dealings, does appear from time to time in the later fiction. But it is fragmentary and abortive. It disrupts the discursive, calmly reflective, often nearly random course of the main narrative, but leads nowhere:

In houses where, in place of that sacred, inmost flame of love, there is discord at the centre, the whole household becomes hypocritical, and each lies to his neighbor. The husband (or it may be the wife) lies when the visitor comes in, and wears a grin of reconciliation or politeness before him. The wife lies (indeed, her business is to do that, and to smile, however much she is beaten), swallows her tears, and lies to her lord and master; lies in bidding little Jackey respect dear papa; lies in assuring Grandpapa that she is perfectly happy. . . .

Much of the quarrels and hatred which arise between married people come in my mind from the husband's rage and revolt at discovering that his slave and bedfellow, who is to minister to all his wishes, and is church-sworn to honour and obey him—is his superior; and that *he*, and not she, ought to be the subordinate of the twain. . . .

[I, xi, 122]

This kind of generalizing response to Rachel Esmond's unhappiness in her marriage, which acknowledges in the manner and the blatant terms of *Vanity Fair* the gross imbalance of power built into the traditional marriage system, not only appears infrequently; it has no consequence for the novel's plot, for the development of its characters, or for the social and psychological themes that emerge from plot and characterization. In *Vanity Fair* the fraudulent, oppressive nature of the marriage system is exposed through the failure of Amelia's marriage, and Becky's, through the ugliness of any number of open sales of female sexual goods, in and out of marriage, and through the increase in frequency and intensity of the narrator's bitter assaults on the system. This wholesale corruption is reflected in the moral and emotional corruption of the characters: Steyne and old Osborne, the chief tyrannical patriarchs in the novel, are left in bitter, impotent rage at the failure of their sexual schemes; Dobbin is driven to see the unworthiness of Amelia and the consequent futility of his years of devotion to her, a realization that is not obliterated—for him or for us—by their ultimate marriage; and Amelia herself becomes an emotional parasite and an idolator rather than the domestic goddess she seemed designed to be at the novel's outset. (She fashions Georgie into a living icon of the same corrupt sexual values she worships in George, a virtual caricature of his father's arrogance and selfishness.)

In sharp contrast to this integration of narrative commentary with the novel's social and psychological material, *Henry Esmond* leaves the narrator's sporadic recognition of fundamental flaws in the whole system of sexual relations as unexplored fragments. In fact, plot and characterization move steadily away from the potentially rich and potentially explosive sexual material presented in the novel's opening chapters.

Esmond's whole life (at least the life recorded in the novel) is determined by a pair of hopeless infatuations that keep him, as the narrator and the character both remind us repeatedly, from ever participating fully in the social world around him. And, even more important, he remains in a repressed emotional state, static and subdued precisely where we expect most novels to show activity and some measure of development.

He is, throughout the novel, a son devoted to a saintly mother, neither of whom can either acknowledge or develop beyond this emotional relationship that defines their lives. Rachel both invites Henry's ardor and severely limits its expression. Under the sway of emotions that her severe piety prevents her from acknowledging to herself, she intermixes relationships with Henry that are usually considered incompatible: son, lover, brother, surrogate husband, guardian of ideals of sexual purity, even father (when she passes over her own son to treat Henry as the moral head of the household, the arbiter of all the family affairs). The young Henry almost literally reels before this onslaught of seductions, obligations, and prohibitions, but Lady Castlewood always—in each of the roles she grants him—fends off sustained intimacy of any sort. Her occasional frenzied outbursts of emotion toward him, erratic emotion as likely to express itself in condemnation and banishment as tenderness and gratitude, only arouse desires that neither character can admit to, much less fulfill.

When, in an almost grotesque completion of this pattern, Rachel urges him to court Beatrix, the daughter and "sister" serving as surrogate for the mother, there is almost a sense of relief that the emotional impasse between Henry and Rachel has been ended. Acknowledgment, however covert, of the impossibility of a more open erotic relationship seems better than continuation of the repressed desires that have essentially paralyzed the emotional lives of both. It is a false sense of relief, though. His obsessive love for Beatrix becomes even more futile, more directly frustrating than his love for Rachel. (At least he could find some satisfaction in venerating her saintly devotion to her family.) In a tortuous intermixture of characters' and author's sublimations, Beatrix serves as Rachel's and Henry's assurance that he will not marry, that he will remain in hopeless but secure erotic thrall to her surrogate.[8] At the same time Thackeray has substituted a stereotypically heartless coquette for the threatening complexities he created in Rachel. This inadequate Beatrice can not guide Henry or the novel toward any resolution of the suppressed eroticism that charged the first third of the novel.

Her husband's death rescues Rachel from the contempt and abuse he has increasingly directed toward her. But this plot contrivance, unlike George's death, causes the novel to retreat from the implications of the heroine's psychological nature rather than explore them. So long as the marriage persisted—and steadily deteriorated—Rachel's awareness of her own stronger will, intelligence, emotional nature, and moral virtue increased. At the same time, she was agitated by the volatile interaction of incompatible emotions: piety toward traditional religious and marital dogma that preached submission, suffering, and silence as a condition of female life; devotion to that curious, conservative political faith, Jacobitism, which nevertheless urged conspiracy and rebellion (although the novel's symbolic patterns are shadowy and incomplete, here as elsewhere, Father Holt is clearly a rival to Lord Castlewood as both father to Henry and lover to Rachel); the erotic and at least semi-incestuous attraction toward Henry, the young man she has treated as a son; the contrary image of him as a pure, ideal, noble, self-sacrificing *un*erotic antithesis to her husband; and the fear—perhaps in some way the desire—that Henry is also a tainted male (suggested by Rachel's distraught association of the smallpox he brings into the family with his supposed sexual impurity). Her erratic behavior suggests the strength and troubled nature of the desires she represses through her severe marital discipline. Passages like the one quoted above, and Lord Castlewood's consistently callous treatment of his wife, suggest how much these desires are created and driven by a marriage that first confines, then finally torments her.

Once the marriage has ended, however, and she is rescued by authorial fiat, this intriguing, convincing psychological process is suppressed, just when circumstances are so arranged that it might find more direct expression and development. Rachel blames Henry for her husband's death in a duel and banishes him from association with her. The novel hints, though it does not clearly suggest, that guilt is the primary impulse she feels, guilt for loving Henry and despising her husband. She learns that Henry actually tried to prevent the duel and welcomes him home, after a year's absence, in the most powerful and candid scene in the novel:

". . . I knew you would come back—I own that. That is no one's fault. And to-day, Henry, in the anthem, when they sang it, 'When the Lord turned the captivity of Zion, we were like them that dream,' I thought, yes, like them that dream—them that dream. And then it went, 'They that sow in tears shall reap in joy; and he that goeth forth and weepeth, shall doubtless come again with rejoicing, bringing his sheaves with him;' I looked up from the book and saw you. I was not surprised when I saw you. I knew you would come, my dear, and saw the gold sunshine round your head."

She smiled an almost wild smile as she looked up at him. The moon was up by this time, glittering keen in the frosty sky. He could see, for the first time now clearly, her sweet careworn face.

"Do you know what day it is?" she continued. "It is the 29th of December—it is your birthday! But last year we did not drink it—no, no. My Lord was cold, and my Harry was likely to die: and my brain was in a fever; and we had no wine. But now—now that you are come again, bringing your sheaves with you, my dear." She burst into a wild flood of weeping as she spoke; she laughed and sobbed on the young man's heart, crying out wildly, "bringing your sheaves with you—your sheaves with you!"

[II, vi, 232–33]

The emotions expressed in this dramatic scene, which occurs about a third of the way through the novel, are simply left unresolved for the remainder of the narrative. After moving so near to liberating the complex emotional life that both Rachel and Henry have repressed, the novel relentlessly turns attention away from it. In doing so, it also relinquishes the opportunity to explore further the nature of repressive sexual roles in the society it describes or to search for more satisfying and liberating sexual roles.

Rachel is kept—until the coy ending of the novel, which reveals abruptly the marriage of Henry and Rachel—in the sort of desexualized, semireligious, sentimental harem that Helen Pendennis and Laura Bell inhabit in *Pendennis*. All these women serve the disguised erotic needs of the narrative—needs of the narrator, the hero, and the author—until the plot releases them for a final climax of death or marriage that is as thematically distasteful as it is psychologically evasive.

Rachel's erotic desires (the desire to rebel against her condition of sexual servitude as well as her love for Henry) might well be repressed from her consciousness through the force of religious and sexual prohibitions. But this is not the issue; it is the *novel's* suppression of this material that is disturbing. *Esmond* might have shown, as *Vanity Fair* does, the heroine's retreat into a condition of mind that denies her own possibilities for psychological growth by feeding on sentimental illusions of masculine virtues and feminine duties. But it does not. Instead the novel—through the two Henry Esmonds, narrator and character, who together work to evade the implications of the fictional material—pushes Rachel back into the stereotypic role of maternal angel from which she has been struggling to escape. Her self-martyrdom after her husband's death remains unexplored, along with her substitution of her daughter for herself as the *dea certe* Henry should pursue but never embrace.[9] Both Henry the passive actor and Henry the obtuse commentator conspire to enshrine Rachel in frozen pieties as they direct their attention instead to the stereotypically heartless and wordly coquette Beatrix.

In a similar atavistic process, *Pendennis* retreats from the initially intriguing relationships among Pen, his mother, and his adopted sister. The novel replaces Helen and Laura with a whole series of stereotypic love objects, who tempt Pen into fits of rather desultory desire: the comic, stage-Irish Miss Costigan; the poor but honest and utterly adoring porter's daughter, Fanny Bolton; this novel's heartless coquette Blanche Amory; and even Warrington's hidden wife, the unscrupulous older woman who seduced him, trapping him in an unsuitable marriage.

The tortuously concealed incest theme erupts for a brief moment at Helen Pendennis' death. She learns that she has falsely suspected Pen of seducing Fanny Bolton; forgives him; and recaptures with him the "tender and confidential" mood they shared in his boyhood. They pray together as they did when he was a little boy, "And once more, oh, once more, the young man fell down at his mother's sacred knees, and sobbed out the prayer which the Divine Tenderness uttered for us, and which has been echoed for twenty ages since by millions of sinful and humbled men"; and she dies in his arms (II, xix, 251). The paroxysm of piety again evades the real sexual issues. Sin is not the problem but rather Pen's and the novel's refusal to acknowledge, much less deal with, the sexual subjugation of Helen and Laura, the confusion of religious and erotic values, the emotional impasse that prevents the development of any of the characters' personalities. And humbled Pen is not; he continues in the selfish and shallow behavior that distinguishes his career in the novel. Despite the narrator's occasional openness about the incest motif ("there was . . . an anguish or rage almost on the mother's part, to think that she was dispossessed somehow of her son's heart"; II, xviii, 229), Thackeray is simply not able or not willing to develop the primary sexual themes of the novel.

The really "unsavoury" quality about *Esmond's* similar incest motifs (Tilford's term for them)[10] is not the erotic situation itself, but the way Esmond the narrator springs his marriage to Rachel on us in the last hurried pages of the novel. It is a fait accompli with no narrative effort to show us, in the psychological terms crucial to this sort of novel above all, *how* it was accomplished. Development of Rachel's character could also have brought Henry out of his own half-alive state of erotic martyrdom, a secretly self-imposed martyrdom that evades the problems of growth and commitment in a complex, corrupt, and confused social world. More than this, it could have served to expose—as Becky's career does—

the destructive psychological consequences of the whole sexual system.[11]

Instead, the novel dithers off into political and military intrigues that are as feckless in action as they are irrelevant to the development of the novel's characters and themes. Like the literary imbroglios and scenes of university life in *Pendennis*, these rambling, superficial episodes are not the result of Thackeray's notorious carelessness about the details of his fiction. *Vanity Fair* proves that he was not constitutionally incapable of producing a tightly integrated plot. They are uneasy retreats from the sexual conflicts adumbrated in the novel but never fully or consistently developed.

Henry Esmond and *Pendennis* thus not only limit the psychological development of the characters, and their erotic development in particular; they also sequester the personal and the public dimensions from each other. As a result neither novel exposes, as *Vanity Fair* does, the intimate interconnections between the inadequacy of the roles the social world offers and the inadequacy of personal relations and personal development.

As Henry the aging hero fixes his hopeless desires on Beatrix, Henry the narrator abandons even fragmentary assaults on the sexual system and indulges in sentimental rhetoric:

> Who, in the course of his life, hath not been so bewitched, and worshipped some idol or another? Years after this passion hath been dead and buried, along with a thousand other worldly cares and ambitions, he who felt it can recall it out of its grave, and admire, almost as fondly as he did in his youth, that lovely queenly creature. I invoke that beautiful spirit from the shades and love her still. . . .
>
> [III, vi, 422]

The satiric jibes that do survive are almost all brief antifeminist asides, unqualified by the contrary perspectives that always challenge the antifeminist comments in *Vanity Fair* ("priests and women, tyrants by nature," "Amongst her other feminine qualities she had that of being a perfect dissembler," and so forth).

Thus, the narrative voice and the narrative values, like the story itself, are erratic, presenting outright contradiction or fragmentary motifs rather than the kind of creative and coherent ambivalence we have seen in Dickens, Trollope, and Collins and see again in *Vanity Fair*. Thackeray's novels after *Vanity Fair* work to isolate the contradictions from each other (*Esmond* develops the metaphor of the religious cloister most fully and explicitly, as Pater saw). The result is an evasion within an evasion. The characters—the hero in particular—take refuge from the disturbing complexities of "the world" and, even more, from their own psychological fears and desires in a kind of protective, passive innocence that pretends to be the product of shrewd experience. The narrator commiserates, empathizes, admires, praises—does everything but expose this fugitive and cloistered virtue for what it is.

Though this fiction claims to vest its values and its ultimate purpose in the idealized woman—mother, daughter, and sister joined in a symbolically incestuous set—it enshrines a kind of male innocence and timidity more than it enshrines feminine purity or submissive devotion. It thus protects itself from the implications of the sexual material it is driven to sketch but afraid to explore. In fact, the pose of resigned disillusionment of the old Esmond who narrates the novel is even more a retreat from the complexity of the sexual world than the exuberant innocence of the young Henry or the young Pen. They are at least energetic, questioning, engaged with the world, however stereotyped their sentiments, while the much-vaunted narrative sense of memory in these novels serves ultimately to embalm the mind and the story it tries to tell.[12]

The selfish neglect or abuse of women that marks all the heroes of these novels, done in the service of sentimental idealization as well as in the service of pleasure and convenience, is downgraded from vice to folly and then, typically, so indulgently treated by the narrator that it becomes almost a mark of nobility. Gradually each of the three novels *Esmond, Pendennis*, and *The Newcomes* moves away from the abused woman who first holds the narrative attention and, in a thorough inversion of initial perceptions, and a thorough inversion of the typical realities of life in Victorian England, focuses on the wronged man. The heartless Beatrix conveniently substitutes for Rachel; Laura and Helen Pendennis, left for years in the suspended animation of Fairoaks until Pen and the novel are ready for them, are made to wrong Pen by suspecting him of seducing Fanny (a very reasonable suspicion, since he does almost give way to his desires).

This plot development causes the narrator to reflect on Pen's character with the kind of shrewd insight that is the staple of *Vanity Fair* but an infrequent luxury in the other novels. As soon as the insight is delivered, however, the narrator slides away into extenuations that stifle the issues it raises for the whole novel:

In a word, Pen's greatest enemy was himself: and as he had been pampering, and coaxing, and indulging that individual all his life, the rogue grew insolent, as all spoiled servants will be; and at the slightest attempt to coerce him, or make him do that which was unpleasant to him, became frantically rude and unruly. A person who is used to making sacrifices— Laura, for instance, who had got such a habit of giving up her own pleasure for others—can do the business quite easily; but Pen, unaccustomed as he was to any sort of self-denial, suffered moodily when called on to pay his share, and savagely grumbled at being obliged to forego anything he liked.

[II, xiii, 157–58]

We might well ask, though the narrator doesn't, why Laura and Helen should doubt the rumors about the sexual indulgence of such a thoroughly self-centered young man. We might ask further what sort of world, what sort of narrator demands unremitting self-sacrifice of the Lauras and turns a blind eye, when he doesn't wink, at the conduct of the Pens? We might ask the most disturbing question of all: why does the novel lavish its main attention on such a callow, uncaring, self-indulgent character as Pen? The answer that seems nearly self-evident is that much of the novel, like the scene of reconciliation between Pen and his mother, is wish-fulfillment for Thackeray and, in all likelihood, for many of his male contemporaries.

The late novels are caught in this kind of arrested thematic development. But they do not simply reshuffle familiar sexual stereotypes. Even at their most bland, smug, dilatory moments, they have the power to arouse frustration rather than boredom because they have made us aware of the underlying disorder within the novel and the culture it reflects (always Victorian culture, whatever the historical disguise). The frustration comes at the failure to develop the inchoate material. When the novels do retreat to familiar stereotypes, the stereotypes still gain special significance and impact because they are such palpable evasions.

Thus, these later novels make us aware of the characters' inadequate sexual development even though the characters themselves remain in a kind of emotional and social limbo, neither quite fulfilling nor quite rejecting the traditional roles. In this context, the incestuous attachments do not suggest a hidden area of sexual desire that must be denied because it violates prevailing social taboos. In fact, Henry does finally marry the woman who has acted as his surrogate mother, just as Pen marries the woman raised as his sister. The incest motif is, instead, another sign of the inadequacy of desire: attenuated forms of a mother's and a sister's love provide a refuge for the heroes from the baffling world of adult sexual relations. This sentimental confusion of desires leaves the heroes and the novels in an uneasy, debilitated state somewhere between childhood and maturity.

All this, so far as it is realized in clear and convincing development, is a condition of mutual victimization by a sexual system that cannot move beyond inadequate roles. Rachel cannot acknowledge the moral and emotional shoddiness of the husband she worshiped and free the rich complexity of her own emotional and intellectual life. Henry cannot shake a similarly constraining pattern of masculine idealization; he worships Rachel for the very qualities that keep her victimized and prevent any satisfying emotional relationship between them. Both characters try to load the relation between mother and son with all the erotic emotions (and desires for a significant spiritual and social life) that normal maturity supposedly satisfies. This strained, inadequate relation reflects a society that cannot fulfill the expectations it raises. Even Beatrix, though her role is more an authorial imposition than a convincing development of character, cannot escape the limits and the obsessive patterns of the coquette.[13]

Although *Esmond's* early sections suggest this state of mutual victimization by forces beyond the control or even the conscious recognition of any character, the novel does not turn its attention toward the anatomy of social corruption that *Vanity Fair*, operating under similar perceptions, accomplishes. Instead, the narrator increasingly admires the emotional heroism of his younger self, rather than recognizing this self-sacrificing devotion as emotional paralysis. And as part of the same process of displacement, it treats Rachel and Beatrix as figures who have somehow failed Esmond—the "wronged man" motif that recurs in all these novels, placing responsibility for erotic failure in the wrong place, deflecting attention away from the basic corruption of Victorian sexual values toward the stereotypic *belle dame sans merci*. Even those critics who have seen *Esmond* as a fully integrated psychological novel have remarked on the narrator's eagerness to displace his own inadequacies onto Beatrix and Rachel.[14]

Esmond and *Pendennis* do begin to suggest the sort of symbolic analogies in sexual role that are much more fully developed in *Vanity Fair*. Warrington, with his ruined marriage, career as a writer, and tutorial relationship toward Pip is both a partial double and a father to the hero. This motif, like the creation of the two Henry Esmonds, allows the older, worldly wise and somewhat cynical figure to evade the complexities of commitment to personal relations, involvement in social action and, in general, all the pressures and contingencies that can produce self-knowledge. Yet he can still enjoy vicarious participation in the young hero's activities, nostalgically revisiting scenes and emotions that supposedly stirred his own youthful career. This splitting of the novel's main character into two, either character and narrator or characters who are doubles, allows the narrator the emotional luxury of blending disillusion and illusion in a particularly hermetic mixture. Romantic ideals can be enshrined, stereotypes can be easily purveyed, generalizations are not brought to the test of contradictory social reality because the arena of the novel's action becomes almost wholly mental. The *narrator's* reactions supplant the characters' actions as the primary focus of the novel, and they move steadily away from the intense and intriguing sexual material set forth at each novel's beginning into a world of spuriously reflective commentary that actually reshuffles the worn terminology of stereotypes. There is a haunting fear throughout *Esmond* that only memory survives to give individual life significance and that memory is a sentimental delusion.

Sexual cynicism as well as sexual sentimentality can be sporadically indulged in in this essentially autoerotic mental landscape. Rather than exposing the general corruption, these bursts of sardonic commentary provide temporary relief from the pressures of ambivalent, often hostile sexual feelings. They thus protect the narrative from the perceptions it can never quite suppress.

Although *Pendennis* does project the older "self," the passive, disillusioned, but indulgently avuncular figure, into a character, the narrator still acts to restrain the potentially exciting psychological material and keep the focus on his own ruminations. Because the action concentrates primarily on Pen's doings, and because he does enough to divert the reader, Warrington can be kept in the background, the pathos of his withdrawal from full participation in the world coyly hinted at but its causes unexplored. Along with his comic counterpart, Major Pendennis, Warrington serves as a surrogate father for Pen, an indulgent father whose criticisms have none of the force of an ordinary father's. This symbolic arrangement serves to further protect the novel from its own material.

By the time of *Esmond*, the hermetic system is more complete. There the fatherless son is allowed, in a sense, to father himself through the first-person narrative.[15] The old Esmond literally creates the young Esmond for us by telling the story. Of course, this is a condition of all autobiographical first-person fictional narratives, but it takes on special significance in the symbolic context of this novel. Lord Castlewood, the temporary surrogate father, is not only killed off reasonably early in the novel; Henry assists in the affair of honor that causes his death. Though the symbolic pattern remains underdeveloped, this episode enacts a curious kind of patricide. Henry is implicated in the death of his foster father, even held responsible for it by Rachel; and through this action he is freed to become first the substitute and then the actual husband of his foster mother. More significant still, a narrative situation results where Henry Esmond is both father and son—father in the role of the old, comfortable, nostalgic narrator; son in the role of young, suffering, active character. The damaging consequence is that the narrative lapses from any independent, critical perspective on its material into a self-indulgent, metaphorically incestuous interplay between two stages of the same personality.

The most interesting and original material in *Henry Esmond* and *Pendennis* is thus kept peripheral and fragmentary. Thackeray's ambivalence toward issues of sexual identity, role, and desire caused him to suppress his shrewdest, most profound, most disturbing insights in favor of stereotypic motifs. It is a familiar Victorian procedure, except that Thackeray's novels intimate and partially explore the sexual issues that are suppressed. The result is imperfectly realized fiction that arouses expectations it fails to fulfill. Yet if this fiction is often perplexing, it is seldom opaque or bland as literature thoroughly in the grip of stereotypic notions usually is. The consciousness of something lacking in the overt narrative, something suppressed into incomplete and shadowy symbolic patterns, regularly ripples through the seemingly casual flow of the narrative's surface.

It is only in *Vanity Fair* that Thackeray managed to fully integrate plot, narrative techniques, psychological insights and social satire in such a way that his ambivalent attitudes toward sexual relations were encouraged—or even forced—into a creative dialectic. Satire and sentiment, sexual stereotypes and cynical perceptions about traditional norms counteract each other and generate new perspectives not only toward the novel's material but toward the whole of Victorian middle-class culture. The new perspective typically emerges through a process in which initial patterns in action, in symbolic configuration, and in narrative rhetoric assume a more extreme, often a more grotesque form. In this way ambivalence is urged to follow the logic of its own implications.

Esmond and *Pendennis* present us with characters set in potentially intriguing erotic opposition and attraction but restrain them from any real interaction. The apparent interaction that occurs in the mental world of the narrative commentary—the resigned, leisurely, reflective mode—actually muffles psychological interplay. At the same time the plot dawdles about, avoiding the sharp dramatic encounters that the initial situations promise. *Vanity Fair*, though it certainly makes us aware of the narrator's presence, uses the narrative commentary to unsettle any complacency about sexual relations we might bring to the novel and then to redirect our attention to the development of character and action. Thus, for all the aggressively fatuous, aggressively satiric narrative asides that appear on virtually every page of *Vanity Fair*, the novel works in a mode that is essentially dramatic rather than reflective. And as the reflective and randomly episodic methods of *Esmond* and *Pendennis* allow Thackeray to give way to the besetting weaknesses in his imagination, so the dramatic methods of *Vanity Fair* stimulate the development of his keenest insights and his most brilliant social and psychological scenes.

Like Dickens, Thackeray is, in Henry James's phrase, one of the "greatest of superficial novelists."[16] James's censorious phrase for Dickens actually describes a fictional achievement that is not less than but simply different from James's own. Thackeray and Dickens at their best exploit the behavioral mannerisms and social interactions of ordinary life for the subtleties they reveal. They never sacrifice the fascinating surface for the mere depths. Just as episodic fictional construction allows them to discover complexities not originally foreseen, and perhaps never fully recognized, in plot and character, so a focus on dramatic enactment rather than characters' state of consciousness allows them to pursue what might be called the psychosymbolism of ordinary life. It is a method particularly suited to revealing the nature of a society severely repressive and basically confused.

Typically, then, the narrator's asides expose the anomalies in the situations he describes and send us back to the drama with quickened and informed interest. When, for instance, Becky taunts Amelia about her seduction of George, while pretending to advise her to keep him home, the narrator comments:

Women only know how to wound so. There is a poison on the tips of their little shafts, which stings a thousand times more than a man's blunter weapon. Our poor Emmy, who had never hated, never sneered all her life, was powerless in the hands of her remorseless little enemy.

[I, xxix, 354]

Even apart from the dramatic context, the passage draws attention to some anomalies in the sexual situation of this society. Amelia's virtues are presented as negations rather than positive forces, and they are already linked with impotence. Similarly, the narrator does not claim that the "bluntness" of masculine sarcasm is a virtue, a matter of nobler intention, but treats it as a defect, a clumsiness in handling the weapons of social warfare. And, like so many of the narrator's generalizations about men and women, this one is disturbing because it shrewdly points to a social fact. Even if we repudiate the stereotype, we are urged to account for the cultural processes that have trained women more than men to use such weapons, both to conceal and to refine the expression of their aggressiveness.

This passage points toward the climax of the Brussels episode, which is not the defeat of Napolean (with very adroit irony, the novel deals only with the first reports of the Battle of Waterloo, which describe it as a debacle for the English forces) but the victorious maneuvers of Becky Sharp and the novel's explicit recognition of her as its heroine: "If this is a novel without a hero, at least let us lay claim to a heroine. No man in the British army which has marched away, not the great Duke himself, could be more cool or collected in the presence of doubts and difficulties, than the indomitable little aide-de-camp's wife" (I, xxx, 366). In a society where sexual relations have largely been reduced to a struggle for power and status, where aggression and disregard for both rights and emotions of others are the only effective forces, the self-regarding wit, emotional control, and persistence Becky so supremely exhibits have indeed replaced the traditional moral virtues. In contrast, Amelia does not even have the powers of an Esther Summerson to "win some love" through unflagging, selfless service to others; she has been displaced from her always dubious eminence as a moral heroine into the realm of idle feeling, the narrator's patronizing pity for "poor little Emmy."

Vanity Fair makes it clear that the character's basic psychological natures are inseparable from the corrupt social world they inhabit. There is no cloister from vulgarity here, no way after the crass sensuality of old Sir Pitt, the sneering brutality of the Marquis of Steyne, and the unwitting collaboration of even the sensitive and generous Dobbin with the prevailing forces of the sexual marketplace, to make any valid distinction between refinement and vulgarity. That Vanity Fair is primarily a place where sexual wares are sold—either openly as Old Osborne attempts to do in his lust to secure the money of Miss Swartz or more subtly as Becky does in her various intrigues—becomes abundantly clear in the novel. The pursuit of money, place, security, power always comes down, in the novel's development of plot and theme, to fundamental sexual issues.

The detached, reflective consciousness, which husbands its emotions and lets them play only over the secure and restricted field of remembered experience, making a gentle erotic disillusionment a means of furthering illusions, simply has no place in this novel. The one figure who attempts to live in this mode, Dobbin, is first made to subserve the interests of his antithesis, George Osborne, and then literally exiled from the novel's main action. And even Dobbin's moment of real power and insight in the novel—like Rawdon Crawley's—comes when he sees the shoddiness of the woman he has idolized. By that point the novel has fully exposed the spuriousness of the masculine ideals that have created the modes in which both Amelia and Becky operate, so that the real shoddiness is in the ideals themselves, not in the women who embody them.

The world *Vanity Fair* reveals is defined by its social operations. The privacy of self-reflection can be fruitful only as a defensive measure or an effort to prepare for some pending social conflict; real self-knowledge can never be gained. Sustained states of reflection rather than action are regularly described as metaphoric death or paralysis; this is true for Amelia's self-lacerating agonies of rejected love, for Dobbin's more stoic suffering, for Jane Osborne's submisssion to her father, for the ruined Sedley's broodings on his misfortune, and for Old Osborne'e bitter grief at the banishment and death of his son. The novel comes close to suggesting that acute consciousness, in the social world that is the novel's subject, can only be a weakness. The only sort that works to advantage is Becky's sort, an intelligence deliberately limited to self-serving stratagems in the sexual battle that defines the society's preoccupations.

Because the novel's male characters are so overpowered by their conscious and unconscious emotional lives (emotions that invariably center on sexual role and sexual power), only female characters can exercise the kind of calculating intelligence that Becky supremely exhibits. This inversion of the traditional stereotype is exemplified by a host of seemingly ill-sorted male characters: Old Osborne, Steyne, Old Sir Pitt, Bute Crawley, George Osborne, Dobbin, Jos Sedley, by every important male character in the novel. While Becky is unsurpassed in her control over her emotional life, she does have some female counterparts: Mrs. Bute Crawley, Miss Crawley, Lady Jane Crawley, and even Miss Pinkerton. Ironically, though, this greater feminine power over emotions comes about through a severing of personal desires from pragmatic intelligence. It starts by relinquishing the hope of sexual fulfillment and the urge for direct control over personal circumstances that the male characters still seek. It implicitly acknowledges and accepts the role of an inferior, a flatterer, a servant to the desires of men. Becky as a child performing before her father and his Bohemian friends, learning to be on stage at all times, succeeding through cynical mimicry of the social world about her, learns a valuable lesson: the one lesson that allows a woman in the novel to keep some independent power to herself. As much as Esther Summerson, though, Becky gains power through relinquishing personal desires and a search for personal identity.

What sustains Becky, for a long while at least, is the exuberance of her own spirit, her ability to take the vicious sexual game as, nevertheless, a game to be played for all it is worth. She pushes a dependent's, a caterer's, and flatterer's power about as far as it can be pushed. To sustain the game she must move from man to man, eluding the efforts of each one to confine her. And so the young Reverend Crisp (briefly) replaces her father in her first effort to become the puppeteer rather than the puppet; he is replaced by Jos Sedley, then Rawdon (and his father), George, Major Tufto, the Marquis of Steyne, and a series of male escorts in the gambling centers of Europe.

She overplays her game with Steyne, as she must overplay it with someone eventually. The inevitability of her defeat is not the result of her greed or arrogance but is built into the game; sooner or later she must submit to the real power that underlies the sexual appearances that she manipulates so adroitly. However little satisfaction this ultimate power brings to the patriarchal figures like Steyne and Osborne who chiefly wield it in the novel, it is theirs to exercise. So Becky must either submit to Steyne's desires—and the desire for sadistic power is stronger than his physical lust, as his treatment of the women in his own family makes clear—or she must move on. Not only is she weary of such a profitless game by this point, near despair at times, the narrator tells us, but she sees no place to go if she refuses Steyne. In terms of the conscious desires she has for social position, for security, even for respectability, he has the power to make her a social outcast even as he has the power to force his wife and daughter-in-law and mother to invite her to Gaunt House. Her "rescue" from this dilemma ironically will plunge her into a still more despairing and openly sordid round of the same sordid game. And, in another irony, the rescue comes through a momentary resurgence of a stereotypic masculine display of physical courage and outraged sexual honor that seems almost wholesome by comparison with the masculine modes of behavior that dominate *Vanity Fair*.

As A. E. Dyson has said of the celebrated question of Becky's guilt or innocence in the Steyne affair: "What Thackeray comes near to suggesting, like Bunyan before him, is that a society based upon privilege and money is rotten in some fundamental sense. The very concepts of Christian morality become, in such a context, an evasion; an attempt to visit upon the underprivileged and unprotected the sins which more properly belong to the society at large." G. Armour Craig agrees substantially with this assessment: the reader's "moral vocabulary is irrelevant" because the novel presents "a society in which market values and moral values are discontinuous and separate."[17]

Dyson and Craig, like most other critics of *Vanity Fair*, recognize that the social world of the novel is not a "sector" of society like the isolated military, political, literary, academic, and variously genteel circles that appear in Thackeray's other novels. It is emblematic of the entire culture, as the allusions to Bunyan and *Ecclesiastes* imply, and the narrator's sweeping condemnations make explicit. The novel is primarily concerned with people who are scrabbling to gain money and status because they epitomize the forces that are taking over the culture. The ruin of Raggles, the former butler of Lady Crawley, by the Rawdon Crawleys' practice of living on nothing a year is an emblem of this spread of corruption. At the other end of the class spectrum, the Marquis of Steyne is himself drawn into Becky's world and overpowered by it for all his personal and class presumptions. The precariously genteel world of Becky, Rawdon, the Sedleys, and the Osbornes holds the novel's focus because it is the unstable center of change; it subjects the traditional values of the whole culture to a crucial test.

Yet the fundamental rottenness that is exposed, the fundamental values that are tested, are not primarily matters of class privilege or the depradations of a market economy but issues of sexual values and sexual abuses. Dyson is quite right that "Becky *belongs* to Vanity Fair, both as its true reflection, and as its victim; for both of which reasons, she very resoundingly serves it right."[18] But shrewd as this observation is, it does not go far enough. What Becky epitomizes, above all, is the workings of the sexual marketplace. Her power and her methods are based upon her sexuality; her intelligence, resourceful imagination, exuberance, courage, and persistence are all subordinated to sexual pursuits.

As Becky gains more of the externals which are the object of her conscious desires—material luxury, status, the fashionable diversions of balls and suppers, even the appearance of respectability—she becomes less and less satisfied. They are not really what she is after:

the poor woman herself was yawning in spirit. "I wish I were out of it," she said to herself. "I would rather be a parson's wife, and teach a Sunday school than this; or a sergeant's lady, and ride in the regimental waggon; or, O how much gayer it would be to wear spangles and trousers, and dance before a booth at a fair."

[II, xvi, 189]

Becky, of course, would soon grow bored with any of those roles, any roles the society allows her to play; she is no more committed to these idle fantasies than she is to the idea that she could be happy in a country estate with £5,000 a year.

But the passage reveals something essential about her desires and the reasons they are inevitably frustrated, for all her tone of idle whimsy. Becky cannot conceive a life for herself apart from a man, and in a social role subordinate to him. She has danced to men's desires since she was a child ("she had never been a girl, she said; she had been a woman since she was eight years old"; I, ii, 14); she will do so until she dies. As the novel pursues the implications of her career, she becomes more and more haggard until finally "there [is] a period in Mrs. Becky's life, when she [is] seized, not by remorse, but by a kind of despair" (II, xxix, 365). In the last pose she assumes in the novel, she has retreated from explicit sexual encounters to the female stereotype that forms the life of Rachel Esmond and Helen Pendennis, the pious lady of charitable works.

It is surely significant that Thackeray has founded his exposure of social corruption on the careers of two women. As they move toward opposite extremes, Becky and Amelia establish the limits for women's experience in *Vanity Fair*. And, more than this, they set the terms for the whole novel. Their careers dominate plot and thematic development in a way that is unique in Thackeray's fiction, for female or male characters.[19] Through the symbolic opposition of the careers of Becky and Amelia, Thackeray exposes a crisis common to all the various social practices and personal relations in the novel.

It is understandable that many readers have taken money, materialism—or the mechanism for the rapid spread of materialism, a credit economy—as the central target of *Vanity Fair's* satire.

Money is what Becky thinks she is after, certainly what she hoards; money disputes precipitate the break between George and his father; money causes the Sedleys to lose their whole world of social relations; and money gives Jos whatever status he has. But in all the major economic dealings of the novel, sexual forces are the real determinants of the action and the deepest source of characters' motivation.

The chief representative of brutal economic power in the novel, that self-made man who has made himself into a virtual Mammon, demonstrates the way that sexual conflicts fuel all apparent economic conflicts. We never see Osborne on the Stock Exchange; all his dealings come down to one project, his effort to buy a wife for George. His attempt to bribe George into marrying Miss Swartz, his default on the marriage contract with the Sedleys, and finally his disinheriting of George are all consequences of this initial project. Even his effort to buy gentility for his son, through schooling and an army commission, is part of a struggle to force his patriarchal will on the entire family. (The blatantly symbolic ornamental clock, depicting the sacrifice of Iphigenia by Agammemnon, that ticks away in the Osborne dining room suits the crassness and violence of Osborne's desires; and it stresses just how much his character is involved in the sacrifice of women to his own desires, first his wife, then Amelia, then Miss Swartz, then his daughter, and finally Amelia again, as he uses his money to blackmail her into giving up Georgy to him.) None of these transactions fulfills his desires though; he is psychologically memorable for his scenes of rage and smouldering violence, both expressing the frustration of desire.

Osborne becomes part of an analogical set in the novel, a group of raging, frustrated old men that includes Sir Pitt, Steyne, and Major Tufto and thus incorporates the novel's chief patriarchs. Their economic power and social status, their own arrogant assumptions that they can dispose of the lives of others at will, are all frustrated by their inability to achieve their sexual desires. Sexual desires encompass, in this novel's searching view of an essentially modern society, the desire to control a son's or daughter's sexual life and the desire to humiliate a wife as well as the more obvious lusts of a Sir Pitt.

In a virtual fusion of Sir Pitt and Old Osborne, the novel produces a third imperious and frustrated patriarch, Lord Steyne. The characterization of Steyne reveals how multiple sexual forces inform what at first seems to be simple lechery. Steyne's sadistic intimidation of his wife and daughters-in-law, in a scene unmatched for brutality in the novel, reveals a desire for power that is regularly expressed through control and humiliation of women:

"Who are you to give orders here? [he says to Lady Gaunt] You have no money. You've got no brains. You were here to have children, and you have not had any. Gaunt's tired of you; and George's wife is the only person in the family who doesn't wish you were dead. Gaunt would marry again if you were." . . . "You may strike me if you like, sir, or hit any cruel blow," Lady Gaunt said. To see his wife and daughter suffering always put his Lordship into a good humour.

"My sweet Blanche," he said, "I am a gentleman, and never lay my hand upon a woman, save in the way of kindness."

. . . "As for Mrs. Crawley's character, I shan't demean myself or that most spotless and perfectly irreproachable lady, by even hinting that it requires a defence. You will be pleased to receive her with the utmost cordiality, as you will receive all persons whom I present in this house. . . . Who is the master of it? and what is it? This Temple of Virtue belongs to me. And if I invite all Newgate or all Bedlam here, by —— they shall be welcome."

After this vigorous allocution, to one of which Lord Steyne treated his "Hareem" whenever symptoms of insubordination appeared in his household, the crest-fallen women had nothing for it but to obey.

[II, xiv, 164–65]

Though Lord Steyne's relations with Becky are broken off by Rawdon's assault, there is little doubt that they could, and in all probability would, deteriorate to this sort of contemptuous torment once he tired of her. Just as we are shown Old Osborne directing the impotent rage of a whole futile life toward his son and daughter, so Steyne, when he encounters Becky years after his humiliating failure to impose his will upon her, gapes at her "with a livid face and ghastly eyes" and threatens to have her murdered. Steyne has been duped by Becky, his lust unfulfilled and his money taken; he has been insulted and struck by Rawdon; and has been forced to back away from a duel. Virtually all the masculine powers and prerogatives Steyne prides himself on— control of money, shrewd wit, a cynical manipulation of women for his own pleasure, courage, pride, honor—are overthrown in this encounter. When we see him for the next and last time after this episode, he is a ghastly ruin: "Hate, or anger, or desire, caused [his eyes] to brighten now and then still; but ordinarily they gave no light, and seemed tired of looking out on a world of which almost all the pleasure and all the best beauty had palled upon the worn-out wicked old man" (II, xxix, 381).

Steyne is also haunted, like Osborne, by a horrible image of his son that threatens him in a way he cannot defend himself against. Osborne's bitter, raging anguish results from George's death, which seals forever his father's guilt at banishing him, and perhaps even more from his failure to force his will upon George. Steyne is haunted by his son's madness, the result of a hereditary illness that might attack Steyne himself. Both situations come about through sexual corruption that has nothing to do with simple lust. Osborne's effort to force a moneyed wife on George and the inbreeding which has produced the stain of madness in the house of Gaunt both suggest far more insidious and pervasive corrup- tions of patriarchal power than the sexual cravings of old Sir Pitt. After the horrible examples of Steyne and Osborne, Sir Pitt seems relatively decent. At least he neglects his wife rather than sadist- ically tormenting her; his lust is open and he pays his mistresses for it openly; and he is a scandal to the world rather than an honored aristocrat or merchant prince.

The only important father in the novel who does not quite fit this group is Sedley, the only one who does not attempt to force his will upon his family, to determine sexual roles and relations. (For all his cruel tormenting of Jos for his girth, vanity, and "feminine" traits, Sedley is quite willing to let him live as he likes, marry whom he wants: "Why not she as well as another, Mrs. Sedley? The girl's a white face at any rate. *I* don't care who marries him. Let Joe please himself"; I, iv, 35). The racism is ugly, and Sedley surely bears some responsibility for Jos' grotesque substitution of food for sex and the fear of masculine sexual roles which it suggests. But Sedley has the most decent relations with his family of any man in the novel, except Dobbin. And the Sedleys have the only marriage in the novel that is not, sooner or later, a failure. Sedley's economic ruin is a symbolic, if not exactly a logical consequence, of this distinction (though the easy, trusting, essentially nonaggressive relationship he has with his wife, son, and daughter may have some bearing on his inability to survive in the rapacious economic world of the novel).

In sharp contrast to the later novels' discursive presentation of multiple careers, Osborne and Steyne are not seen engaged in the economic and political activities that supposedly underlie their social power. The exercise and the frustration of their power in the novel almost totally involve sexual dealings, and these center on the buying, selling, and emotional abuse of women. Lévi-Strauss' theory that social organization began with the exchange of women by men may be an inaccurate, or at least an untestable, hypothesis; like Freud's theory of the primal horde, it may be an extrapolation backwards of an insight into contemporary culture. But it does describe a dominant pattern in sexual relations in Western culture, flourishing in Victorian England and scarcely altered today.[20] As *Vanity Fair* abundantly demonstrates, the deferential attitudes toward women, the sentimental idealization of women, the protective masculine displays toward women are wholesale hypocrisies. As in *Martin Chuzzlewit*, disputes over the possession of women underlie nearly all the dealings between men in the novel. The abuses are so systemic that the most self-sacrificing of Dobbin's transactions on Amelia's behalf have something of the taint.

All the characters' motives and pursuits cannot be collapsed into one pattern of sexual desire, insecurity, hostility, and frustration. The pursuit of money, social status, military glory, and so forth have a reality in themselves that resists such programmatic assimilation. One of Thackeray's most brilliant and convincing dramatic effects, in fact, is to present the mixed and often sporadic motives that determine his characters' behavior. Yet the novel insists on the multitude of ways that sexuality so informs the other manifest business of *Vanity Fair* that it becomes an inseparable element of every other preoccupation. Thus sexual fraud is a major element in every other kind of fraud in the novel.

We have seen how the overbearing patriarchal figures of the novel are drawn into the prevailing sexual pattern through their own obsessions; their desire to dominate the barter of women is its own undoing, leaving them in frenzies of impotent rage. But the character whom the narrator holds up as the novel's one instance of a true gentleman also illustrates the prevailing masculine dilemma. Dobbin loses interest in his military career just as he has lost his one friend (through disillusion about George's character even before George's death) because he has set his heart on the hopeless pursuit of Amelia.

Dobbin is the most admirable character in the novel, by traditional moral norms and by the standards of a traditional masculine sexual ethic (epitomized by Austen's George Knightley); he is also the most frustrated character in the book. He has neither the protective illusions about himself that even Jos Sedley can rebuild after every humiliation, nor the temporary accomplishment of provisional goals that sustains most of the characters. Dobbin acts, but only in the interests of others. In *Vanity Fair* this ethic, based upon secularized Christian precepts and older, more general ideals of friendship, can only intensify hypocrisy and viciousness and the destruction of the self; for the people and the system it serves are so caught up in corrupt practices that furthering their interests is furthering corruption. This is fully exemplified in the marriage of Amelia and George that Dobbin arranges. Dobbin's supposed virtue, like Becky's supposed vice, is thus nearly nullified by its consequences in the world at large.

Dobbin's folly is underscored by the narrator from the beginning and is finally brought home even to Dobbin himself. His dependence on a woman is thoroughly incapacitating, through its own sentimental distortions and not through Amelia's flaws. His own false sentimentality blinds him to the weakness, inanity, and self-mortifying devotion intrinsic to the stereotypic feminine virtues that Amelia incarnates. The presentation of his situation is not tinctured with the excessive narrative pathos of *Esmond* and *Pendennis* that washes over and obliterates the fundamental errors in the sexual attitudes of their heroes. As a result Dobbin is not only a more balanced character but a more admirable one. His generosity and decency are made more attractive because the narrator is not always there to camouflage his limitations. We are likely to value his real virtues all the more, as we are the virtues of Becky, because we have been shown the destructive sexual forces they must necessarily struggle against.

Vanity Fair also avoids the obsessive, though often disguised, preoccupation with the sentimentally erotic relation of son and mother that subverts the development of character and theme in Thackeray's late novels. There is no saintly self-sacrificing mother, to start with. Instead we are presented with the refreshingly ordinary and worldly Mrs. Sedley, the thoroughly abject and demoralized Lady Crawley, and so on. George's mother has died long before the narrative begins; Dobbin's is kept out of the direct narrative. This not only allows a clearer focus on the fathers who struggle to dominate the world and the patriarchal system that is corrupted by its victimization of women; it also allows Thackeray to avoid entrapment in the complex of emotions that clearly dominated his own personal life and frustrated some of the finest potential developments in his late fiction.

Amelia does become a self-abnegating mother, of course, so much so that the narrator describes her existence as "a maternal caress." But the destructive effects of her development, on Georgy, on her parents, and on Amelia herself, are so thoroughly exposed by the novel that she becomes a parody of the ideal that incapacitates *Esmond* and *Pendennis*. The parody is unmistakable when the narrator describes her as an agonized Hannah relinquishing her Samuel. Her Samuel is as selfish and as snobbish as they come in *Vanity Fair*, and he is delivered up to Mammon, the money power of Old Osborne, not to God. The response of a contemporary reader of the novel, Mrs. Jameson, was shrewd: "No woman resents Rebecca . . . but every woman resents his selfish and inane Amelia."[21]

The demolition of stereotypes about sexual relations in the family, in courtship and marriage, and in society at large accompanies the novel's focus on Becky Sharp. She eventually succumbs to the power of the traditional stereotypes, and we are led to see how they have shaped her course all along. But she is, like Emma Woodhouse and Catherine Earnshaw, a woman who acts not just to achieve her own personal aims but to give the world about her coherence, purpose, and energy. She is in this sense the chief actor in *Vanity Fair*, as well as its most accomplished performer of manipulative and deceptive rituals.

Becky's goals and her modes of operation are, however, essentially no different from those of the world about her; they are merely pursued with a remarkable wit, energy, resourcefulness, and dramatic skill. It is not that the world cannot live up to her expectations but that she lives down to the standards of the world. If this saves her from the arrogance of Emma and Catherine, it also prevents her from participating in an effort like theirs to reshape the world to a finer ideal of human existence.

Becky is certainly in many senses the heroine, as she is the chief projection of the author—the creator of dramatic scenes and a brilliant satirist. But she, like the novel at large, serves to scuttle the very idea that personal heroism is possible in such a thoroughly corrupt social world. Both she and Dobbin, antitheses in most ways, demonstrate that even a moderately decent life is nearly impossible in the scrabble for money, security, and status that characterizes the surface life of this society.

Though Becky has unusual intelligence, a robust spirit, and a remarkable ability to mimic and manipulate social mannerisms, her whole career is based on her sexual attractiveness. Without her youth, her figure, her status as both a licit and illicit object of male desires, she would have remained a governess. However she turns the stereotypic notions against themselves, however she exposes the fatuous bravado and sentimentality of a vicious sexual world, she has no other conceptions of what life is or might be than the very stereotypes she so adroitly uses to her advantage. The advantage is only temporary, and it is ultimately not only unsatisfying but degrading. The degradation that matters most is not Becky's soiled social reputation in the novel's closing European episodes but the degradation of her spirit. A fashionable world whose arbiters of decorum are figures like the Marquis of Steyne has lost all right, all ability to make distinctions.

The novel's own traditional moral norms, represented by Dobbin and by one set of impulses in an ambivalent narrator, are rendered irrelevant to Becky. The supposedly sordid Becky, so distasteful to Dobbin and so unfit, in his opinion, to associate with Amelia, provides the one resurgence of vitality and humor in the increasingly despondent, bitter mood of the novel's close. This is the wonderful scene that returns us to the opening episodes of the novel, where Becky courts Jos once more while the brandy bottle, rouge pot, and plate with scraps of a meal on it—all of which she has shoved under the bedspread in hasty preparation for her visitor—clink away merrily in counterpoint to the arts she once more exercises over Jos. Although this scene already contrasts sharply, to Becky's advantage, with the increasingly somber and even pompous moral tone of Dobbin, with his dog-like devotion to Amelia, the narrator enlarges Becky's virtues much more than this:

Becky liked the life. She was at home with everybody in the place, pedlars, punters, tumblers, students and all. She was of a wild, roving nature, inherited from father and mother, who were both Bohemians, by taste and circumstance; if a lord was not by, she would talk to his courier with the greatest pleasure; the din, the stir, the drink, the smoke, the tattle of the Hebrew pedlars, the solemn, braggart ways of the poor tumblers, the *sournois* talk of the gambling-table officials, the songs and swagger of the students, and the general buzz and hum of the place had pleased and tickled the little woman, even when her luck was down, and she had not wherewithal to pay her bill. How pleasant was all the bustle to her now that her purse was full of the money which little Georgy had won for her the night before!

[II, xxx, 385]

If Becky enjoys this sort of world, so did Chaucer and Shakespeare. Becky might well sigh with one of her great progenitors, "It tikleth me about myn herte roote . . . That I have had my world as in my time." For she does experience exuberantly, and reveal to us, much more of the world than any other character in the novel. In this passage the narrative presents a sector of the world that might well leaven the sterile hypocrisies of the fashionable society that excludes Becky, and the more subtle hypocrisies of the moral world of Dobbin and Amelia. It is, of course, still inevitably a world of pretensions and self-serving, but it is rich, varied, bustling; it includes all who come to it, even when they can't pay their bills, rather than excluding them like the would-be genteel world that has been the novel's primary subject. Clearly it is more attractive in every way than the viciousness of Gaunt House and the self-absorbed, timorous, inbred little house where Amelia lived with her parents and Georgy. Dobbin makes a great deal of Becky's abuse of little Georgy when she has him gamble for her. But the narrative analogies, though not the narrator himself, are pointedly there to undercut Dobbin's moral censure. Becky induces Georgy to gamble; Amelia sold him to his grandfather, whose riches can only further Georgy's progress in the ways of Vanity Fair.

The novel's plot is brilliantly contrived to reinforce this point. Becky returns Dobbin's enmity by acting to fulfill his desires. When she exposes George Osborne's true sexual nature to Amelia, Becky does the one thing that can make Amelia accept Dobbin's offer of marriage. Ironically, the necessary proof, the note that George wrote her, is the result of the very sexual wiles that both Amelia and Dobbin piously condemn. Once again the moral and sentimental world is made the beneficiary of the sordid sexual world that it alternately ignores and disdains but that shapes it at every turn.

When Dobbin has just openly condemned Becky to Amelia in Becky's presence and has tried to prevent any contact between them, the narrator gives us her reflections: "'What a noble heart that man has,' she thought, 'and how shamefully that women plays with it.' She admired Dobbin; she bore him no rancour for the part he had taken against her. It was an open move in the game, and played fairly" (II, xxxi, 409). Becky's generosity will seem surprising only if we have failed to recognize that she has been, together with Dobbin and Rawdon, one of the very few characters in the novel who has consistently acted with generosity and good humor (when such behavior did not directly conflict with her self-serving plans, of course). Her metaphor of life as a game is a much more accurate reflection of the world both she and Dobbin inhabit, and a much surer guide to conduct in it, than Dobbin's sentimental idealizations and moral norms. It is, in fact, the metaphor Dobbin himself uses during his one moment of real lucidity and creative strength, when he declares his intention to leave Amelia: "I have spent enough of my life at this play" (II, xxxi, 409).

The novel does not make this the single, final perspective on Becky, of course. There is no single comprehensive resolution of any of the contradictions in the world the narrator describes or in his own ambivalent attitudes toward it. But the narrator's urge to condemn Becky and all the disturbing things she represents exposes its own strains increasingly in the novel, so that the most lurid description of her vices also appears in the final episodes:

it has been the wish of the present writer, all through this story, deferentially to submit to the fashion at present prevailing, and only to hint at the existence of wickedness in a light, easy, and agreeable manner, so that nobody's fine feelings may be offended. . . . In describing this Siren [Becky], singing and smiling, coaxing and cajoling, the author, with modest pride, asks his readers all round, has he once forgotten the laws of politeness, and showed the monster's hideous tail above water? No! Those who like may peep down under waves that are pretty transparent, and see it writhing and twirling, diabolically hideous and slimy, flapping amongst bones, or curling round corpses; but above the water-line, I ask, has not everything been proper, agreeable, and decorous, and has any the most squeamish immoralist in Vanity Fair a right to cry fie?

[II, xxix, 364–65]

The satire here is obviously directed at the hypocrisy of that sort of reader whose squeamishness is actually a cover for unacknowledged voyeuristic and sadistic urges—the "squeamish immoralist."

The real emotional excesses on the part of the narrator do not appear in passages like this where he contemplates Becky, but in passages where he revels in the self-lacerating torments of little Amelia ("O you poor secret martyrs and victims, whose life is a torture, who are stretched on racks in your bedrooms . . . [E]very man who . . . peers into those dark places where the torture is administered to you, must pity you. . . ."; II, xxii, 275–76). This is scarcely less lurid than the passage on Becky, but here the narrator is an excited participant, as voyeuristic as any of his readers.

The qualities of temperament that make Becky so compelling and so attractive must either struggle for sporadic and usually fleeting expression (her generosity toward Dobbin, her genuine fondness for Rawdon, her realization that he is "worth twenty George Osbornes") or they must subserve the warped sexual values that control the whole society's behavior. It is to her credit that she exposes the system's corruption even as she uses it to her own advantage and even when she succumbs to its power over her. This is the real nature of her rebellion: persistent mockery of the only world she knows, a mockery that allies her with the satiric narrator.[22]

Arnold Kettle has written of her rebellion:

Only two courses are open to her, the passive one of acquiescence to subjugation or the active one of independent rebellion. . . . And so she uses consciously and systematically all the men's weapons plus her one natural material asset, her sex, to storm the men's world. And the consequence is of course morally degrading and she is a bad woman all right. But she gains our sympathy nevertheless—not our approving admiration, but our human fellow-feeling—just as Heathcliff does, and she too gains it not in spite but because of her rebellion.[23]

We would qualify this fine perception a little: Becky's sexual assets, her power to gain what she thinks she wants and to expose what the whole society is after, are highly artificial—not natural—products of a deeply divided patriarchal society, and they operate most profoundly in a psychological and spiritual, not a material, context. Her rebellion can only reveal what is wrong with the world even as it ensnares her more and more tightly in corruption. The despair that settles increasingly over her own spirit shows how futile for her own life are the services she performs for the reader's enlightenment.

Kettle is absolutely right about Becky's basic appeal, however. She does not exercise the traditional feminine charms over the reader, neither the charm of open seduction nor the more furtive erotic appeal of coy innocence. Her attraction is based upon rebellion against a system that subjugates the oppressors as well as the victims, and it arouses a *human* fellow-feeling—the only way that the novel can escape the stereotypes that crush its characters. Her chief weapon is ridicule, forcing the snobs and hypocrites, the self-righteous and the vicious, to see themselves, for a moment, as they are.

As a consequence of a thoroughly disoriented sexual world, none of the main characters in the novel is able to pursue a "normal" sexual career. Amelia, Dobbin, and Jos are all kept in a condition of enforced celibacy and frustrated erotic desires. Becky uses her marriage as a means to gain the social advancement she wants, first as a front for a virtual gambling house and then as a cover for sexual adventurism. Though Becky has the physical desires most of the characters repress or sublimate (the narrator suggests that her relationship with Rawdon is physically satisfying to both) she destroys the marriage by using her sexual attractiveness as a stratagem to gain money and status. In the world of Vanity Fair, as Becky knows best, female sexuality can retain some measure of independence only by delaying or denying the desires it arouses; personal sexual satisfaction is at best an expendable luxury. Women who attempt some direct fulfillment of direct physical desires must accept the victim's role, as Amelia illustrates. Women who retain some control over their lives all work outside the standard erotic expectations: Miss Crawley, Mrs. Bute Crawley, Miss Pinkerton, and so forth.

George Osborne is the only character who follows, until his early death, a fairly standard sexual career; and it serves as a satire of romantic norms. The first stage is submission to family arrangements for marriage, whose chief criterion is social status. In the second stage he is ready to submit to his father's will, to abandon Amelia if not to marry Miss Swartz, until Dobbin shames him into momentary romantic heroism. Even this heroism is disastrous—not because it fails but because it succeeds: because there is no firm love or commitment to sustain George's impulse, and because Amelia's love is founded on romantic illusions, the marriage is doomed whether he lives or dies. (In fact its life is prolonged far beyond all likelihood by his death, as Amelia enshrines his spurious virtues in her memory.) The point is made by the plot, which has him on the verge of an adulterous relationship with Becky as the summons to Waterloo occurs.

George's strong sensual desires appear only in this adulterous context. This is typical of the novel, where the rare expressions of direct physical sexuality always occur in a context of deception and betrayal. It is also typical that the affair is not consummated. Because sexual roles and rituals are so warped and inadequate, sexual desires are manifested in frustration, not fulfillment. Although *Vanity Fair* displays the swaggering of rakes and the seductive enticements of both demure and brazen coquettes, this display is as phony as every other social pretense. What we remember, what the novel creates most vividly, are scenes of erotic impasse and erotic failure: George defying his father's effort to force Miss Swartz upon him, in ugly racist terms ("Marry that mulatto woman? . . . I don't like the colour, sir. Ask the black that sweeps opposite Fleet Market, sir. *I'm* not going to marry a Hottentot Venus" (I, xxi, 225); Emily deserted in her funereal marriage bed, "nursing the corpse of love"; Sir Pitt, Major Tufto, and Lord Steyne maddened by balked desire; Rawdon outraged at Becky's infidelity; Dobbin self-martyred by his hopeless love for Amelia; Jane Osborne sacrificed to her father's tyranny and, even more, to a sexual system that condemns her to a life of grim celibacy.

The frustration of the conscious sexual desires of the characters and the pressures of unconscious sexual conflicts work together to *transform* the characters into stereotypes. They become, in the course of the narrative, the puppets that the narrator initially describes them as; but the force that controls them is not the manipulation of an arbitrary authorial presence but the "unseen hand" (to borrow Adam Smith's phrase) of the society's sexual economy. George is transformed into a paragon of martial and marital virtue by Amelia's imagination; Amelia narrows her own life to the faithful widow and selfless mother; Dobbin becomes the rejected but faithful lover who suffers in silence; Rawdon Crawley—for all the real nobility of his action—plays the part of the gallant hero defending his wife's honor against the wicked aristocrat; Mr. Sedley shrinks to the ruined merchant harping on the injustice he has suffered, almost a humour character. All the young characters, but Becky in particular, begin with richer possibilities than the world can accommodate. The exterior roles that society forces on them become interiorized. They are subdued to what they work in. And their mannerisms, habits of mind, and ideas about their motives become more habitual, until we have Amelia the "tender little parasite" clinging to Dobbin the "rugged old oak," and then the narrator puts his puppets away and shuts up the box.

Stereotypes have this impact because the novel insists on their predominant power in the struggling social milieu it takes as the epitome of Victorian society. The complexity of the characters persists, but it is more and more repressed from their consciousness and from other characters' attitudes toward them. The complexity reveals itself in unconscious, symbolic behavior that the novel discloses through a brilliant rendering of the nuances of dramatic action and its interconnection of related scenes through symbolic analogy. Thackeray's well-known idea that character is static is yet another way of stressing the tremendous power of social conditioning. In Thackeray's bleak but persuasive view, only a very few people manage to turn the quirks of their behavior into a unique personality. The persistent delusion in the later fiction that characters like Esmond and Warrington *might have been* something great except for the tragic force of circumstances is already in *Vanity Fair* exposed to the most cynical scrutiny.

The narrator of *Vanity Fair* makes the stuff of stereotypes into a provocative means of unsettling and enlightening the reader, working to achieve more directly what the plot, symbolic configurations, and dramatic action achieve implicitly. The narrator does not attempt to turn contradictions into comprehensive resolutions that are themselves stereotypic or even platitudinous— as too often happens in Thackeray's later fiction. Contradictions, festering emotions, and the deforming nature of stereotypes are thrust before us by the extreme form in which they are cast and by their juxtaposition with contradictory stereotypes:

The illness of that old lady [Mrs. Sedley] had been the occupation and perhaps the safeguard of Amelia. What do men know about women's martyrdoms? We should go mad had we to endure the hundredth part of those daily pains which are meekly borne by many women. Ceaseless slavery meeting with no reward; constant gentleness and kindness met by cruelty as constant . . . all this, how many of them have to bear in quiet, and appear abroad with cheerful faces as if they felt nothing. Tender slaves that they are, they must needs be hypocrites and weak.

[II, xxi, 271]

The male narrator presumes to tell us what men don't know about women. Amelia's attack on her mother for dosing George with patent medicines (Amelia accuses her of poisoning Georgy) is hardly the expression of "constant gentleness"; it causes a rift between them that is never joined. But even apart from these ironies developed through the dramatic context, the passage reveals contradictory attitudes toward women through its own substance and its own rhetoric. Somehow the enormous strength of women (not as the strength of ten but of a hundred men) and their meekness, gentleness, and kindness become weakness and hypocrisy by the end of the passage. And, of course, the passage evades, and makes its evasion obvious, the question of who is responsible for the "martyrdom" the narrator tries to simultaneously lament and praise—surely not dying old ladies. The simple categories of traditional sentimental pathos and traditional antifeminist patronization cannot contain the character of Amelia or the responses of the narrator to her; but the passage does imply how much the two stereotypic attitudes have in common.

This sort of juxtaposition of contradictory attitudes within the narrative appears regularly through the novel. The narrator's generalization about "that secret talking and conspiring which form the delight of female life" is almost sure to be followed or preceded by a comment that does not qualify but contradicts it. In this case, it is the narrator's revelation that "that young whiskered prig, Lieutenant Osborne" has been secretly conspiring against Becky by warning Rawdon to be on guard against her (I, xiv, 171–72).

The narrator of *Vanity Fair* is certainly caught up in contradictions but not in the confusion or even incoherence that obscures and limits the later novels. The blatantly contradictory views have disturbed readers from the time *Vanity Fair* appeared because they call attention to their own inconsistencies. The narrator "encapsulates" absolute statements about the sexual world (women are made, by instinct, either to scheme or to love; men are as vain as women about their personal appearance) that *rhetorically* treat the world as if it were a stable and consistent thing. These comments take a momentary foothold in words but they are continually contradicted by the dramatic and symbolic substance of the novel. Was Lady Crawley made to scheme or to love? How vain is Dobbin about his personal appearance? What we see in nearly every instance when the narrator smugly delivers an absolute judgment is an effort transparently born of the failure of all traditional categories to encompass the complexity that the novel describes. Winslow Rogers has complained that "no event in a Thackeray novel can have a stable meaning; no character can be finally known."[24] But this is surely one of the most profound insights that Thackeray had about Victorian culture. Many critics who find Thackeray's methods disturbing seem to be asking, through discussion of aesthetic issues, for a more reassuring view of the modern world than Thackeray can be expected to give.

6

TROLLOPE

O F course, everyone knows how, along with the Queen, Trollope disapproved of the "mad, wicked folly" of Women's Rights. After all, he tells us often enough: in his lecture on higher education for women, in an unequivocal letter stating that the "supremacy of men over women" is "as certain to me as the eternity of the soul," and most significantly, over and over again in his novels.[1] "What," asks the narrator on behalf of Alice Vavasor, "should a woman do with her life?" Why, he answers sententiously, "Fall in love, marry the man, have two children, and live happily ever afterwards. I maintain that answer has as much wisdom in it as any other than can be given;—or perhaps more" (*Can You Forgive Her?*, 11).

Certainly there is abundant evidence of antifeminism in Trollope's novels: strong women like Mrs. Proudie are punished or have their folly exposed; the female world is universally concerned with getting, being, and staying married; and there are any number of warm-hearted, brown-haired, wren-like young women who are exemplars of all the domestic virtues. Moreover, from the sixties on, when women's rights had become the subject of much public debate, jesting references to the subject are scattered through Trollope's novels. In *Phineas Finn*, Violet Effingham replies to Phineas' comment that "a man should try to be something" by saying, "And a woman can be content to be nothing—unless Mr. Mill can pull us through!" (59). In the midst of the tangle created by Ferdinand Lopez in *The Prime Minister*, Lady Glencora characteristically defends herself from her husband's scolding by retorting, "Really you are becoming so autocratic that I shall have to go in for women's rights" (32). Madame Max lists women's suffrage with the radical political stands of the day such as "manhood suffrage, . . . unlimited right of striking . . . [and] education of everybody. . . ." (*Phineas Finn*, 40). "You don't advocate the rights of women, Madame Goesler?" Phineas asks in *Phineas Redux*. "Oh, no," Madame Max replies, tongue in cheek, "knowing our inferiority I submit without a grumble. . . ." (32).

In two novels, this joking disparagement of the Woman Question turns into full-fledged satire: with the strident feminists Wallachia Petrie of *He Knew He Was Right* and Olivia Q. Fleabody and the Baroness Banmann of the Female Disabilities Institute in *Is He Popenjoy?* But whether it surfaces as a running joke, as a subplot, or as the major direction of the novel, Trollope's hostility to the Woman Question seems evident.

Despite the narrator's hostility, however, readers frequently find Trollope sympathetic to women and concerned about the same problems troubling Victorian feminists. Pamela Hansford Johnson has claimed, "the woman who reads his work must do so with the overwhelming impression that she is receiving fair play." Trollope's women, she goes on to say, are "whole creatures instinct with life and with energy."[2] This is not the impression the reader expects to receive if led by Trollope's pronouncements on women, but certainly many readers receive it—particularly from the later novels. A number of critics, in fact, have found the later novels not just vaguely sympathetic to women but a "particular source of information regarding women's role in Victorian society."[3] We have, then, two Trollopes—the seemingly hostile critic of the Victorian women's movement and the sympathetic Victorian sociological novelist capturing in fiction the tensions being felt by upper-class men and women of his day.

Trollope clearly was not interested in the specific forms the debate about women assumed in the nineteenth century: the problem of "redundant" women, economic independence for women, reform of the married women's property laws, opening up the professions to women, education, and suffrage for women. When these issues make their rare appearances in his novels, they are almost invariably ridiculed.

A second obstacle to readers' perceptions of Trollope's sympathetic presentation of women is the tendency of his narrators to make judgments partially or sometimes totally belied by the narrative. The narrator of *He Knew He Was Right*, for instance, says of the American feminist, Miss Petrie:

Miss Petrie was honest, clever, and in earnest. We in England are not usually favorably disposed to women who take pride in a certain antagonism to men in general, and who are anxious to shew the world that they can get on very well without male assistance. . . . The hope in regard to such women,—the hope entertained not by themselves, but by those who are solicitous for them,—is that they will be cured at last by a husband and half-a-dozen children.

[77]

Miss Petrie seems either silly or fanatical to the narrator in her commitment to "that contest which she was determined to wage against man" (77). Yet the novel presents just such a contest— and a deadly one—between men and women throughout English society. Though some characters arrive at a measure of accommodation, none are untouched by the conflict. Even in the casual conversation of a barmaid and a potboy at a pub, the issue surfaces:

"[I]t's two to one the young 'ooman has the worst of it," said the barmaid.
"They mostly does," said the potboy, not without some feeling of pride in the immunities of his sex.

[32]

The central irony is that while the narrator extols marriage as a "cure" for female problems, the novel persistently details the destructive effects of unlimited male power in patriarchal marriage. Trevelyan's increasingly insane determination to force his wife to obey him destroys him and makes his wife miserable. So the events of the novel and the narrative commentary are ironically juxtaposed. In dozens of other instances, Trollope's narrators make pat judgments whose inadequacy only becomes apparent when seen in relation to the complexities of character and theme.[4]

Another kind of inadequacy arises from the narrator's reluctance to draw the conclusions that the events of the novel insist upon. The treatment of women's rights in *Is He Popenjoy?* is an example of such refusal. The feminists connected with the Institute for Female Disabilities, Lady Selina Protest, Dr. Olivia Q. Fleabody, and Baroness Banmann, are smugly caricatured as women whose feminism is a response to their lack of sex appeal. George calls the institute women, "Two old maids who have gone crazy about Women's Rights because nobody married them" (18). Mrs. Jones, who dismisses them contemptuously as "American she-doctors," exclaims: "Women's Rights! Women are quite able to hold their own without such trash as that" (30). The narrator himself calls the women who attend the lectures at the institute

strongly-visaged spinsters and mutinous wives, who twice a week were worked up by Dr. Fleabody to a full belief that a glorious era was at hand in which women would be chosen by constituencies, would wig their heads in courts of law, would buy and sell in Capel Court, and have balances at their bankers.

[60]

The narrator thus refuses to see any connection between "women's rights" and the events of the plot. Similarly the heroine, Mary Germain, cannot see the relevance of the issues raised at the institute to her own life and finds a lecture she attends at the "Disabilities" duller than a sermon. Yet the legal, economic, and marital disabilities these women seek to remove are the same issues fought over by the Germains—the right of a married woman to retain her identity and exert power over her own life. George wants a traditional wife, content to be a reflex of her husband; Mary wants her will and desires recognized. Neither characters nor narrator are willing to perceive the analogies that are apparent to the reader.

A similar case of the narrator's reluctance to draw conclusions occurs in the handling of Ruby Ruggles' story in *The Way We Live Now*. After a brief flirtation with Felix Carbury, Ruby is coaxed, scolded, even driven to marry her first suitor—the well-meaning but countrified and inarticulate John Crumb. Ruby seldom moderates her scorn for her "mealy" suitor, and the analogous plots of the other women—Lady Carbury, Marie Melmotte, Georgiana Longstaffe, Hetta Carbury, and Mrs. Hurtle—certainly do not imply that marriage is always and unequivocally good for women.

The narrator refers to "poor" Ruby and explains that she is "tamed and quelled by the outward circumstances of her position" (94). The proud John Crumb points to Ruby with his whip, and Joe Mixet refers to the couple as "Mars and Venus," while Ruby "would have run away and locked herself in an inner chamber had she not been certain she would be brought back again" (94). Yet the narrator does not commit himself to explicit support or condemnation of Ruby's resistance. J. Hillis Miller has written of Trollope's narrator: "he took upon himself the role of spokesman for the general judgment of the community of English ladies and gentlemen. There are, however, strata, distinct levels of awareness, within that collective consciousness. These account for the persistent tone of irony in Trollope's narratives."[5] With Ruby Ruggles, as with Melmotte and many other characters, Trollope presents conventional judgments, allows the characters themselves to present intolerant opinions, and causes events—rather than explicit narrative commentary—to suggest the narrow-mindedness of community judgments. For the modern reader, at least, the result may be the feeling of being goaded into denying the conventions of the community.

This sort of evasive tactic of Trollope's narrators, when confronted with the troubling sexual conflicts in the novels, has caused many readers to see him as a bland apologist for orthodox sexual relations. We do not have in Trollope (as we do in George Eliot, for instance), a wise, controlling, exploring, and synthesizing narrative voice; readers instead are forced to do the exploring and synthesizing for themselves. In lieu of an actively synthesizing narrator, Trollope substitutes patterning by analogy—sometimes through significant contradictions in action and characterization. Thus, though Trollope's personal hostility to feminism and his misleading narrators cloud the reader's understanding, the novels' "interior" arrangements can guide us to recognize the complexity they depict.

What matters in a Trollope novel, as Jerome Thale has pointed out, is not so much the sequence of events as their grouping, the "parallels, contrasts, repetitions with slight variations" that become the "method of organization" of the work.[6] In the earlier novels that are more concerned with courtship, for example, the multiple plot structure helps delineate the central courtship by contrast to variant minor courtships. In *Doctor Thorne*, Mary Thorne's fidelity to her own love for Frank, in spite of their economic and social differences, is counterpointed by Augusta Gresham's blind obeisance to notions of "blood" and Miss Dunstable's strong-minded refusal to marry any man who wants only her money. These limited analogies still manage to extend our understanding of the central heroine and, at the same time, permit the narrator to explore a range of sexual options without making a direct narrative commitment.

In the early novels the focus on one central plot, with only limited analogical counterpointing, is a sign of Trollope's faith in a stable and secure value system. By the time of the later novels, *Is He Popenjoy?* (1878), for example, the multiple plots are necessary to reflect the fragmentation Trollope finds in his society. The stable centrality of a story like Mary Thorne's is gone. In its place are fragmented and unstable sexual roles reflected in multiple plots that clash with each other and resist a final resolution. Counterpoint has become unresolved dissonance.

In the process, plot motifs have taken on a distinct symbolic significance. There are no comprehensive descriptive symbols in Trollope—no dust heaps, fogs, not even an Iphigenia clock. But from the parallels, contrasts, and variations among his characters' situations (particularly in novels of the mid-sixties and the seventies) symbolic patterns quietly emerge and alter the very substance of the surface narrative.

In *Popenjoy*, for example, symbolic analogies transform a melodramatic plot into a means for ridiculing the pretensions of the patriarchal class structure. On the surface, the question about Popenjoy's legitimacy sounds merely melodramatic: has the syphilitic Marquis of Brotherton married his Italian wife legally so that his sickly son is the legitimate heir? But, as James Kincaid points out, Trollope directs the reader's attention away from the melodrama by turning the question into a dead end in the plot: the marquis never really discovers whether his son was legitimate or not, and the major action of the story does not directly depend upon the Popenjoy question.[7] Yet the underlying issue about young Popenjoy, far from being irrelevant, helps establish the theme that binds the plots together. We are not merely asked to consider who the legitimate heir is, what loyalty George owes his elder brother, what service the elder brother owes his female relatives, and so forth. The trivialization of the question in the novel's title allows symbolic implications to gather into a more profound and comprehensive question: what legitimacy does the whole system of male dominance have?

Power, in fact, is the subject of *Popenjoy*—the power given men in a hierarchical and patriarchal society. The various plots of the novel reveal the damage done to the men and women who live by its values. This issue is raised within the marriage of George and Mary Germain, in the satiric "Female Disabilities" subplot, and within the Germain family itself when George, his mother, and his sisters must decide whether to honor the marquis's capricious and even malicious decisions.

Both the marquis and his mother, the dowager marchioness, give slavish allegiance to a hierarchical concept of human relationships. The marquis is the highest ranked male in the novel and gains his authority wholly through his rank. He is outrageously insulting to almost everyone he encounters, but people generally react in a subvervient manner. When by "condescending" to visit the shops of Brotherton he wins over the formerly hostile town, the narrator comments ironically: "A little kindness after continued cruelty will always win a dog's heart; some say, also a woman's. It certainly seemed to be the way to win Brotherton" (24). The marquis's contemptuous abuse of authority disfigures all his sexual relations: his midnight affairs with disreputable women; his syphilis; his son's consequent ill health; his estrangement from his wife; and his callous attitude toward the women of his family.

At the opposite extreme, the marquis's mother has so absorbed the patriarchal values of her culture that she totally abases herself before her son. The marquis always seems right to her simply because he is the eldest son. Even when he evicts her and his sisters from the family home, she submits meekly. She blames herself for living in her own house, criticizes her daughters, and takes sides with the marquis whenever he insults his younger brother George. She is convinced of the marquis's "right to be unreasonable" (22). Her behavior is as extreme a version of traditional feminine submissiveness as the marquis's is of traditional masculine authority.

Only one member of the household, the marquis's sister, Lady Sarah, has the clear vision and strength to oppose him. She does not rebel against the traditional male prerogatives, but she does refuse to pay homage to the outrageous abuse of masculine power that others meekly or blindly tolerate: "If we are to be miserable, let us at any rate tell the truth about it," she declares to her mother (48). Although her defense of her mother's rights and, finally, of Mary's right to depart from the Germain traditions have no effect on the inflexible males who rule the household, Sarah helps tell the truth about the corrupt system to the reader.

George Germain is also the victim of his own belief in a patriarchal hierarchy. He suffers from his relation to his older brother and hasn't, like Sarah, the self-confidence to assert his feelings or his mother's and sisters' rights in the face of his brother's opposition. He also believes that his wife Mary is inferior to him in both class and gender; that "She had to struggle upwards, so as to be able to sustain properly the position and dignity of Lady George Germain, and the possible dignity of the Marchioness of Brotherton. She ought not to want playfellows" (19). And so, although he has his playfellow in Adelaide Houghton, George allows Mary's innocent (if thoughtless) friendship with Jack de Baron to become a source of such conflict between them that their marriage is nearly destroyed.

Since George never really does recognize his flawed conceptions of marriage, sexual roles, and class structure, the novel's happy ending is more a tribute to Mary's vitality than to the validity of the system George believes in. He is simply lucky that the wife he marries for money turns out to be a good wife (even by his standards), that his older brother dies, and that his first child is a son. The elements of his world that do not fit the patriarchal system—unfaithful or insubordinate wives, unruly older brothers,

questionable heirs, girl babies—seem to be wished away by the
novel's ending, but at best the resolution is atypical and precarious.
Implicit thematic patterns gradually take shape in *Is He Popenjoy?* as these interconnected relations of power and powerless-
ness brings the novel's true theme into focus: the inevitable warp-
ing of marriage and family life when society attempts to give
material dominance and psychological authority exclusively to
men. These patterns do not form the elaborate, minute, precisely
detailed network of analogies typical of Dickens' novels—and to
a lesser extent of Collins' and Thackeray's. They are subtle variations radiating outward from a thematic center, a center only
gradually defined by implicit resemblances and contrasts in characters' roles, situations, and action.

This method of fictional construction distinguishes Trollope's
novels after the mid-1860s. Plot patterns are often the surest guide
to discovering the thematic richness of his work and the fullest
definition of his characters. In this light, the hostile critic of the
women's movement and the conventional defender of the way
things are give way to the novelist capturing the tensions of men
and women living in a society whose traditional values were breaking down. In his understanding of the oppressive nature of patriarchal values he merits Rebecca West's conclusion: "Trollope
was a feminist."[8]

TROLLOPE'S WOMEN: THE POLITICS OF COURTSHIP
AND MARRIAGE

There is a picture by Pavel Tchelitchew, "Hide-and-Seek," that
from a distance looks like a brooding forest scene; one dark tree
dominates the canvas. From closer up, however, red-veined heads
and bodies of fetuses emerge, intertwined among the branches.
With the change in perspective, a world of surrealistic clarity is
revealed. Anthony Trollope's middle and late novels can have just
such an effect on the reader. Read casually, they look like the most
traditional Victorian novels, complete with love triangles, multiple marriages, and battles fought in the drawing room. But when

we look more closely, these novels about courtship and marriage convey an intense, searching examination of the relationships between men and woman.

In *Victorian Ladies At Work*, the historian Lee Holcombe claims that "In its essence, the women's movement of the late nineteenth century was an attack on the 'patriarchal ideal' of Victorian society and the special role of domesticity and dependence, of subjection, which is assigned to the perfect woman." This "revolt against the prevailing patriarchal ideal" is documented in Trollope's later novels.[9] Although their ostensible subject is courtship and marriage, they simultaneously depict the rebelliousness and dissatisfaction of women confined within traditional roles and their struggle to retain some measure of freedom and power within the restrictions of mid-Victorian family life.

Because Trollope's novels retain the old courtship and marriage plots of romantic comedy, they can be seen as the most Victorian of "closed form" novels. At the same time, as James Kincaid has pointed out, they persistently subvert the closed form and "open" the form of the novel:

The result is an exposition of the traditional values of, say, Jane Austen, with a running counter-exposition which casts doubt on the validity or existence of these values; the secure formal pattern, correspondingly, is made fluid, pried open in various places and with various tools.[10]

This sort of subversion is present in *Barchester Towers* in Madeline Neroni. Through her unconventional past, her sexuality, and her cynicism about Barchester pieties, Madeline manages to unsettle most of the major characters; even though—after accomplishing her work of embarrassing Slope and bringing together Eleanor and Arabin—she returns to Italy, leaving the Barchester values essentially intact. Even within the conventional courtship plot of the early novels there is a pattern of incipient female rebellion in which the heroine refuses to have her emotions dictated to her. By the novels of the sixties, the heroine's rebellion is increasingly in the foreground and remains there in the later novels.

Beginning with the genre of the domestic novel in the Barchester series, Trollope gradually transforms his courtship stories until they belong more properly to the tradition of the apprenticeship novel; they trace the education of a young woman—or two or three—in the social and psychological dynamics of male-female relationships in a male-dominated marriage system. In the earlier novels the courtship plot is often independent of the theme of female self-development. Early heroines like Mary Thorne and Lucy Robarts are not simpering or passive; in fact they hold fast to their own feelings and refuse rather forcefully to be converted by others. Mary and Lucy do not renounce their own emotional needs or their particular romantic desires, but they do renounce their right to marry Frank Gresham and Lord Lufton, or even to influence Frank and Lufton into acting against family desires. The only rebellion permitted them is their refusal to falsify their own feelings. Later heroines like Marie Melmotte in *The Way We Live Now* (1875) act very differently. Marie asserts her right to have the husband she chooses even if she has to steal from her father and coax the young man. But the heroines of *Doctor Thorne* (1858) and *Framley Parsonage* (1861) hardly even affect their own fates. The happy endings are decided by chance and by benevolent older people like Doctor Thorne and Lady Lufton. Mary Thorne's marriage is not a culmination of her "education" in the apprenticeship novel tradition. Rather, it serves to revitalize the Gresham blood through an infusion of Mary's natural vitality, virtue, and money, in a way that almost erases her individuality.

By the mid-1860s and later, Trollope is much more likely to treat courtship as an apprenticeship to the difficult career of marriage. Of Dorothy Stanbury in *He Knew He Was Right* (1869) Trollope writes:

Her life at Nuncombe Putney had been of such a nature, that though she knew that other girls . . . got married and had children, no dim vision of such a career for herself had ever presented itself to her eyes.

[22]

The choices during courtship and the marital conflicts that follow are invested with significance and intensity in these novels because Trollope views marriage for a woman as a choice involving status, security, autonomy, and power—her very identity. For the Victorian woman, Trollope realized, marriage was indeed a career. This conception underlies the story of Nora Rowley in *He Knew He Was Right* (1869) and Violet Effingham in *Phineas Finn* (1869). In the latter novel, in fact, Trollope insistently parallels Phineas' apprenticeship to the career of politics and Violet's apprenticeship to the career of marriage.

In the love triangles of the traditional courtship plot, the heroine faces an either/or choice. Of course the Trollope novels present many such choices: should Alice Vavasor marry George Vavasor or John Grey; should Violet Effingham choose Oswald Chiltern or Phineas Finn; will Lady Glencora stay with her husband or run away with Burgo Fitzgerald; will Nora Rowley choose Mr. Glascock or Hugh Stanbury? But underlying these either/or plots is a much more fundamental question: whether to marry at all. Female independence is a tantalizing daydream for Trollope's most intelligent heroines. In *He Knew He Was Right* Nora Rowley and Priscilla Stanbury debate the possibility of independence for women:

"Sometimes women despise men," said Priscilla.
"Not so very often;—do they? And then women are so dependent on men. A woman can get nothing without a man."
"I manage to get on somehow," said Priscilla.
"No, you don't, Miss Stanbury,—if you think of it. You want mutton. And who kills the sheep?"

[25]

The cramped and ascetic life of self-denial that Priscilla Stanbury leads is a recognition of the impossibility of such a choice for most Victorian women, because they are economically dependent on men and lack any real alternative to marriage. As aware as Trollope was of the basic economic needs that drove a woman to marriage, he saw that marriage was also the only way most women could acquire status, relative freedom from parents' domination, and occupation in nineteenth-century England. When Emily Trevelyan expresses her wonder that Nora still wants to marry after being exposed to the misery of the Trevelyan marriage, Nora replies simply, "What is a girl to do?"

Stereotypes of Victorian domesticity have little to do with Trollope's depiction of marriage, however. His primary female characters are more likely to be presented as politicians than as mothers and homemakers. Although critical attention has focused recently on the parallels the Palliser novels draw between politics and marriage, it is not merely the analogies between the two institutions these novels insist on, but the politics of marriage itself.[11] Indeed, the chief parallel between the political plots in the Palliser novels and the romantic plots is the struggle for dominance both involve.

Trollope repeatedly shows that marriage provides potentially greater areas of conflict than other kinds of relationships because the husband is—whether by custom, law, economics, or education—superior to the wife. Thus marital conflict and the conflicts within courtship leading up to marriage provide a microcosm of all the disputes—between lovers, between brothers and sisters, between elder and younger brothers—arising in a patriarchal system where some people automatically count more than others. Yet Trollope also delights in the forms of accommodation, tolerance, adaptation, and sympathy through which people learn to make life easier for others and for themselves. If marriage epitomizes the problematic nature of social interaction, marriage can also provide some measure of reconciliation.

Trollope's attitudes toward marriage become increasingly complex and ambivalent. His narrators' pronouncements on marriage as the "natural" destiny of women are well-known:

When a girl asks herself that question,—what shall she do with her life? it is so natural that she should answer it by saying that she will get married, and give her life to somebody else. . . . Nature prompts the desire, the world acknowledges its ubiquity, circumstances show that it is reasonable, the whole theory of creation requires it. . . .

[*Vicar Of Bullhampton*, 37]

But, as Hillis Miller has recently pointed out, Trollope also suggests that marriage is nearly as important for Victorian men:

At the center of this novel [*Ayala's Angel*], as of so many others by Trollope, is the idea that a man's substance is his love for another person. . . . [Selfhood] must be embodied in marriage and in assimilation into the community's structure of roles and relationships.[12]

Through all his explorations of marriage as the inevitable focus of Victorian society's deepest conflicts and longings, Trollope persistently emphasizes that a woman's condition in this patriarchal society is utterly dependent on the males she is associated with, and that in such a society, women really have few very pleasant options but marriage. In *He Knew He Was Right*, Nora Rowley reflects bitterly,

The lot of a woman, as she often told herself, was wretched, unfortunate, almost degrading. For a woman such as herself there was no path open to her energy, other than that of getting a husband. Nora Rowley thought of all this till she was almost sick of the prospect of her life.

[4]

This perception of "the hardness of a woman's lot . . . called upon to decide her future for life in half a minute" (13), this awareness of the economic, social, and psychological position of women is so acute that the "condition of women" is the underlying issue of most of the stories involving women in these novels.

The same social tensions that led to the women's movement after 1850 also underlie Trollope's middle and late novels. No matter how Trollope himself argued against feminism and insisted upon the propriety of woman's traditional role as wife, his novels reflect the rebelliousness and dissatisfaction of women at a time when alternatives to women's dependence were energetically debated but were actually available to only a very few women. That is why his courtship novels turn out to be apprenticeship novels and why the "domestic scene" in the Trollope novel, as R. C. Terry has pointed out, is "seething with disturbed, anxious, rebellious womankind. . . ."[13]

Because marriage is so crucial in the society Trollope depicts, his novels explore not large gestures of rebellion (refusing to marry, choosing a career, leaving a husband) but smaller ones within the context of courtship and marriage. The significance of Alice Vavasor's question, "What shall a woman do with her life?" lies less in the narrator's exasperated response than in the fact that the question is raised insistently, in novel after novel, by Trollope's woman characters. Though Lady Glencora or Alice Vavasor or Nora Rowley arrive at what may be conventional marriages, they have grappled with issues of female identity within Victorian social structures. They may, like Alice, be confused about their own motivation, and their rebellion may, like Glencora's, take devious forms, but they are all deeply involved in assessing and, to the degree they can, changing the basic roles allotted to them. Their confusion, perplexities, and even perverseness, in fact, are the surest signs that they are trying to change their roles.

Individualized as they are, the women central to these courtship/ marriage plots of Trollope's middle and late novels can be placed in certain recognizable groupings. Trollope's method of parallels, contrasts, and repetitions even demands this kind of analysis, since it is through this patterning that the novels' themes emerge. There are women who make a business of husband hunting: the desperate Arabella and Camilla French of *He Knew He Was Right*, with their deadly sibling rivalry over the few available males; Georgiana Longestaffe of *The Way We Live Now*, caught in the sexual tensions of a society in transition between aristocratic and mercantile dominance; and Arabella Trefoil of *The American Senator*, who has been busy at the "work" of finding a husband for years and who is "sick of the dust of battle and conscious of fading strength" (20).

Trollope is hard on such women; his narrators are quick to stress the immorality of marriages contracted for wealth and security instead of affection. But Trollope also details with minute attention and great sympathy the plight of these victims of the marriage market and assails the parents who bargain to sell them. The novels also present his understanding of the conditions that produce frantic husband hunting and give it far-reaching social significance.

With Georgiana Longstaffe, for example, Trollope depicts the dependent daughter in a patriarchal family—stripped of all power, without status unless she marries, her life and income at the mercy of her father. Her father forces her to spend the London season with the family of Melmotte—whom he despises as a racially tainted adventurer—yet reacts with outrage when Georgiana snares a Jewish fiancé. The analogies among the stories of Marie Melmotte, Georgiana Longstaffe, and Hetta Carbury in *The Way We Live Now* make the condition of the dependent daughter under patriarchal capitalism a major theme of the novel.

Georgiana desperately tries to sell herself in the marriage market. But despite the narrator's urge to condemn her behavior, Georgiana's deficiencies and sufferings are distinctly related to the socioeconomic forces that drive the novel's social world. Her father is, as she recognizes, the "natural adversary" of her mother, her sister, and herself. She endures rituals of husband hunting without any thought of pleasure; but despite her ignorance and mercenary training, she still asserts some right to a life of her own: "I will do something. I'm not going to be cheated and swindled and have my life thrown away into the bargain" (21). Trollope's husband-hunting woman is a victim before she is a victimizer.

Then there are the women who regard men and marriage with fear and dislike, for whom a relationship with a man is a violation of their integrity; Lucinda Roanoke in *The Eustace Diamonds* so loathes Sir Griffin Tewett and the implications of martial and sexual dominance that she is pushed to madness as her only means of escape; Priscilla Stanbury in *He Knew He Was Right* sees that she must remain single in order to retain her independence. In a number of novels, Trollope examines the ways in which the unchecked exercise of masculine power produces this fear and hatred, as it does in Emily Trevelyan of *He Knew He Was Right* and Laura Kennedy of *Phineas Finn* and *Phineas Redux*. Miss Todd, who appears in *The Bertrams* and in *Miss Mackenzie*, is described in the latter as a "stout jolly-looking dame, with a red face" (3) who refuses to marry not because she dislikes men but because she dislikes dependence: "Now for me, I'm so fond of my own money and my own independence, that I've never had a fancy that way— not since I was a girl" (13). But Miss Todd is unique in the Trollope novels.[14]

In some women (Alice Vavasor, for example) distrust of marriage leads to self-loathing or disparagement of the very state of womanhood. "The curse," as Lady Laura says in *Phineas Finn*, "is to be a woman at all" (51). A number of mothers in these novels, most notably Lady Carbury of *The Way We Live Now*, Lady Fawn of *The Eustace Diamonds*, and the Dowager Marchioness of *Is He Popenjoy?*, belong with this group in their devaluation of their daughters and themselves. Trollope says of Lady Carbury, "In regard to her daughter, she was always influenced by a vague idea that Hetta was an unnecessary trouble" (36). Lady Carbury, like many of the other mothers in these novels, is willing, indeed eager, to obliterate herself and her daughter in order to help her son.

Lady Carbury has lived through marriage with a tyrannical husband (whom she married because she was poor) and is again threatened with poverty because of a tyrannical son. She has internalized Victorian values that tell her a title is more important than a profession and a man more important than a woman; in her marriage she accepted "suffering and servility" (36) and continues to abase herself before her son:

That all her interests in life should be made subservient to him was natural to her. . . . In everything she had spoilt him as a boy, and in everything she still spoilt him as a man. She was almost proud of his vices, and had taken delight in hearing of doings which if not vicious of themselves had been ruinous from their extravagance.

[2]

The kind of sexual inequality the Carburys believe in has far-reaching consequences—the mother's inability to protect herself and her daughter; the son's inability to work or to respect any woman; the son's need to prey on other women in hopes of marrying money; and the habit of self-denigration that the daughter inherits:

Henrietta had been taught by the conduct of both father and mother that every vice might be forgiven in a man and in a son, though every virtue was expected from a woman, and especially from a daughter.

[2]

Some women in Trollope's novels have so accepted and internalized the debasing sexual values of their culture that they see themselves as Dorothy Stanbury does, "born to eat and drink, as little as might be, and then to die" (*He Knew He Was Right*, 30). The poor but genteel governesses and companions like Miss Cassawary of *The Eustace Diamonds* are such women. Self-denigration is so deep-seated in many of these women that they feel called into existence only when given identity by male recognition. Dorothy Stanbury, for instance, has never recognized her beauty or her strength of character because she lives in a society where poor spinsters, as she seems destined to be, are of little importance. However, once Brooke Burgess loves her, she can recognize herself as an attractive young woman, not a dowdy and diffident girl.

Other women try to live vicariously, attaching themselves to a male figure through whom they can gain excitement and purpose in life. Alice Vavasor is such a woman, as is Laura Kennedy, who feels that "a woman's life is only half a life, as she cannot have a seat in Parliament" (*Phineas Finn*, 60), and who tries to enter political life through her husband. Lizzie Eustace also cannot conceive of a woman's life without a man; she looks to men to create a romantic drama of her life and permit her to play the heroine. Mabel Grex, despite all her wit, charm, and courage, feels that her fate depends utterly upon whether she marries well, and she misses her chance to marry Silverbridge partly because of her conventional image of masculinity. Dorothy Stanbury expresses the feelings of all these women when she says:

A man who is a nobody can perhaps make himself somebody,—or, at any rate, he can try; but a woman has no means of trying. She is a nobody, and a nobody she must remain. She has her clothes and her food, but she isn't wanted anywhere. People put up with her. . . . She doesn't earn anything or do any good. She is just there and that's all.

[*He Knew He Was Right*, 51]

Some of the older women seem to be struggling against this perception of a woman's being nobody by attempting to gain power in unpleasant or perverse ways. Mrs. Proudie—comic and unlovable as she is—is clearly frustrated by wanting to be taken seriously and yet having to work through her husband and other men in order to have power.[15] Mrs. Bolton of *John Caldigate*, more ascetic and evangelical than Mrs. Proudie and seemingly less interested in power, nevertheless wants power over her daughter as a form of recompense for all that she sees wrong with the world—and all the thwarted feelings she herself is unable to analyze. In the climax of the scene where Mrs. Bolton tries to save Hester from the sinfulness of men by keeping her prisoner in the house, the following passage makes clear the complexity of motives driving this tormented woman: "'I will not let you go,' said the mother. . . . 'I too can suffer, I too can endure. I will not be conquered by my own child.' There spoke the human being. That was the utterance natural to the woman. 'In this struggle, hard as it is, I will not be beat by one who has been subject to my authority'" (36).

Other women, like Lady Carbury, have suffered from abusive, or simply capricious husbands. Lady Mason of *Orley Farm* is an essentially good woman made wretched by an uncaring husband and the forgery she feels driven to by love for her son. In *The Claverings* two sisters with very different personalities both marry sadistic husbands; Julia Ongar's husband dies, but for most of the novel Hermione Clavering lives in fear of a husband so "hard" that he seems to reproach her for their child's death. (Hugh Clavering is drowned, however, by the merciful novelist.) All of these married women's lives have been perverted or made miserable in some way by woman's subordination in marriage and society.

Trollope's heroines in the later novels are distinguished by their struggle to preserve some integrity of the self, some sense of their own worth. For many of these women, this means a refusal to submit to the demands of the family and society. Hester Bolton in *John Caldigate* opposes her entire family, including her fanatically religious mother, when her husband is tried and convicted (mistakenly) of bigamy. Hetta Carbury remains faithful to Paul Montague despite her mother's, her brother's, and Roger Carbury's disapproval of Paul's relation to Mrs. Hurtle. Mary Masters of *The American Senator*, Lucy Morris of *The Eustace Diamonds*, Emily Wharton of *The Prime Minister*, and Lady Mary Palliser of *The Duke's Children* act similarly. However, though they resist domination, they are seldom moved to reflect on the general condition of women in their society.

In contrast, other heroines—especially Violet Effingham, Lady
Glencora, and Madame Max—clear-sightedly perceive the realities
of the condition of Victorian women, rebel against them, and
ultimately work out an accommodation between their own needs
and their society's demands.

As Trollope's views of women, marriage, and the whole nature
of the Victorian patriarchy grow more complex and more ambivalent, he creates pairs of heroines to embody his divided perceptions. Their analogous circumstances allow him to explore a
richer field of psychological and social conflicts and, even more
important, to suggest through the interplay of analogies a devastating critique of Victorian sexual practices that he could not
directly express. These paired heroines are often quite different
in temperament, desires, scruples, and social circumstances, but
each is, in an essential way, a rebel against the stifling routines
prescribed for respectable Victorian women.

His first interesting pair in the Palliser novels, Alice Vavasor
and Glencora Palliser, in *Can You Forgive Her?*, confront sexual
dilemmas in which the alternatives the women face are unsatisfactory.[16] Alice, though she has money of her own, leads such
a constricted life that she must look to men to provide meaning
and excitement. Yet the two men she has to choose from are no
match for her energy or ambition. George Vavasor offers danger
without real passion or real political achievement. John Grey offers
a "love" that conceals condescending mastery and a prospective
married life of placid country retirement, with Alice relegated to
the roles of wife and mother. Alice, however, never really understands what it is she wants or why each choice is unsatisfactory;
so her rebellion is spent in unconsciously creating the drama she
lacks by forcing George and John into active competition for her.
By jilting John Grey and then perversely refusing to forgive herself
for doing so, she forces him into activity and into a pleading
posture—both foreign to him. She never admits to herself that
his smug quiescence and disregard for her opinions are what she
dislikes about him. At the same time she forces George to live up
to his own romantic posturing about his superior, unrecognized
capacities by funding his purchase of a parliamentary seat. His

corrupt and thoroughly inept behavior as a candidate and an M.P. expose him as both a mock-Byron and a mock-Machiavel. Alice's rebellion finally comes down to a kind of unwitting satire of masculine pretensions as she forces both her suitors to reveal their inadequacy, shallowness, arrogance, and—in George's case—brutality.

Unlike Alice, who is free not to marry at all, Glencora has already been forced into an unhappy marriage when the novel begins. As Trollope wrote in his *Autobiography*:

She had received a great wrong,—having been made, when little more than a child, to marry a man for whom she cared nothing;—when, however, though she was little more than a child, her love had been given elsewhere. . . . [It] must ever be wrong to force a girl into a marriage with a man she does not love,—and certainly more so when there is another whom she does love.[17]

Can You Forgive Her? and much of the rest of the Palliser series focus on Glencora's reactions to the fact of her situation. The novel records the failure of her escapist dream of romantic love and her recognition that she must accommodate herself to her marriage—and yet also somehow shape her marriage to her own desires.

While Alice acts unconsciously, Glencora's rebellion is more conscious and direct. Her intelligence and her wit provide her with whatever freedom she achieves, and force Palliser to become aware of her needs and adapt to them. Glencora uses her wit and vivacity to create the interest otherwise absent in her life. She succeeds better than Alice in maintaining her self-esteem and in simply enjoying life because Alice expects fulfillment from men while Glencora only tolerates the vicarious life she is forced into. Glencora wants—and later in the series almost achieves—power and significance in her own right.

By the time of *The Prime Minister*, Glencora has made peace of a sort with her society. No longer thinking of romantic escape as an alternative to the confines of a traditional marriage, she has accepted her identity as mother and duchess (though she never accepts the identity—and limitations—of wife). And she has become, as Trollope makes clear in *Phineas Finn*, an "inveterate politician" (37). She has also developed a strong sense of self: "She already possessed all that rank and wealth could give her, and together with those things, a peculiar position of her own, of which she was proud, and which she had made her own not by wealth or by rank, but by a certain fearless energy and power of raillery, which never deserted her" (*The Prime Minister*, 6). "I am myself, too," she says, "Glencora M'Cluskie that was, and I've made for myself a character that I'm not ashamed of" (37).

The real issues between Glencora and her husband, however, remain the same—independence and power. Two themes emerge clearly from the story of Glencora in *The Prime Minister*: woman's search for autonomy instead of subjection and her struggle for equality in marriage. Mr. Gresham, seeing Glencora and Mr. Monk whispering together at a party, asks what they are up to. "Making men and women all equal," answers Glencora (*Phineas Finn*, 14). Glencora brings to this worthy struggle her immense vitality, intelligence, candor, and wit.

The title of *The Prime Minister* is ambiguous, for there are two ministerial careers traced in the book, not one—the duke's and Glencora's. Sometimes she is jokingly referred to as "Prime Ministress," but most of the references made to her political career are more straightforward. "I mean," Glencora says, "to have a cabinet of my own" (6), and the duke suspects her of "a design of managing the Government in her own way, with her own particular friend, Mrs. Finn, for her Prime Minister" (32).

Lady Glencora, Trollope says, was "essentially one of those women who are not contented to be known simply as the wives of their husbands" (6). The power struggle between the two in this novel centers on her urge for a life beyond her domestic duties. "I like to be busy" (6), she says, first asking her husband for an appointment as Mistress of the Robes and then turning to what seems to be the only significant activity open to her—political hostess. Clearly Glencora wants occupation; her energy and intelligence demand something to do. But her husband makes plain his horror over his wife's having "any duties unconnected with our joint family and home" (7).

In a chapter entitled "The Beginning of a New Career," Glencora assumes her new political functions. "I begin to find myself,"
she says later, "filled to the full with political ambition" (11). At
first, she thinks of her efforts only as a prop to her husband's
career, but soon it becomes clear to her that she is ambitious for
political power. "She, too, wished to be written of in memoirs,
and to make a niche for herself in history" (28). "And why should
she not have her ambition in life as well as he his?" (32). Plantagenet, who holds fast to the old, wants her to have a traditional
life within traditional boundaries. Glencora's ambition and her
desire for equality are both incomprehensible to him.

Trollope emphasizes the parallels between the political careers
of both husband and wife. He juxtaposes Glencora's recognition
of her own desire for power with Plantagenet's discovery of his.
Gradually Palliser sees that his original sense of unworthiness as
prime minister, his acceptance of it merely to do his duty to his
country, has been superseded by a desire to hold on to the job
and the power it confers. He has acquired "the gradual love of
power created by the exercise of power" (66). In fact, ultimately
the same emptiness overtakes both, the same sense of failure and
of lost power.

Robert Polhemus places Glencora with Emma Woodhouse,
Diana Vernon, Emma Bovary, Becky Sharp, Dorothea Brooke,
Anna Karenina, and Isabel Archer, all of whom, he says "show
their authors' concern with woman's rebellion against convention,
her conscious quest for individuality, and the effects on society."
"Glencora Palliser," he continues,

is one of the greatest of these nineteenth-century women in European
fiction. In her, Trollope expresses carefully and fully, not only the frustration, flightiness, passion, and courage of a single high-spirited Victorian woman in all her complexity, but also a kind of universal feminine
plight.[18]

Yet Trollope is at pains to show that Glencora is not a glorious
freak of nature, that her rebellion has significance for the specific
Victorian plight of women. Once again, he extends his essentially
feminist perceptions through an analogous heroine. Though

Emily Wharton of *The Prime Minister* is quite unlike Alice Vavasor personally, her circumstances counterpoint Glencora's rebellion as Alice's did earlier in *Can You Forgive Her?* In fact, the entire Wharton/Lopez subplot mirrors the battle for marital power between the duke and the duchess.

Glencora has resisted marriage—both before and after the enforced marriage to Plantagenet. In direct contrast, Emily Wharton "has been taught to presume that it was her destiny to be married" (5), the narrator declares. But Trollope makes clear that even such a soft woman as Emily, possessing that "feminine sweetness which has its most frequent foundation in self-denial," is driven to exert her will against a husband who regards her as totally subordinate to him, a creature of his will (5). Although Lopez, the unscrupulous adventurer, and Plantagenet Palliser, the overscrupulous aristocrat, are seemingly very different, Trollope draws sinister parallels between their views of marriage. Lopez says to Emily's father, "She belongs to me,—not to you or to herself" (52). "[I]n all things there must at last be one voice that shall be the ruling voice," declares the duke, and that usually is the man's (32). Both men expect their wives to be subordinate to their power; both women rebel against this assumption.

While subject to social rules that deny her a name, identity, and money separate from the man—father or husband—who controls her, Emily contrives to increase her options and to produce a certain amount of "vassalage" in Lopez, Mr. Wharton, and Fletcher by pitting them against each other. Like Alice Vavasor, Emily compensates for her lack of real power by a combination of unconscious manipulation and strong, impulsive emotional attachments. By first wanting to marry Lopez and then refusing to marry Fletcher after Lopez dies, Emily manages to have everyone in the Fletcher/Wharton social circle consulting her wishes and aware of her importance. Marrying an outsider and not marrying an insider seem to be the major options available to her for asserting that she is not simply a subordinate part of the clan— and for rebelling against respectable Victorian notions of the sort of man a woman ought to love.

As marriage relations in Trollope's later novels appear ever more complex, his expansive methods of thematic development cause him to extend the analogical relations among his heroines beyond the limits of a single novel. In *Phineas Finn* (1869) and *Phineas Redux* (1874), he juxtaposes another set of heroines whose extended careers present opposed efforts to achieve a common goal: true female independence. Violet Effingham resists marriage as the inevitable end to her freedom, while Laura Standish tries to exploit the power relations of the marriage system to gain personal power. Their attempts reveal the unjust power relations that make independence virtually unattainable for most Victorian women.

The urge for female independence is very much alive in *Phineas Finn*. To remain single, to live happily independent of men and male power, however, is presented as a dream that, no matter how tantalizing, cannot be realized in the society the novel presents. There are two confirmed unmarried women in the novel: Augusta Baldock, who must become a nun in order to escape the tyranny of her mother, and Aspasia Fitzgibbon, who, though she "walked about sturdily by herself, and spoke her mind about everything," is characterized by "the violence of her jokes and the bitterness of her remarks" (5). Violet Effingham speaks wittily of her aunt's Female Protestant Unmarried Women's Society. (Trollope refers to the associations established to address the problem of the surplus population of women, documented by the census of 1861.) "My aunt," Violet says, "wants me to go out as a sort of leading Protestant unmarried female emigrant pioneer myself" (41). To Violet, the idea of escaping men and marriage altogether is a wistfully attractive notion and one she spends a good deal of time thinking about in the face of the questions "Who?" and "When?" that the world badgers her with. "I think I shall set up a little house of my own, and let the world say what it pleases" (22). She makes a number of joking references to John Stuart Mill throughout the novel: "I shall knock under to Mr. Mill, and go in for women's rights, and look forward to stand for some female borough" (51). But Violet's wit only half masks her serious doubts that marriage and female independence are compatible. Lady Laura's marriage seems to her "terrible. This makes me feel that I will never be married" (51). "Matrimony,"

she says, "never seemed to me to be very charming. . . ." (51).
At the very moment when she accepts Oswald Standish, the legal
consequences are very clear to her: "Do you not know," she asks
him, "that in these new troubles you are undertaking you will
have to bid me in everything, and that I shall be bound to do your
bidding? Does it not seem to be dreadful? My wonder is that any
girl can ever accept any man" (52).

Phineas Finn details Violet's

dream that she might escape, and live alone if she chose to be alone; that
she might be independent in her life, as a man is independent, if she
chose to live after that fashion; that she might take her fortune in her
own hand, as the law certainly allowed her to do, and act with it as she
might please.

[73]

But *Phineas Finn* also traces Violet's recognition that "though she
could talk about remaining unmarried, she knew that that was
practically impossible" (51). Though the law would allow her to
do so, she feels the force of "another law," a social code, that
makes independence no more than a wistful dream. Violet's only
real alternative, as she comes to realize, is to choose a suitor. In
this regard, Violet is contrasted to Mme. Max Goesler. Madame
Max, though she lives alone and is independently wealthy, is a
woman who wants her life involved with another's—as friend,
companion, wife. She has no interest in or desire for Violet's
solitary kind of independence.

Violet realizes that the choice of a suitor must be made very
carefully. She has loved Oswald Chiltern since they were children
together. Chiltern, his father, and his sister Laura all want Violet
to marry him, but as *Phineas Finn* begins, Chiltern has been virtually outlawed by good society. Trollope, who is simultaneously
portraying Laura's marriage to the seemingly bland Robert Kennedy, takes care to make Chiltern seem a most dangerous man
(by the canons of Victorian respectability)—red of face, violent,
a lover of horses, a man given to excess. Violet at one point says
to Laura, "Your brother, Laura, is dangerous. He is like the bad
ice in the parks where they stick up the poles. He has had a pole

stuck upon him ever since he was a boy" (52). Laura's theory is that Violet should save Chiltern by marrying him, but Violet says,

I don't know that I have any special mission for saving young men. I sometimes think that I shall have quite enough to do to save myself. . . . If I were a man myself I should go in for everything I ought to leave alone. I know I should. But you see,—I'm not a man, and I must take care of myself. The wrong side of the post for a woman is so very much the wrong side.

[10]

Later she says,

I do not believe in girls being saviours to men. It is the man who should be the saviour to the girl. If I marry at all, I have the right to expect that protection shall be given to me,—not that I shall have to give it.

[19]

The heart of the difference between Violet's and Laura's rebellion is that Violet—like Glencora—refuses to abandon herself or to hope for fulfillment from a man, while Laura—rather like Alice Vavasor—hopes to live vicariously through either Kennedy or Phineas and thinks Violet might do the same through Chiltern.

Violet does love Chiltern and finally agrees to marry him because of her love and because she has at least half-satisfied herself that she will be safe as his wife. The rest of the novel and the contrasting Kennedy marriage give the reader grounds for also believing that her venture has been prudent. Violet's success— and she is, with Madame Max, perhaps Trollope's most successfully married woman—comes from a combination of qualities: intelligence, love, prudence, the ability to fight for her rights, and the refusal to live vicariously.

Laura is less fortunate, however. A bright and capable woman, she is first introduced as the self-assured and self-contented mistress of her father's house, feeling very much her own power and potentially troubled only by her love for Phineas Finn. Laura, who had "resolved that she would use the world as men use it, not as women do" (39), desires political power and status. Somewhat inconsistently she combines male traits (using her hands and sitting as men do; seeking political power) with an unthinking conventionality about female roles. The narrator comments significantly that "the cause of the Rights of Women generally was odious to her" and that she wished to "be brought as near to political action as was possible for a woman without surrendering any of the privileges of feminine action" (10). She says, "I tried to blaze into power by a marriage, and I failed . . ." (*Phineas Redux*, 12).

Laura feels superior to ordinary women with romantic entanglements—"nearly free from the dangers of those rocks upon which other women make a shipwreck of their happiness" (*Phineas Finn*, 17)—yet her combined denial of and susceptibility to romance cause her failure in marriage.[19] She denies her love for Phineas because of her rather confused ambition and then discovers she has chosen a husband with Calvinistic notions of women's duties. He wishes her to live by his rigid notions of how a Christian wife should live and utterly subordinate herself to him. "There are moments, Robert," Laura bursts out, "when even a married women must be herself rather than her husband's wife. . . . You cannot make a woman subject to you as a dog is so" (39).

In the story of Lady Laura, as in that of Mabel Grex in *The Duke's Children*, Trollope deals with a woman who saw no other way to acquire status and power politically, socially, and economically than to marry for it. "She had married a rich man," Laura admits to herself, "in order that she might be able to do something in the world, and now that she was this rich man's wife she found she could do nothing" (*Phineas Finn*, 32). Both Laura and Mabel refuse to admit the folly of denying their own feelings until they have lived to experience the consequences. The husband Laura chooses with seeming prudence turns out to be the least prudent of choices. Had Laura been as clear-sighted about her own emotions as she is about politics, she would not have made such a mistake, and had she not tried to live through others, she might not have thrown herself away.

Trollope's analogous stories of women's marriages make clear his awareness of the limited and oppressive options the social structure permitted women. Though an occasional Glencora or Violet emerges with exuberance from her difficulties, the condition of most of his female characters is not so fortunate. Increasingly in the later novels Trollope also comes to explore the psychological limitations placed on men by the system they uphold, so that oppressive sexual situations come to seem inevitable and largely uncontrollable in the Victorian upper-class society he depicts.

TROLLOPE'S MEN: THE COSTS AND LIMITS
OF PATRIARCHAL POWER

As Trollope discloses his heroines' struggles for identity, power, and freedom, he raises equally important questions about their husbands and fathers: are the men freer and happier because they are more dominant? Or does their power over their wives and daughters create just as many obstacles to male happiness as the women's submissive roles raise for women? By the time of the novels of the sixties and seventies, Trollope persistently shows that the stereotypic masculine posture—masterful but not gentle, righteous but not tolerant—damages men themselves. In extreme cases like Robert Kennedy (the "*Phineas*" novels) and Louis Trevelyan (*He Knew He Was Right*), it causes psychic disintegration and madness.

Just as the difference between Violet Chiltern and Laura Kennedy is crucial for understanding Trollope's heroines, the difference between Chiltern and Kennedy is crucial for understanding his husbands. Chiltern seems violent and self-assertive, but there are indications in *Phineas Finn* that he might make a good husband for Violet. First of all, he has loved her deeply from childhood. In the childhood episode repeatedly alluded to in the novel, Chiltern took her away on a pony without bringing her back until teatime (a comic parody of melodramatic males—both heroes and villains). But Violet remembers only his goodness to her:

"I think it was the happiest day in my life. His pockets were crammed full of gingerbread and Everton toffy, and we had three bottles of lemonade slung on to the pony's saddlebows. I thought it was a pity we should ever come back. . . . You took off my shoes and dried them for me at a woodman's cottage."

[11]

Now that they are both adults, however, Chiltern's potential for carrying off maidens becomes more threatening: "It looked as though he would not hesitate to wring his wife's neck round, if ever he should be brought to threaten to do so" (11), the narrator says. His potential for violence raises the question of the underlying cause that arouses a sense of the danger in marriage for women like Glencora, Alice, Violet, Laura, and Emily Trevelyan. It is emphatically not physical sexuality that is frightening in a Ferdinand Lopez or a Chiltern. In discussing Chiltern with Laura, Violet is quite candid about his sexual attractiveness and about her own unconventional desires:[20]

"I like a roué myself. . . . I prefer men who are improper, and all that sort of thing. If I were a man myself I should go in for everything I ought to leave alone. But you see,—I'm not a man, and I must take care of myself. The wrong side of a post for a woman is so very much the wrong side. I like a fast man, but I know that I must not dare to marry the sort of man that I like."

[10]

Masculine sexual identity that has been frustrated by narrow social restrictions seems to be the danger the prospective wives of the Chilterns and Lopezes perceive. A restrictive, snobbish, male-controlled system of power and status is the fundamental source of discord in this area of courtship too.

Chiltern's treatment of horses gives a clue to his personality and the social roles that distort its expression. His violence comes from his excess of energy and his inability to find a meaningful occupation into which to channel it. As a horseman he likes to be active: "My horses," he says to Phineas, "all pull like the mischief, and rush like devils, and want a deal of riding. . . . I like it. I prefer to have something to do on horseback. When a man tells me that a horse is an armchair, I always tell him to put the brute into his bedroom" (19). When he has Phineas ride his horse Bonebreaker for the hunt, Chiltern explains that "you want a horse to rush in that country . . . you want a little force, or you're apt to be left up a tree" (24) and tells Phineas "Just let him have his own way at everything" (24). So although Chiltern prizes power and even violence, he is interested in riding with the horse rather than breaking its will to his own. (When Phineas gives Bonebreaker his head, he does indeed come to no harm.)

By the time of *Phineas Redux* these features of Chiltern's personality—his kindness to Violet as a child and his gentleness with horses—have grown into qualities that subdue and temper his excessive energies. In his role as Master of the Hunt, Chiltern combines a measure of nurture and protection (of his hounds, his horses, even of the foxes) with "male" qualities of power and force. Chiltern's balanced personality is stressed in the following passage:

> And he understood hunting, not only as a huntsman understands it . . . but he knew exactly what men should do, and what they should not. In regard to all those various interests with which he was brought in contact, he knew when to hold fast to his own claims, and when to make no claims at all. He was afraid of no one, but he was possessed of a sense of justice which induced him to acknowledge the rights of those around him. . . .
>
> [7]

Later, when Phineas is accused of murdering Bonteen, Chiltern is one of the few men who has not lost touch with the kind of intuitional or emotional perception often considered "feminine"; when the men of the novel are proved wrong in their suspicions of Phineas, Chiltern is ranked with the women who are able to judge Phineas according to a richer sense of humanity.

In *Phineas Finn* Chiltern's brother-in-law, Robert Kennedy, is his opposite—cold rather than passionate, proper and religious rather than disreputable. He appears a safe enough man for Laura to marry, though she does not love him. But he turns out to be far more dangerous and despotic than Chiltern. Chiltern's violent energies are not used to subordinate his wife, but Kennedy's coldness and propriety are:

> The threat [of leaving him] which she had held out to him was very dreadful to him. He was a man terribly in fear of the world's good opinion, who lacked the courage to go through a great and harassing trial in order that something better might come afterwards. His married

life had been unhappy. His wife had not submitted either to his will or to his ways. He had that great desire to enjoy his full rights, so strong in the minds of weak, ambitious men, and he told himself that a wife's obedience was one of those rights which he could not abandon without injury to his self-esteem.

[51]

When Laura leaves him, Kennedy in his madness sounds like a religious version of Louis Trevelyan:

Life is not to me a light thing, nor are the obligations of life light. When I married a wife, she became bone of my bone, and flesh of my flesh. Can I lose my bones and my flesh,—knowing that they are not with God but still subject elsewhere to the snares of the devil, and live as though I were a sound man? Had she died I could have borne it.

[*Phineas Redux*, 10]

Religious rigidity and patriarchal rigidity join in Kennedy. Unable to bend, he is driven mad, Trollope suggests, by the role he has forced on himself.

Trevelyan and Kennedy are not Trollope's only crazed and disappointed men; they are akin to Mr. Gilmore of *The Vicar of Bullhampton*, Ferdinand Lopez, George Germain, George Western (of *Kept in the Dark*), and to other intractable men whose unyielding qualities sometimes pit them against men instead of women (Mr. Tappitt of *Rachel Ray*, Mr. Crawley of *The Last Chronicle of Barset*, the Vicar of Bullhampton, and so forth).

Trollope's tyrannical men are fundamentally weak and self-destructive. Kennedy dies insane while Chiltern leads a full life, satisfying his needs for occupation, love, and pleasure. Maleness itself is not the danger that Laura Kennedy discovers in marriage; the danger comes from the desire for power over others that the system breeds in certain men.

Mr. Gilmore in *The Vicar of Bullhampton* (1868) cannot accept Mary Lowther's desire to break their engagement because she loves another man. But it is not love that motivates him so much as his sense of male dominance and self-esteem: "He held her still by the hand, not with a grasp of love, but with a retention which implied his will that she should not pass away from out of his power" (64).

Trollope wrote in his *Autobiography* that the Brattle plot of *The Vicar of Bullhampton* was most important to him and that he had forgotten what Mary Lowther did in the novel (237). Critics in general have also preferred the Brattle plot to the Lowther-Gilmore plot, but there is an important link between the two. Mary's offense against Mr. Gilmore is like the "fallen" Cary Brattle's offense in that both have been disobedient to men's ideas of what they should do and have followed their own impulses instead. The link between the two women becomes clearer when Mr. Gilmore speaks of Mary's "shameful" refusal as if it were a sexual sin: "If you were my sister, my ears would tingle with shame when your name was mentioned in my presence" (64).

Trollope complains in the preface, and the characters echo the same complaint, that men's transgressions are punished far more leniently than women's. The novel implies one reason: men's sexual misconduct does not put them outside the control of the men who run their immediate family or community, whereas women who "sin" deny the control of their fathers and brothers and put themselves in the power of men who are outsiders. Women's sins are thus a more serious challenge to the local patriarchal authority.

Trevelyan of *He Knew He Was Right* shares Kennedy's desire to subordinate his wife and his fate of dying insane. Although both Emily and Trevelyan like to have their own way, their initial quarrel arises from more than a problem of individual temperament; Trevelyan unquestionably accepts the idea that a husband should be superior. Even when his personal impulses would lead him to act in a loving, tender, or forgiving manner early in the novel, he feels obliged by the demands of his role to be stiff, masterful, and, above all, right. Emily does not feel this same pressure. Though some characters see the role of submissive wife as acceptable for her and she toys with various sorts of submission, she—and some others—also see her refusal to obey as acceptable behavior. She has options to choose from, and while she undoubtedly causes Trevelyan and herself unnecessary grief, she at least lives through her trials without disintegrating psychologically. Trevelyan disintegrates because he knows only the prescribed authoritarian role, and it does not work for him.

Trevelyan's increasingly psychotic desire to be right and to be obeyed by his wife is a symptom of a problem touching all the characters of the novel. Trollope is interested in how a hierarchically and patriarchally ordered social system functions when the patriarchs find themselves temperamentally incapable of sustaining their rigid roles. Another would-be patriarch in the novel, Sir Marmaduke Rowley, helps develop this theme. Brought back to England from his position as governor of the Mandarin Islands through the intervention of his crony Colonel Osborne, Sir Marmaduke displays his incompetence as governor, father, and father-in-law. His testimony before Major Magruder's committee reveals his ineptitude as governor. In his attempts to govern his daughter, Nora, he repeats Trevelyan's fall on a smaller scale. Just as Trevelyan forbade Emily to see Osborne, Sir Marmaduke forbids Nora to see Hugh Stanbury, warns her not to be "obstinate and disobedient," and then says, "I do not for a moment suppose that you dream of carrying on a communication with this gentleman in opposition to our wishes" (70). And when Nora says she does, Sir Marmaduke "assumed an air of increased authority, in which he intended that paternal anger should be visible" and then threatens to throw her off with his curse (70).

Like Trevelyan, Sir Marmaduke has tried to disown a dependent, but in this novel those who abuse the power of their patriarchal status are themselves emotionally banished. In the end Trevelyan feels exiled from England and from society; and Sir Marmaduke considers his post on the Mandarin Islands a banishment. At the beginning of the novel, Trevelyan has prided himself on providing a home not just for Emily but for her sister also; but through his obsessive tyranny, he fails to provide a home for either. Their father fails similarly; Sir Marmaduke is forced to give in to the marriage between Hugh and Nora partly because he cannot provide a better home for Nora himself.

As these inept patriarchs blunder about, making themselves and their dependents wretched (even Miss Stanbury attempts to exercise patriarchal domination), the novel develops what appears to be a benevolent patriarchal figure. Mr. Glascock has all the external marks of his position—land, wealth, and a name—and is regularly assailed by the doctrinaire Wallachia Petrie as a representative of an oppressive aristocracy; but he is almost comically unassuming and passive—a most atypical patriarch. (When asked what he is fond of, he says, "Of sitting at home and doing nothing"; 76). Despite Glascock's apparent fecklessness, however, the novel suggests that the true area of significant action lies precisely in those messy and unpleasant domestic problems with which he copes admirably. Because Glascock is so strong, personally, he does not need to spend time like Trevelyan (or Robert Kennedy) demonstrating how masterful he is; most of the time we see him as social, gentle, agreeable, hospitable, undoctrinaire, and generally benevolent.

Glascock is one of the two men chosen to handle Trevelyan and is also chosen for the more "maternal" task of transferring young Louis from one parent to the other. In the chapter "Mr. Glascock as Nurse" (86) Mr. Glascock successfully achieves this mission, persuades Emily to take over the function of nurse to Trevelyan, and then marries Caroline Spalding. This combination of events is subtly suggestive; the focus of the chapter is not really upon Glascock's handling of the child but upon his handling of the adults involved. Trevelyan trusts him and asks that neither the boy's mother nor his grandfather, Sir Marmaduke Rowley, be allowed to come for young Louis. Glascock is thus asked to perform as a substitute mother and grandfather without having any strong personal ties to the Rowleys or Trevelyans.

When Glascock urges Emily to return to Trevelyan, he does not stress wifely duties but simply Trevelyan's need as a suffering human being. He prompts her change of heart where others have failed, because he appeals to human responsibility rather than patriarchal authority:

But now she felt that she might not return and leave that poor, suffering wretch behind her. . . . Emily Trevelyan was forced to tell herself that all that [romantic love and worship of her husband] was over with her. . . . But still he was her husband, and the father of her child; and though she could not dare to look forward to happiness in living with him, she could understand that no comfort would be possible to her were she to return to England and to leave him to perish alone at Casalunga.

[86]

By acting benevolently rather than egocentrically, by using persuasion rather than flaunting authority, Glascock exemplifies a kind of behavior that has nothing really to do with prerogatives of sex or class.

Glascock is no paragon; when Caroline Spalding tries to break their engagement, he treats her "almost as a child." But this is a brief patronization; usually he is sensible, tolerant, and kind. As his roles of nurse and surrogate parent suggest, Glascock is admirable because he is capable of incorporating traditional feminine traits of love, nurture, and tolerance and because he is uninterested in exercising traditional masculine modes of domination. Thus he does not illustrate a perfection of a patriarchal ideal but a virtual abandonment of patriarchal claims.

This abandonment of patriarchal claims is a motif running through Trollope's novels. In *Barchester Towers* and later in *The Last Chronicle of Barset*, Mr. Harding's persistent gentleness, refusal to engage in power struggles, and renunciation of both self-righteousness and material rewards make him, James Kincaid writes, "essentially feminine."[21] The novelist who created Mrs. Proudie and Mrs. Bolton was too intelligent to imply that all women are essentially gentle and tolerant and all men harsh and intolerant. But Trollope does create novels in which "female" qualities like gentleness, tolerance, and flexibility in making decisions are brought into dialectic relation with "male" qualities of hardness, judgmental rigidity, and reliance on abstract logic.[22] Mr. Glascock softens a stereotypically "masculine" mode with a "feminine" one, as do Mr. Harding in *The Last Chronicle* and Chiltern in *Phineas Redux*. In those two novels Trollope uses trials to explore the dialectic. In both cases women are sure of the innocence of the accused—Mr. Crawley and Phineas—even though they rely upon intuition and ignore seeming evidence. But except for Harding and Chiltern, the men usually judge Crawley and Phineas guilty. The male legal system in *Phineas Redux* is stereotypically masculine; it is impersonal and ruthlessly logical, and the characters' varying responses to it show the degrees to which their emotions and perceptions are fragmentary. In solving the question of who killed Bonteen, Madame Max shows she is that rare person who combines "female" sympathy for and belief in Phineas with a rational and active, "male" approach to exonerating him.

The Trollope novels contain many portraits of intractable men, unyielding, rigid, often crazed. Whatever reasons they offer for their positions, Trollope clearly suggests that the underlying source is the love of power or dominance over others, a stance encouraged by their patriarchal society but a stance that often cripples them emotionally.

In many of the later novels, individual instances of the abuse of masculine power are drawn together by a central crime or fraud—much as Dickens uses the Merdle swindle in *Little Dorrit* to indict a whole system of patriarchal abuses.[23] In *Phineas Redux*, for instance, the trial of Phineas for the murder of Bonteen haunts the whole novel. Though *Phineas Redux* is ostensibly a political novel, it is clear that the struggle for dominance and the underlying fraud Trollope depicts in the political world permeate religion, marriage, and family relations as well. Motives are not quite what they seem. Bonteen and Phineas quarrel about power in their political world, but Bonteen cloaks his attack on Phineas with the fraudulent charge of sexual misconduct, based on Phineas' aid to Lady Laura. In a similar way, Laura and her husband struggle for power in their marriage, but Kennedy disguises his desire for power through religious rationalization. Daubeny appears to support Church disestablishment, but does so only because it is politically expedient, and the real murderer, the "Reverend" Emilius, is guilty of bigamy, religious hypocrisy, and disguise. London society is permeated with a corruption that contaminates seemingly innocent bystanders like Phineas. And when Phineas is shot at by Kennedy, attacked by a political rival, accused of sexual misconduct, religious hypocrisy, and then murder, the claims of the male political system and male dominance under the system of patriarchal marriage and family are substantially undermined.

In *The Way We Live Now* (1875), Trollope draws insistent analogies between exploitive capitalism and exploitive family relationships. Melmotte comes to symbolize the basic corruption of both systems that are controlled by a masculine hierarchy. Melmotte the capitalist has sought money, prestige, political power, and aristocratic connections through a financial system that depends upon credit and economic coercion rather than substance. Similarly, as a father, he has maintained power over his daughter, Marie, by force rather than love. His downfall comes partly because he forges her name on a document she refuses to sign, as fraudulent capitalism and coercive family relations intersect.

We cannot dismiss Melmotte as a non-English adventurer, a boorish criminal who thrusts himself into a company of gentlemen, as the genteel speculators in the novel wish to do. For the aristocratic Longstaffes deal with him eagerly for their own gain while they hypocritically despise him as a dubious gentleman and probable Jew. And they are quite as willing to defraud him as he is to defraud them.

Initially the Longstaffes and Melmottes are dissimilar in birth, class, religion, and values, but their similarities draw them closer and closer until they exchange first a house and then a daughter. Georgiana's attempt to get herself married, in fact, parallels Melmotte's economic activities; the latter tries to advance himself and gain money by the appearance of already having it, while Georgiana tries to vend herself (like fraudulent stock) in the marriage market, with no intrinsic value—no love, no money. Her bargains with Lady Julia Monogram resemble Melmotte's deals with aristocratic men. She has abandoned the possibility of marrying for affection, so she is utterly incapable of understanding Brehgert long enough to keep him engaged to her. Brehgert, whom she sees as a fat, greasy, aging Jew, is externally deficient in all but money by Georgiana's standards; she cannot understand that he— almost alone in the novel except for Roger Carbury—is intrinsically so good, understanding, intelligent, and even humorous that the externals might not mean very much. In all this the Longstaffe daughter is far inferior to Melmotte's own daughter Marie. The parallels between monetary and sexual fraud suggest that in a society where appearances, money, titles, and gender are more important than intrinsic qualities, all forms of human relationships will be similarly tainted.

In the Lopez plot of *The Prime Minister*, the social outsider's fraudulent sexual and economic dealings are overshadowed by the coercive, exclusive, snobbish power of the respectable establishment:

[Glencora] knew enough of such people as the Whartons and the Fletchers to be aware that as a class they are more impregnable, more closely guarded by their feelings and prejudices against strangers than any other. None keep their daughters to themselves with greater care, or are less willing to see their rules of life changed or abolished.

[77]

Lopez certainly intermingles sexual and economic fraud in his efforts to get at the Wharton money through his marriage to Emily Wharton. But he is more desperate than devious; and he pursues the standard rewards of Victorian masculine enterprise, money and prestige, through one of the most standard methods, marriage to an heiress.

Lopez cannot conduct his life in an unruffled and gentlemanly way like Arthur Fletcher (the suitor approved by the Wharton clan) because Lopez is starting without money or status and must struggle in a rapacious economic world. While Lopez's struggles are never very admirable, they do demonstrate how the uglier aspects of capitalistic economics and sexual dominance result from social inequality. To secure a place in his society Lopez needs money; to get money he needs power, but power is also the result of already having money. So from the beginning he faces a dilemma like Melmotte's of trying to appear to have money in order to gain money.

One method that established people like the Whartons and Pallisers recognize as legitimate for their own class is to marry money. But while such a system within a homogeneous class merely helps maintain an equilibrium of money and power, it works quite differently if a daughter's money may pass out of the hands of her father, brothers, cousins, or neighbors into those of an outsider. Just as the stories of Carry Brattle and Mary Lowther in *The Vicar of Bullhampton* suggest that part of the system of sexual roles is to keep family females from escaping control of family males and coming under the control of outsiders, so in the Lopez plot we see the whole Wharton-Fletcher clan aroused to action by the threat that Emily might leave the clan and become a Lopez.

They try persuasion and then ostracism. When all else fails, Mr. Wharton simply keeps control over his money.

Lopez's tyranny over Emily is restrained, not by inner scruples, respect for women, or fear of the law, but by his economic dependence on another man, Mr. Wharton: Lopez "was most desirous to make her subject to his will in all things, and quite prepared to exercise tyranny over her to any extent,—so that her father should know nothing of it. He could not afford to quarrel with Mr. Wharton" (37).

After Lopez dies, the reaction to his widow's last name again indicates how the struggle for male dominance is involved in the struggle between outsider and insiders. Mr. Wharton pays money to Mrs. Parker, hoping never again to hear the name of Lopez (69); when Emily is visiting the country Whartons and Fletchers, they do not call her by her last name. Her father even sends letters to her in care of Everett so that they may be addressed simply to "Emily" (70). When Arthur Fletcher visits her intending to propose, the sound of Mrs. Roby addressing Emily as "Mrs. Lopez" drives him away. A woman's name tells which man she belongs to—her father or her husband—and though Emily is to be brought back into the fold, the family does not want to acknowledge that she once belonged to Lopez. Looked at in one way, Emily is only a pawn in the struggle—first destined for Fletcher, then caught by Lopez, struggled over by Lopez and Mr. Wharton, quarreled about by Fletcher and Lopez during the Silverbridge election, and finally recaptured to keep Lopez out of power.

When sexual relations—in particular, a woman's status and desires—are so subordinated to a family's economic and class interests, and when those interests are so boldly directed by self-serving, bigoted desires for power and prestige, it becomes difficult to distinguish between the fraud of the outsider and the fraud of the respectable establishment. It is significant that *The Prime Minister* offers no identifiable crime as the culmination of its exposure of economic and sexual corruption (as *The Vicar of Bullhampton, Phineas Redux,* and *The Way We Live Now* have all done); instead there is Lopez's suicide—a more chilling emblem of what the patriarchal sexual economy may come to.

In his exploration of the oppressive and constricting patterns of sexual relations under the patriarchy, Trollope can be said to have developed feminist themes. But although the integrity of his perceptions led him to explore the patriarchy, he never directly questioned its fundamental claims. Rather, he was consciously absorbed in the ways people accommodate themselves to society, the efforts of men and women to find a viable balance between the demands of the self and the claims of society. The social and psychological conflicts that prevent such accommodation—or make it possible only for a fortunate few, and even then only in a most imperfect form—assume increasing prominence in his later novels, however. The inner contradictions of the Victorian sexual system are implicitly exposed, elaborated, and given such essential force in shaping characters' behavior that they constitute, as we have argued, a coherent counterplot in many of his novels.

Conservative plot and radical counterplot clash with each other, generating still more thematic conflict but also more discoveries; neither cancels out the other. Trollope, like Dickens, Collins, and Thackeray, remained essentially ambivalent about his culture's sexual relations. The sympathy that all four novelists felt for the plight of men and women victimized by Victorian sexual practices was reluctant, divided, troubled, imperfect; and these terms ought to qualify Rebecca West's characterization of Trollope as well. Yet the essential insight and sympathy outweigh all qualification: they all were feminists.

7

TOWARD BETTER RELATIONS

IKE any of us, Dickens, Collins, Thackeray, and Trollope were shaped by the culture they lived in; they achieved no transcendence or resolution of the conflicting loyalties or divided impulses that characterize the Victorian period. But to a remarkable degree they succeeded in exposing their culture's contradictions in sexual relations by making that conflict into a principle of fictional creation.

As we have tried to show in the chapters on each novelist, their ambivalence is expressed through oppositions between directly articulated fictional material and implicit networks of symbolic motifs that differ from and often contradict the overt narrative. Fundamental issues in these novels often come into existence only when the reader perceives (and pursues) the interplay between manifest and implicit design. For this reason, we have been concerned primarily with making the implicit explicit through analysis of the texts themselves. The "interior" worlds of these novels—and equally important, the often paradoxical interactions between interior and exterior—are so complex, subtly varied, and disguised, and have been so little recognized in their full significance by most critics, that simply to try to disclose what is there has occupied most of our attention.

Of course, to try to say what is there is to report what we see there. As readers are often reminded today, "Different literary critics necessarily . . . discover different meanings, meanings which reflect not so much the *text qua text* but the *text as shaped by* the particular questions or analysis applied to it."[1] But as Myra Jehlen has said in a recent assessment of feminist critical theory, we can at least try to avoid a simple superimposition of our own biases on the literary subject by seeking "to ask the text what questions to ask."[2] Our collaborative work on these four novelists began—as we noted in the preface—when we discovered that intriguing anomalies in their presentation of sexual relations had appeared to each of us independently. In effect, it seemed that the texts themselves were insistently prompting questions about their own apparent purposes.[3] We have tried to show how inconsistencies form a dialectic, how a plot development is followed by a variation that shifts the ground of fictional discourse rather than simply elaborating the original motif, how a narrator's assured assertion is countered by an implicit or even an explicit challenge to its validity.

But there are more comprehensive questions aroused by these novels, especially in the context of recent discussions of critical theory and methodology. For all the perplexities in these authors' treatment of sexual relations, their fundamental perceptions support a feminist analysis of literature and culture; hence recent developments in feminist critical theory seem especially relevant. Though, as a number of critics have noted, feminist literary theory is multiform—most generative where it avoids a narrow dogmatism—it is possible to sketch a part of the larger context in which these novelists might be placed. The sketch will be tentative and incomplete, since it deals with border areas and frontiers rather than established settlements.[4]

We agree with critics such as Jehlen and Elizabeth Able that feminist literary studies seem to have "shifted from recovering a lost tradition to discovering the terms of confrontation with the dominant tradition."[5] To assume that we can recover a suppressed tradition of purely female experience is to forget how compromised all relations in a patriarchal culture are: "there can be no writing or criticism totally outside of the dominant structure; no publication is fully independent from the economic and political pressures of male-dominated society . . . women's writing is a 'double-voiced discourse' that always embodies the social, literary, and cultural heritages of both the muted and the dominant."[6] This means, for Jehlen, Kolodny, Auerbach, Gilbert and Gubar, and other feminist critics, that we must increasingly adopt a method of "radical comparativism" between men's and women's writings, in recognition that the traditions of women's writings have always been themselves relational, and that their relation to the dominant male traditions has usually included a deforming dependence. Another benefit of this comparative methodology will be to demonstrate "the contingency of the dominant male traditions,"[7] "to show that the maxims that pass for the truth of human experience, and the encoding of that experience in literature, are organizations, when they are not fantasies, of the dominant culture."[8]

We have tried to explore a neglected, essential term of this comparison: the world of sexual relations as perceived by four of the most perceptive and inventive of Victorian male novelists. Beyond this, we find that the novels *in themselves* offer a "radical comparativism"—revealing through their subtle dialectic both the deforming dependency of most female roles and the deforming authority of most male roles. And they insist upon the tortuous interdependence of all male and female experience in the social worlds they describe.

These narratives are distinguished by those gaps, anomalies, divergences, contradictions, uncertainties, and anxieties that have provided the points of entry for structuralist, semiotic, neo-Freudian, Marxist, and deconstructionist critics. Undoubtedly this rage for disorder is a reflection of a modern culture whose corrosive doubt reflects the cumulative assaults on every area of authority that broke into open awareness in the Victorian period (and that are basic to works such as *Sartor Resartus*, Mill's *Autobiography*, and most of Arnold's poetry). Undoubtedly in some of its manifestations, this fascination with contraries is a fugitive and cloistered enterprise—retreating into a scepticism that is as sacerdotal as any of the narrow orthodoxies it seeks to demolish. But it does seem true that crucial issues for our culture manifest themselves precisely at points of contradiction.[9]

In pursuing the points of contradiction in our culture that feminist studies have progressively disclosed, Jehlen, Kolodny, Showalter, Auerbach, and others have found how frequently a developed feminist perspective intersects the dominant (and predominantly masculine) schools of contemporary literary the-

ory.[10] The very metaphors that recur in recent feminist criticism—
"double-voiced discourse," "palimpsest," "dominant" vs. "muted"
stories, and so forth—suggest this common ground with intellectual methodologies that assume a radical dualism in our culture,
with one entire set of terms deeply repressed. And these same
critics have shown how feminist perspectives—far from being
mere subdepartments of the dominant enterprises—can invigorate
and redirect disciplines that can easily become "arid and falsely
objective, the epitome of a pernicious masculine discourse."[11]

Most feminist critics insist that the real energy and acumen of
our modern sensitivity to paradox and contradiction are inseparable from the relations between the individual and the social world.
The world can indeed appear as a palimpsest, an overdetermined
symbolic script, a tissue of intertextuality; but to read it as if it
were actually and only a piece of writing is to risk the worst sort
of irrelevance to the lives of most readers—who continue to read
in some sense to discover alternative ways of living. Some of the
finest practitioners of various new theoretical disciplines have
powerfully affirmed this basis for writing and reading. Geoffrey
Hartman, for instance, writes:

> The truth of art and the useful mediation of the critic are the argument,
> explicit or implicit, of all books of criticism, including mine. . . . I prefer
> to *confess* what art has meant to me. It shapes my consciousness as if that
> were as material as language, and makes eyes and ears brood. . . . It
> gives words and takes them away. Through it I can feel in touch with
> myself, and sometimes with others. . . . In oppressive social systems it
> has always found a way to create a form of expression.[12]

Where Hartman, Bloom, Derrida, Lacan, and other theorists
of the dominant schools tend to acknowledge the place of literature
in their lives in terms of an isolated ego, most feminist critics insist
on seeing the self as intimately, essentially defined by social relations as well. This is, of course, also the commitment of Dickens,
Thackeray, Trollope, and Collins, whose most adroit verbal ar-
tifices also serve a social, moral intent. They all shared, as did
most Victorian writers, some version of George Eliot's creed:
"Art . . . is a mode of amplifying experience and extending our

contact with our fellow men beyond the bounds of our own personal lot."[13]

Without trying to conflate all the diverse ideologies of contemporary criticism into one megalotheory, we can see that the most influential of them share some fundamental perceptions with feminist thought: that modern culture often rests its authority on the suppression of a great part of the individual's vital experience; that this suppression is a form of tyranny, whether we see its primary victims as libidinal impulses, certain social classes, or an entire gender; that denial of the very existence of the suppressed forces becomes essential to the maintenance of the dominant system; and that language itself becomes infected and deformed by this massive dissimulation.

Marxist, Freudian, deconstructionist, and much semiotic theory share with feminist theory the belief that culture is largely determined by the action of hidden forces, not just acknowledged but forcibly suppressed from common awareness by a massive effort of collective will. This conspiracy is not necessarily conscious, of course; in fact, it is usually unconscious—and for that reason, all the more difficult to comprehend or counteract. Although the common ground becomes disputed territory as soon as we descend to specific causes and consequences of this disguised authoritarianism, it seems important to acknowledge that we have not yet become, like the academicians of Swift's Lagado, thorough solipsists.

Still, feminist thought rests on a distinctive perception that cannot be assimilated into other ideologies; it can only join them as a transforming principle. This is, of course, the insight we have found central to the novels of Dickens, Thackeray, Trollope, and Collins: whatever its particular ideological variations, modern culture is undergirded by the pervasive ideology of patriarchal authority.

Jehlen has written that feminist criticism needs to disclose "not just any point where misogyny is manifest but one where misogyny is pivotal or crucial to the whole. The thing to look for is . . . the meshing of a definition of women and a definition of the world. And insofar as the former is deleterious, the connection will be contradictory; indeed . . . one may recognize a point of connection by its contradictions."[14] These four novelists not only show how every feature of their society meshes with the sexual ideology that victimizes both men and women; they develop this understanding as the core of their fiction. In part because they inherit a dominant rather than a dependent role—both as authors and in their more ordinary social roles—they are driven to explore and expose the abuses of that power to a degree that no women novelists of the period did. They are implicated in the oppressive system, and this involvement becomes a powerful motive to understand and, finally, to reject both its imperatives and its seductions.

But even as the exposure of the systemic nature of sexual corruption develops in their novels, we are confronted with a perplexity that continues to trouble recent feminist literary criticism. How do we even speak, how did these novelists even convey a sense, of a deformed sexual system when the whole culture seems so massively conditioned by patriarchal values that we do not know our proper nature, and the language through which we seek it is tainted by pernicious and arbitrary sexual implications? And how, lacking a language and frame of reference, can we conceive of an alternative system that might truly satisfy us?

John Stuart Mill's conviction that we simply cannot know the natures of men and women "in their present relation to one another" reflects this impasse.[15] And the desire for a thorough transformation appears in other writers on social issues, such as Florence Nightingale, and in fictional characters like Charlotte Brontë's Shirley:

Why have women passion, intellect, moral activity—these three—and a place in society where no one of the three can be exercised? Men say that God punishes for complaining. No, but men are angry with misery. They are irritated with women for not being happy. They take it as a personal offense. . . .

And women, who are afraid, while in words they acknowledge that God's work is good, to say, Thy will be *not* done (declaring another order of society from that which He has made), go about maudling to each other and teaching to their daughters that "women have no passions." In the conventional society, which men have made for women, and women have accepted, they *must* act the farce of hypocrisy, the lie that they are without passion—and therefore what else can they say to their daughters, without giving the lie to themselves?

[Nightingale][16]

'Men, I believe, fancy women's minds something like those of children. Now that is a mistake. . . .

'If men could see us as we really are, they would be a little amazed; but the cleverest, the acutest men are often under an illusion about women: . . . they misapprehend them, both for good and evil: their good woman is a queer thing, half doll, half angel; their bad woman almost always a fiend. Then to hear them fall into ecstasies with each other's creations, worshipping the heroine of such a poem—novel—drama. . . . Fine and divine it may be, but often quite artificial—false as the rose in my best bonnet there. If I spoke all I think on this point; if I gave my real opinion of some first-rate female characters in first-rate works, where should I be? Dead under a cairn of avenging stones in half an hour.'

[*Shirley*][17]

Victorian women novelists frequently create characters like Shirley, or narrators, who appeal for an alternative way of life (in *Mary Barton, Middlemarch, Wuthering Heights*, and *Villette*, for example). And they often imply what Mill and Nightingale declare explicitly, that the need is not for a change in this or that social practice, not a need for meliorism, but for a change in the basic sexual mythos that structures the whole culture.

In Shirley's youthful composition *La Première Femme Savant*, for instance, she momentarily senses through her persona Eva her own potential power but also recognizes her alienation in a world that offers no creative form or material for that power to work in:

She felt the world, the sky, the night, boundlessly mighty. Of all things, herself seemed to herself the centre,—a small, forgotten atom of life, a spark of soul, emitted inadvertent from the great creative source, and now burning unmarked to waste in the heart of a black hollow. . . . Could this be, she demanded, when the flame of her intelligence burned so vivid; when her life beat so true and real, and potent; when something within her stirred disquieted, and restlessly asserted a god-given strength for which it insisted she could find exercise?

[457–58]

Eva's (and Shirley's) questions are prompted by an unreconcilable contradiction in her emotions: she feels that she is simultaneously the center of the world and a "small forgotten atom." Her nascent revolutionary impulse—revolutionary not because she envisions some grandiose plan for world reformation, but because she accepts herself as a center, not as a satellite—soon subsides into the traditional forms. Eva does not become the source of a new mythos, an Eve self-created by self-awareness ("declaring" what Nightingale passionately desired, "another order of society than that which He has made"). She is declared a "Daughter of Man" by a "glorious Bridegroom," an awesome "Son of God" who "claims" her. And we discover that Shirley's youthful composition was "corrected" by her tutor Louis Moore in a way that intimidated her into silence—a version of Brontë's own experience with her teacher Héger, recreated again and again in her fiction. At the novel's conclusion, in an account written by Moore himself (who now takes command of the novel's language as well as Shirley's) he narrates Shirley's submission to him:

"'Now, then, I have you: you are mine: I will never let you go. Wherever my home be, I have chosen my wife. If I stay in England, in England you will stay; if I cross the Atlantic, you will cross it also: our lives are riveted; our lots intertwined."

"'And are we equal then, sir? Are we equal at last?" Shirley asks.

"'You are younger, frailer, feebler, more ignorant than I."

"'Will you be good to me, and never tyrannize?"

[578–79]

Though not always with such a blatant reversal, all these novels regularly return to the traditional value system, the traditional ways of life. And the fortunate women are frequently informed, in one way or another, by their patronizing spouses, "You are younger, frailer, feebler, more ignorant than I." It is as if these Victorian women novelists lack a starting place, a framework on which to build a new conception of relations between men and woman. They can find a language of protest and plea but no language or action that is truly founded on an alternative vision.[18]

The male novelists we have explored in this study seldom even speculate—directly or indirectly—on alternatives to the world whose corruption they anatomize so thoroughly. In fact, their narratives ridicule or shrink in horror from the characters who venture to suggest some radical alternative—significantly, these are female characters such as Wallachia Petrie, Miss Wade, and Lydia Gwilt. The more indulged and admired rebellious women, the Becky Sharps and Magdalen Vanstones, remain within the prevailing sexual system, however much they offend against its moral standards.

When these four novelists turn to the predictable resolution through marriage, we do not sense a retreat from the possibility of an alternative world (the sort augured in the relationships of Catherine Earnshaw and Heathcliff, Shirley Keeldar and Caroline Helstone). We sense rather that they have struggled to find some sign of regeneration within the system and have failed. Their exposure of sexual corruption comes close to suggesting that the present system simply cannot satisfy human needs for creativity, growth, physical and emotional satisfaction, and some integration of personal desires with social roles. The infernal misery of Tom's-all-Alone's, the despair that lies just under the tawdry bustle of *Vanity Fair*, the fraud and crime that spread to taint the most respectable characters in *Phineas Finn* and *No Name*—these are not thematic hyperboles but such inescapable consequences of the novels' social vision that a return to a domestic enclave is a tempting refuge. At the very best, these four novelists offer a melioration of traditional oppression that, in a way typical of the paradox, serves to mute the outrage against the whole system that the novels have generated.

Amy Dorrit and Arthur Clennam, Rochester and Jane Eyre, Lydgate and Rosamond, Laura Fairlie and Walter Hartright, Alice Vavasor and John Grey, all the impaired couples who salvage some measure of personal contentment and humane relationship from the devastation of sexual relationships are absolutely typical of the Victorian novel. A more promising fulfillment (including perhaps some resolution of personal and social aspirations beyond the exchange of marriage vows) is lacking not because of a failure of the novelists' own imagination or will but because of a flaw in the whole culture's imagination. The women novelists can more easily frame an *appeal* for a radical change in their characters' or narrators' thoughts, but they often endorse a heroine's ultimate submissiveness to male-controlled values more thoroughly than do the creators of Mrs. Joe, Glencora Palliser, Becky Sharp, and Magdalen Vanstone. And both male and female Victorian novelists make their strongest, most searching appeals for a radical reformation of culture through symbolic action that challenges the orthodoxy of the direct narrative. Whether we express this as a counterplot, a double voice, a palimpsest, or a subtext, we are acknowledging the presence of a fictional method that seeks to make of the culture's destructive contradictions a true dialectic to revalue fundamental sexual myths and practices.

For a number of reasons, assessed by a number of recent feminist critics, Victorian women novelists often attempt to redeem the traditional dominance of their heroes (usually after a period of chastening affliction) through a transformation of arrogance into a form of virtuous authority. The domineering cruelty of Grand-court, Casaubon, Harry Carson (*Mary Barton*), and Brocklehurst leads to their own self-destruction, as it does for the more savage and maddened patriarchal figures in Dickens, Thackeray, Trol-lope, and Collins. But the authoritarian excesses of Rochester, Paul Emanuel, John Thornton (*North and South*), and St. John Rivers receive far more tolerant treatment and are even rewarded.

Charlotte Brontë's personal adulation of the Iron Duke Wel-lington, and its apparent basis in the power that the males of the Brontë family possessed over the daughters who were actually more imaginative and strong-willed than either Patrick or Bran-well, certainly help account for her novelistic redemption of mas-culine authoritarianism (and for the countervailing humiliation and punishment that regularly precede redemption).[19] But as Terry Eagleton has argued, there is a greater cultural force at work here, at work in all the Brontës' fiction, an attraction to the workings of the "myths of power" in Victorian society.[20] When we realize that Elizabeth Gaskell, with a very different temperament, background, mode of life, and religious and political beliefs than Charlotte Brontë, created similar tyrannical figures—and a similar mode of punishment followed by reward—we can see that something beyond the accidents of personal environment is at work. Even George Eliot follows a complex transformation of the pattern in characters such as Lydgate and Tom Tulliver.

The heroines typically suffer the hero's tyranny and even admire this "strength of character." Readers' reactions are understandably much more ambivalent. In the clearest versions—again Charlotte Brontë's—the "nobility" of the male character is established through the revelation of his own long-suffering endurance of an affliction that has blighted his life. The narrative revelation of a secret "curse" on his life transforms him (or at least attempts to transform him) into a victim rather than a tyrant and makes him a figure who appeals to the heroine of the novel for a merciful rescue, as erotic patterns undergo the moralization typical of the Victorian novel. And, quite significantly, the curse on the hero has been inflicted by a woman (true for Paul Emanuel as well as Rochester and Heathcliff, though the death of an angelically pure woman rather than the fearsome passions of an unruly woman causes his suffering).[21] In simple terms that make clear the presence of a pattern of symbolic action here, the good woman redeems the bad woman. Sin and redemption have been displaced from the tyrannical male onto a bifurcated version of femininity; and these terms suggest Eve and the Virgin Mary in addition to the wicked stepmother and Cinderella or Gretel.

As the heroes are punished through near death (occasionally through actual death—Tom Tulliver and Heathcliff, for instance), maiming, public humiliation, psychological torment, and loss of career or fortune, a catharsis seems to occur that restores them to virtue, nobility, and inevitably, to dominance. In this process, the reader is encouraged, by the heroine's own responses, to transfer empathy from the heroine's quiet endurance to the more violent torments of the heroes.

One element of this attempted catharsis is an unacknowledged need in the fiction to reestablish the culture's pattern of female dependence. We can see more clearly how the force of this unconscious need operates *through* the novelists, despite all variations of personal temperament and aesthetic objective, if we realize that it even appears, despite several symbolic displacements, in Eliot's treatment of the relationships among Rosamond, Lydgate, and Dorothea. Rosamond (and Laure before her) is the "bad" willful woman who causes the man's secret torment, of course. Lydgate's "tyranny" lies not in personal abuse of women (he is actually kind and patient) but in his stereotypic notions of feminine subservience. Although his rescue through Dorothea's noble generosity does not lead to the standard resolution through their marriage, this catharsis does prepare for Dorothea's marriage to Will and for the patching-up of Lydgate's and Rosamond's marriage. (And many readers have felt that Dorothea and Lydgate were "designed" for each other.) Despite the complex displacements here, the pattern of dependency is reinforced: Dorothea is subordinated to Will's parliamentary career even though, the narrator tells us, "Many who knew her, thought it a pity that so substantive and rare a creature should have been absorbed into the life of another, and be only known in a certain circle as a wife and mother."[22]

It is only women novelists who seem called upon to make the fictional ratification of the culture's myths of power and dependence—and who respond to the call. By contrast, the four male novelists, as we have seen in earlier chapters, regularly undercut the authoritarian postures of their central male figures, romantic heroes and benevolent patriarchs as well as romantic villains and domestic tyrants. In direct opposition to the pattern we have seen in the women's novels, this exposure of inadequacy and injustice occurs even when the character—John Harmon, say, or Pen, or Plantagenet Palliser—is lauded by the narrator. The interior power shift in their novels is away from the male figures and toward the female figures: toward Becky, not Dobbin; toward Miss Barbary and Lady Dedlock, not Jarndyce, Sir Leicester, Woodcourt, or, finally, even Tulkinghorn; toward Alice Vavasor and Glencora, not John Grey, Palliser, or George Vavasor; and toward Lydia Gwilt, not Midwinter or Allan Armadale.

But as this power is transferred (again with an effort to engage the reader's own emotional participation in the psychological action) a revealing transformation occurs. The women who exercise the power are characterized as morally corrupt or weak, and emotionally deformed or excessive. This directly inverts the pattern of the woman novelists; it debases the female characters who have real power, while the women novelists elevate the male characters who do not. The empowering of wicked or supposedly aberrant women, like the redemption of the tyrannical heroes, radiates the unresolved psychological and moral discord at the core of all these texts. Where the women novelists follow the culture's urge to sustain masculine power, the male novelists are impelled to punish feminine power.

In another set of contrasts the women novelists are drawn to "feminize" the brutality of the system by substituting a woman's conscious, moral self-sacrifice for an automatic, routine, romantic submission (Jane Eyre for Bertha Mason, Dorothea Brooke for Celia). The contrasting tendency for the male novelists is to redeem masculine brutality by substituting a virtuous domination for a sadistic domination (Henry Esmond for Lord Castlewood, Pip for Bentley Drummle and Orlick, John Grey for George Vasor, Hartright for Glyde and Fosco). This may seem to amount to the same thing: a restoration of masculine dominance. But the way the restoration is brought about is quite different. The Rochesters and the Thorntons are sustained by the powerful, virtuous admiration of the self-sacrificing heroines, whereas the heroines of Dickens, Thackeray, Trollope, and Collins grow more pallid and weak as the virtuous hero replaces the sadistic oppressor. For all their outward ratification of female submissiveness, the women's novels assert a feminine power. For all their outward glorification of virtuous masculinity the men's novels reveal a masculine debility. The psychological homeostasis that occurs in both fictional systems implicitly condemns the cultural system it seems to support, however, by exposing the arbitrary, compulsive, and mutually destructive nature of the whole process.

Jehlen has argued that the interior life still associated in our culture with women is not at all suppressed by the tradition of the English novel, even though that tradition falls under the sway of the patriarchy. Rather, she writes, "the interior lives of female characters are the novel's mainstay. Instead it is the women's ability to act in the public domain that the novels suppress." And in keeping with her salutary belief that we must always be attentive to the relational context of any sexual motif—the way that masculinity and femininity are defined by their difference from each other—she proposes that the novel "demands androgynously heroic males [that is, males with significant interior and significant public lives] and prohibits androgynously heroic females."[23]

We have seen, though, how the interior lives of both male and female characters are narrowed and impoverished in the novels of Dickens, Thackeray, Trollope, and Collins. Where Victorian women novelists do seek to provide an enclave apart from the active social world where the interior lives of their heroines can flourish, these male novelists only fitfully, imperfectly, and almost reluctantly develop the interior lives of their characters. At the same time, though, they do not provide their heroes with a robust and successful public life. Even Plantagenet Palliser, who was designed by Trollope to exemplify the importance of a public career, finds his role as prime minister empty and unsatisfying.

The possibilities for interior and public life both dwindle in their novels, so much so that we find a number of nominal heroes who are almost a parody of Jehlen's androgynous hero: Pip, Arthur Clennam, Walter Hartright, Ozias Midwinter, Dobbin, Henry Esmond, George Vavasor, and Plantagenet Palliser. Another sort of interior world displaces the development of the characters as the center of fictional interest in these novels: that secret nexus of sexual relations that binds the whole society together, a sociopsychic interior world expressed through the behavior of a number of characters rather than the subtle consciousnesses of a few central characters.

This absorption in the psychodynamics of the sexual system, in the way it dominates and reduces both the social and the private experiences of most individuals, distinguishes these novelists from the major women novelists of the period. The women create characters like Caroline Helstone and Gwendolyn Harleth whose interior lives grow in subtlety, range, and depth as their options for external action are constrained into the narrowest scope. There is often, as Gilbert and Gubar copiously document and subtly argue, a crippling, diseased, claustrophobic quality to this world in a narrow cell; but the heroines are remarkable and heroic in their resistance to almost intolerable pressures, both severe social restrictions and that urge toward self-denigration that women in this culture are conditioned to feel. Beyond this somewhat negative virtue, and despite the tacit support for a kind of quietism in the face of massive sexual oppression, the interior worlds of these heroines become sustaining, imaginatively varied responses to an environment that seemed intolerably bleak—an alternative to that despair voiced by so many male Victorian writers over a world that offered "neither joy, nor love, nor light, / Nor certitude, nor peace, nor help for pain" (Arnold, "Dover Beach").

The male novelists, despite the predilection for an introspective imaginative life that they share with most modern poets and novelists, are drawn rather to explore the interiority of the whole system, the precondition and constant modifier of conscious life. In this they are also writing about and for people whose mental lives are more typical than the brilliantly subtle characters of Austen, Brontë, James, and Joyce. Either they use a limited account of their character's consciousness as part of a largely symbolic method (as Dickens usually does); or the record of conscious life is fragmentary and compulsive in its fits of introspection and flashes of insight (Trollope's preferred method); or the presentation of conscious life is disingenuously confessional and less subtle or candid than it pretends to be (Thackeray's practice in *Esmond, Pendennis,* and *The Newcomes*). The narrators of all four novelists, as we have shown earlier, also tend to obscure a direct representation of characters' mental lives through their own interpretive rhetoric.

The dominant tradition of the English novel that Jehlen describes is indeed centered on a feminine model of the interior life, identifying the culture's ideal of women's nature with the ideals of a conscious moral introspection and of spiritual self-development that are a heritage of the Reformation. This allows the novel to sustain "the distinction between the private self and the world out there that is the powerful crux of middle-class identity."[24] This helps to explain why Dickens' most introspective male characters, such as Copperfield, Paul Dombey, Pip, and Arthur Clennam, are regularly associated with "feminine" traits, as are Thackeray's Esmond, Hardy's Jude and Angel Clare, James's Strether, Joyce's Bloom, and so forth.

But the interiority of the novel form was not, from the beginning, limited to Richardson's identification of interior life with a certain model of femininity, as *Don Quixote* and *Tristram Shandy* attest. The novel's chief subject, the individual caught in perplexing transactions with the social world, can be "interiorized" in quite different ways.

Male authors do frequently write with a greater initial confidence than women authors, in the Victorian period and today. The debilitating prohibitions against authorship that confront women writers can create the sense that their very gender incapacitates them from a full participation in imaginative creation. Although the male novelists faced the sort of prejudice against novel writing that James combatted in his prefaces and reviews, and although they all felt a measure of alienation from their society that is shared by most modern writers, they did not begin with the sense of disability that deeply troubled writers such as Charlotte Brontë and George Eliot.

In fact, their careers began confidently, even exuberantly. *Sketches by Boz* and Thackeray's Yellowplush pieces illustrate this blithe beginning, in their boisterous humor and their easy caricature of familiar social types. With the exception of Collins, they all began with an acceptance of the traditions they were later to challenge so profoundly. Only as they begin their major novels do they gain an awareness of how deeply sexual status infiltrates every area of social and personal life. And they come to realize their own ineluctable personal involvement in this process. We can see this sort of growth (not unique to these authors, of course, but especially significant for them because so many of their imaginative discoveries ran counter to their conscious intentions) clearly in Trollope's relationship with his Palliser characters:

By no amount of description or asseveration could I succeed in making any reader understand how much these characters with their belongings have been to me in my latter life; or how frequently I have used them for the expression of my political or social convictions. . . . I do not think that novelists have often set before themselves the state of progressive change,—nor should I have done it, had I not found myself so frequently allured back to my old friends [the Pallisers]. So much of my inner life was passed in their company, that I was continually asking myself how this woman would act when this or that event had passed over her head, or how that man would carry himself when his youth had become manhood, or his manhood declined to old age. It was in regard to the old Duke of Omnium, of his nephew and heir, and of his heir's wife, Lady Glencora, that I was anxious to carry out this idea; but others added themselves to my mind as I went on, and I got round me a circle of persons as to whom I knew not only their present characters, but how those characters were to be affected by years and circumstances.

[*Autobiography*, 264–65]

What is extraordinary in this passage is that Trollope responds to his characters as an old friend rather than as their creator; he wonders how they will react to changing circumstances and remains open to possibilities he has not yet anticipated. While a later writer like Gissing in *The Odd Women* drew his women with the conscious intention of showing the wrongs done to women, Trollope and the other novelists of our study were more likely to imagine their characters first, then find them in distress, try to show how they might have reacted, and not consciously ponder the theoretical implications of the situations they describe.

The anxiety that influences these authors grows from a grappling with a whole culture's traditions rather than with a single progenitor. (This is probably true for most novelists; and it may distinguish them from poets who work within genres dominated by great individual predecessors.) In this struggle, originally static and simple forms—sexual stereotypes in particular—become fragmented, polymorphic, and fluid.[25] The system these writers inherited might be described as Ruskinian in its view of women, seeing woman as the sex whose moral sensitivity and sympathy for others could help to right the wrongs of their culture. The creators of Esther Summerson, Marian Halcombe, Amelia Sedley, and Eleanor Bold were certainly schooled to hold such opinions. Yet these same writers created Caddy Jellyby, Magdalen Vanstone, Rachel Esmond, and Violet Effingham, who work to undermine the brittle Ruskinian view. In fact, the novels that set such antithetical female characters into a dialectical relation with each other help to show how much this stasis is not a sluggish complacency but a terrified defense.

We have tried to sketch some areas where a relational study of men and woman novelists of the Victorian period might be fruitful. The goal of such study probably should not be, however distant in prospect, a "promised land in which gender would lose its power, in which all texts would be sexless and equal, like angels." In her wry rejection of this illusory ideal, Elaine Showalter has argued that "We may never reach the promised land at all; for when feminist critics see our task as a study of women's writing, we realize that the land promised to us is not the serenely undifferentiated universality of texts but the tumultuous and intriguing wilderness of difference itself."[26] Our counterargument is that feminism in practice is still rare enough that we should welcome it wherever we find it, in however unexpected a guise. And difference is always difference *from*, which need not mean (though it usually has meant) the rigged hierarchy of dominance and submission. If we are indeed to explore the "intriguing wilderness of difference itself," we cannot afford to banish the creative works of either gender. Seeing them in relation to each other makes all the difference.

NOTES

1. THE PERPLEXING ANGEL: THE WOMAN QUESTION AND DICKENS, THACKERAY, TROLLOPE, AND COLLINS

1. For fuller treatment of women's struggles for economic, legal, and social reform see Martha Vicinus, ed., *Suffer and Be Still* (1972) and *A Widening Sphere* (1977); Rachel Strachey, *The Cause* (1978); and Josephine Kamm, *Rapiers and Battleaxes* (1966).

2. Frances Power Cobbe, "The Final Cause of Women," p. 26.

3. "*Women's Rights and Duties*, considered with reference to their Effects on Society and on her own Condition, *Woman's Mission*, the fourteenth Edition" read a typical publisher's advertisement of the era (included in a copy of *The Englishwoman's Review of Social and Industrial Questions*, 1877). The "Woman's Mission" controversy of the forties alone, for example, generated a furious series of replies and counter-replies: Sarah Lewis, *Woman's Mission* (1839); Mrs. Craik, *Women's Rights and Duties* (1840); Mrs. Hugo Reid, *A Plea for Women* (1843); Ann Lamb, *Can Women Regenerate Society?* (1844) are just a few.

4. Among the critical works that treat the literature of the nineteenth century in the light of recent women's studies scholarship are: Françoise Basch, *Relative Creatures*; Ellen Moers, *Literary Women*; and Elaine Showalter, *A Literature of Their Own*. Nina Auerbach in "Women on Women's Destiny" considers a number of feminist scholars—Kate Millet, Patricia Meyer Spacks, and Elaine Showalter among them—who have generally treated the male Victorian novelists as straightforward purveyors of stereotypes about women. Auerbach argues, as we do, that this is a mistaken judgment. See also Carolyn Heilbrun, *Reinventing Womanhood*. We will return to this subject in the last chapter.

5. Trollope's remark was made in a letter to Adrian H. Toline, April 2, 1879, *The Letters of Anthony Trollope*, p. 418.

6. In his discussion of sexual themes in Dickens, Alexander Welsh argues that this sort of disguised sexuality is as fascinating and as representative of actual experience as more explicit presentations: "Oddly enough, we wish just as much to read about passions in their multiform disguises as we do of passions in naked genital embraces; passions are more often than not disguised in real life, and their extraordinary complexity, and even their universality, are often a function of the disguise"; *The City of Dickens*, pp. 154–55.

7. In *He Knew He Was Right*, p. 34.

8. Vicinus, *Widening Sphere*, p. xii.

9. Tony Tanner, *Adultery in the Novel*, p. 15.

10. Ibid, p. 17. "Patriarchal" in this context is not a recent feminist coinage, as Tanner makes clear in his references to the Victorian jurist, Sir Henry Sumner Maine. Maine not only used the term "Patriarchal Power" but also declared "I feel sure that power over children was the root of the old corruption of Power" (ibid., p. 5).

11. During the last decade, there has been an explosion of research concerned with the history of marriage and the family and the role and status of women within the family and society in general. A great deal of this research bears on the understanding of women in the nineteenth century. Essay collections such as Berenice Carroll, ed., *Liberating Women's History*; Mary S. Hartman and Lois Banner, eds., *Clio's Consciousness Raised*; Renate Bridenthal and Claudia Koonz, eds., *Becoming Visible*; and the two collections edited by Martha Vicinus, *Suffer and Be Still* and *A Widening Sphere* contain much important material. Relevant book-length studies such as Lee Holcombe, *Victorian Ladies at Work*, Patricia Branca, *Silent Sisterhood*, and Mary S. Hartman, *Victorian Murderesses* are referred to elsewhere in our text. Another significant source is material from periodicals: the *Journal of Social History*, the *Journal of Family History*, the *Journal of British Studies*, and *Victorian Studies* as well as the work in sex role research and on the social roles and status of women to be found in the psychological and sociological journals. The new periodicals that have come into being with the establishment of women's studies as a field of research have been particularly drawn to the examination of women in the nineteenth century: *Signs, Feminist Studies, Women's Studies*, the *International Journal of Women's Studies* are among a growing number of such journals. Barbara Bellows Watson's "On Power and the Literary Text," Helene E. Roberts' "The Exquisite Slave: The Role of Clothes in the Making of the Victorian Women," and Sister A. Martha Westwater, "Surrender to Subservience," are examples of the investigations that have extended our understanding of nineteenth-century women and their depiction in literature.

12. "Of Queens' Gardens," in *The Works of John Ruskin*, 18:123, 140.

13. Walter Houghton, *The Victorian Frame of Mind*, p. 343.

14. Simone de Beauvoir, *The Second Sex*, trans. H. M. Parshley, p. 197.

15. Alexander Welsh in *City of Dickens*, pp. 180–95, writes perceptively about a complex of essentially religious functions that Dickens' female characters perform in the guise of familial and romantic roles. In other variations of the father-daughter relationship, according to Welsh, the "transference of loyalty from father to husband becomes a ritual of salvation" (p. 171).

16. Sandra M. Gilbert and Susan Gubar, *The Madwoman in the Attic*.

17. Ibid., pp. 73, 64.

18. Ibid., p. 51. See also Carolyn Heilbrun, *Reinventing Womanhood*, pp. 71–92, for a discussion of what she calls a "failure of imagination" in women writers.

19. Rich, "An Interview with Adrienne Rich," p. 59.

20. As Raymond Williams has argued, the presentation of desire in *Wuthering Heights* moves from an erotic to a political context: the novel conveys "the central feeling that an intensity of desire is as much a response . . . to the human crisis of that time as the more obviously recognisable political radicalism. Indeed, to give that kind of value to human longing and need, to that absolute commitment to another. . . . is to clash as sharply with the emerging system, the emerging priorities, as any assault on material poverty. What was at issue really was relationship itself." *The English Novel from Dickens to Lawrence*, p. 61.

21. Myra Jehlen, "Archimedes and the Paradox of Feminist Criticism."

22. J. S. Mill, "On the Subjection of Women," pp. 367–68.

23. See, for example, Robert Garis, *The Dickens Theatre*.

2. THE AMBIVALENT NOVELISTS: THE QUESTION OF FORM

1. Wayne C. Booth, *The Rhetoric of Fiction*, pp. 4f. and 51.

2. Wolfgang Iser, *The Implied Reader: Patterns of Communication in Prose Fiction from Bunyan to Beckett*, p. 108.

3. Iser, *The Implied Reader*, p. 119.

4. Robert Polhemus, *The Changing World of Anthony Trollope*, p. 40.

5. Joan Fetterly in *The Resisting Reader: A Feminist Approach to American Fiction* examines American writers who have a strong antifeminist bias but nonetheless produce fiction that is "sub-intentionally feminist." Her analysis of James's *Bostonians*, which presents "a massive documentation of women's oppression" (p. xxv), or Faulkner's "A Rose for Emily," in which "the power of men over women is an overt subject" (p. xv), suggests that many American writers may warrant the kind of examination our book gives to male Victorian novelists.

3. DICKENS

1. Although characters in the novels of Trollope, Collins, and Thackeray may have little more real autonomy than Dickens' characters, they are usually able to shake free of the intense emotional relationships that bind parent and child. In many of Thackeray's novels, like *Henry Esmond* and *Pendennis*, fundamental conflicts between parents and children do remain unresolved, but the main narrative action serves to conceal and evade them. In Dickens' novels, the main action underscores the symbolic family relations.

2. This relation between fathers and daughters does not hold true for mothers and daughters. No daughter is forced to assume a parent's role toward her mother. Most often, in fact, the reversal of roles between father and daughter occurs in a family where the mother has died. Although the daughter is forced to act as both mother and wife to her father, this does not mean that she is free from patriarchal domination; the roles of mother and wife have been fashioned according to masculine standards.

3. Washington Irving, for example, praised the story of Nell for its "exquisite pathos" and "moral sublimity" (J. A. Hammerton, *The Dickens Companion* [New York, 1910], p. 298; quoted in George H. Ford, *Dickens and His Readers*, p. 56). Ford's discussion of this phenomenon, pp. 55–71, is very useful.

4. Steven Marcus, *Dickens: From Pickwick to Dombey*. Marcus uses the term as his title for the book's first chapter.

5. Walter E. Houghton, in *The Victorian Frame of Mind*, pp. 341–93, refers to a number of Victorian writers who seek, through an idealization of womanhood, an alternative to the male-dominated value system. Ann Douglas presents an excellent account of the comparable process in the United States during the nineteenth century in *The Feminization of American Culture*.

6. As Alexander Welsh writes, "The good people of Dickens's novels dwell in the earthly city without being of it . . . they are only sojourners." *The City of Dickens*, p. 118. Welsh's entire discussion of the intermixture of religious and secular motifs in Dickens is very perceptive, and one of his major conclusions seems unarguable: "Christianity apparently contributes more to the complexity of social questions [in Dickens' novels] than it does to their solution" (p. 141).

7. Carolyn Heilbrun, *Toward a Recognition of Androgyny*, p. 52; Angus Wilson, *The World of Charles Dickens*, p. 98; Katherine M. Rogers, *The Troublesome Helpmate: A History of Misogyny in Literature*, p. 195.

In "Murderous Mothers: The Problems of Parenting in the Victorian Novel," Joan Mannheimer sees in such aggressive mothers as Mrs. Joe and Mrs. Jellyby "a revolutionary energy." "The Terrible Mother," she argues, "far from being an individual deviant, frequently embodies a radical indictment of her society." Mannheimer examines the "deep ambivalence" the Victorian novelists frequently had about these women, "an ambivalence that asks us to attend them more carefully" (p. 530).

8. For a judicious consideration of the impact that shifting emotional values within a culture may have on literary criticism, see Ford, *Dickens and His Readers*, pp. 55–71.

9. See Welsh, *City of Dickens*, pp. 180–95.

10. Alex Zwerdling, "Esther Summerson Rehabilitated." See also Mannheimer, "Murderous Mothers," on the way in which the "Good Mother" figure "assumes the proportions of the grotesque," p. 531; and Judith Wilt, "Confusion and Consciousness in Dickens' Esther."

11. Ellen Moers, "*Bleak House*: The Agitating Women," p. 13.

12. Mary S. Hartman, *Victorian Murderesses*, p. 125.

13. See Edgar Johnson, *Charles Dickens: His Tragedy and Triumph*, 1:1070–1114.

14. Welsh argues persuasively against the notion that the Victorians' avoidance of explicit sexual discussion can be adequately accounted for as a simple repression of erotic desires (*City of Dickens*, pp. 154–55). As he says, "passions are more often than not disguised in real life, and their extraordinary complexity, and even their universality, are often a function of the disguise" (p. 155).

15. Quoted in Hesketh Pearson, *Oscar Wilde*, p. 208. Jeffrey's response, and the similar responses of figures like Carlyle and Landor, are reported by Ford, *Dickens and His Readers*, pp. 56–57. Few people who quote Wilde's comment have remarked on the sentimentality of his own fairy tales and many of his poems (at the deaths of the nightingale and the selfish giant, for example).

16. A comment Dickens made to Forster about Sairey Gamp and Pecksniff suggests how important intuitive methods of creation were to him: "as to the way in which these characters have opened out, that is to me one of the most surprising processes of the mind in this sort of invention. Given what one knows, what one does not know springs up; and I am as absolutely certain of its being true, as I am of the law of gravitation—if such a thing be possible, more so." John Forster, *The Life of Charles Dickens*, p. 311; quoted in Marcus, *Dickens*, p. 222.

17. Welsh, *City of Dickens* pp. 180–95.

18. This is true, at least, for the novels after *Pickwick*. There part of the exuberant comedy of Sam Weller's romantic involvements is his adroit ability to fend off the addled interventions of both his actual father and his surrogate father, Pickwick.

19. George Henry Lewes, "Dickens in Relation to Criticism"; George Orwell, "Charles Dickens"; Robert Garis, *The Dickens Theatre*.

20. Orwell, "Dickens," pp. 89–90.

21. Forster, *Life of Dickens*, p. 311.

22. Marcus, *Dickens*, p. 258.

4. COLLINS

1. Considering his popularity among Victorian readers, very little criticism has been written about Collins' novels, and, so far as we know, no book-length studies of Collins' feminism. Robert Ashley has written of Collins: "He deserves particular credit for his resolute heroines, unique among Victorian fictional females both for their strong-mindedness and for their undisguised sex appeal. In his recognition of the unjust restrictions imposed on women by Victorian society, his sympathy for the fallen woman, and his audacity in creating women with minds of their own as well as strong physical charm, Collins was ahead of his time" ("Wilkie Collins Reconsidered," p. 271). Even more recently, an isolated comment like Maurice Richardson's that Collins was "a radical feminist" is a rarity; see Richardson's introduction to *The Woman in White* (Dutton ed.), p. vii.

2. For a discussion of Collins' interest in the law, see Dougald B. Maceachen, "Wilkie Collins and British Law."

3. Winifred Hughes's discussion of the conventions of the sensation novel is helpful to readers of Collins—especially her discussions of the moral ambiguity the sensation novelists substituted for the moral certainty of the melodramatic conventions they exploited; see Hughes, *The Maniac in the Cellar: Sensation*

Novels of the 1860s. Hughes also discusses the sensation novel's plot devices of victimized women and loss of identity, but she does not see these plot devices as having the far-reaching thematic significance about women's lives that we do. William Marshall and U. C. Knoepflmacher also discuss Collins' interest in human identity, but neither sees the problem as specifically related to woman's identity; see Marshall, *Wilkie Collins,* and Knoepflmacher, "The Counterworld of Victorian Fiction and *The Woman in White.*" Marshall, for instance, writes of *No Name:* "The question implied, though not pursued, is whether modern man, forced to total self-dependence—without the aid of whatever the past once bestowed upon him—can survive in both the moral and the economic realms of his being" (p. 70). We see *No Name* and *The Woman in White* as far more concerned with the specific problems of women's identity than with general problems of human identity.

4. Collins' "bad" women and his sensationalism in general may have a great deal in common with the "bad" women in the female sensationalists' novels. Although Elaine Showalter sees Collins' novels of the 1860s as "relatively conventional in terms of their social and sexual attitudes" (*A Literature of Their Own,* p. 162), we find that his "bad" heroines like Magdalen Vanstone and Lydia Gwilt ultimately attack Victorian convention in much the same way that Lady Audley does in Braddon's novel *Lady Audley's Secret.*

5. Harvey Peter Sucksmith sees the two women as reflections of "the dissociation between sexual feelings and the sexual instinct" more than as opposed kinds of personalities; see his introduction to *The Woman in White* (Oxford ed.), p. xviii.

6. In *The World* (December 26, 1877, pp. 4–6), Collins said that he received a number of letters from single men who wanted to marry the original of Marian Halcombe; reprinted in Edmund Yates, *Celebrities at Home,* 3d ser. (1879), pp. 145–56 and again reprinted in Appendix C of the Oxford edition of *The Woman in White,* p. 592.

7. Critics also are capable of reacting the way Hartright does. Julian Symons, for instance, asks whether Marian has "Lesbian tendencies"; see his introduction to *The Woman in White* (Penguin ed.), p. 15.

8. Sandra M. Gilbert and Susan Gubar suggest that the pen is a metaphorical penis and the writer in patriarchal Western culture, therefore, a male "whose pen is an instrument of generative power." *The Madwoman in the Attic,* pp. 16ff. Repeatedly in Collins' novels the written word is a source of power associated with men and male institutions like the law, but Collins' rebellious women repeatedly usurp this male power.

9. William Marshall, for instance, interprets the ending as an endorsement of Norah's feeling that identity comes from within (*Wilkie Collins,* pp. 69–70).

10. H. F. Chorley (unsigned review, *Athenaeum,* January 1863) and Mrs. Oliphant (unsigned review, *Blackwood's Magazine,* August 1863); rpt. in *Wilkie Collins: The Critical Heritage,* pp. 131, 143.

11. The link between sexual and racial oppression implicit in *Armadale* is similarly implicit in *Vanity Fair* and *The Way We Live Now*.

12. *Armadale*, according to Nuel Pharr Davis, *The Life of Wilkie Collins*, pp. 243–46, was unpopular with Victorian readers and reviewers in England but very successful in America. T. S. Eliot commended it for its melodrama in a 1927 essay, "Wilkie Collins and Dickens," *Selected Essays*, pp. 300–1. But modern critics have devoted very little attention to it—probably because of its highly complicated plot.

13. Unsigned review (*Spectator*, June 1866) and H. F. Chorley (unsigned review, *Athenaeum*, June 1866), rpt. in *Wilkie Collins: The Critical Heritage*, pp. 150, 147–48.

14. S. M. Ellis, *Wilkie Collins, Le Fanu, and Others*, p. 37. For further details, see Elizabeth Jenkins, *Six Criminal Women*, or William Roughead, *Bad Companions*.

15. For Freudian interpretations of *The Moonstone*, see Lewis A. Lawson, "Wilkie Collins and *The Moonstone*," or Charles Rycroft, *Imagination and Reality*, chapter 9. For a more modern psychoanalytic treatment, see Albert D. Hutter, "Dreams, Transformations, and Literature: The Implications of Detective Fiction."

16. For discussions of the importance and difficulty of interpreting texts within Collins' novels, see Albert Hutter, "Dreams, Transformations, and Literature"; Walter M. Kendrick, "The Sensationalism of *The Woman in White*"; and D. A. Miller, "From *roman policier* to *roman-police*: Wilkie Collins's *The Moonstone*."

17. The reversal of position in which Valeria becomes dominant over Eustace is underscored by the following comments of Dougald Maceachen: "[The] chief weakness [of *The Law and the Lady*] as a novel of 'purpose' was that it failed to make Eustace Macallan, the pivotal character, a person worthy of the reader's sympathy. Eustace is too passive, weak, and selfish to be worthy of Valeria's efforts in his behalf. . . . As usual, Collins paid so much attention to his plot . . . that he failed to see the damage his plot was doing to his most important character. The reader could hardly be expected to see any great injustice in the verdict of 'Not Proven' when it was associated with the kind of person Eustace Macallan is" ("Collins and British Law," pp. 137–38). We, on the other hand, assume that Collins did know what he was doing, that he intended to show Valeria as stronger than her husband, and that we are supposed to see Eustace as partly guilty of his wife's death.

5. THACKERAY

1. Winslow Rogers, "William Makepeace Thackeray," p. 154; idem., "Thackeray's Self-consciousness," p. 153.

2. A. E. Dyson, "*Vanity Fair*: An Irony Against Heroes," in *The Crazy Fabric: Essays in Irony*, p. 73, reprinted in *Vanity Fair: A Collection of Critical Essays*, ed.

M. G. Sundell, p. 77; Mark Spilka, "A Note on Thackeray's Amelia," p. 207; Thackeray's comment was made in a letter to Robert Bell, quoted by Dyson, *The Crazy Fabric*, p. 79; Walter Pater, *Appreciations*, vol. 5 of *Works of Walter Pater*, pp. 17–18.

3. The phrase is Dyson's, "*Vanity Fair*" p. 81; Arnold Kettle, *An Introduction to the English Novel*, pp. 156–70; Kathleen Tillotson, *Novels of the Eighteen-Forties*, pp. 234–56. Dyson's, Kettle's, and Tillotson's essays are collected in *Vanity Fair: A Collection of Critical Essays*. Subsequent page references to these essays will be to this collection.

4. Although Gordon Ray considers the later fiction of Thackeray more mature, he provides a clue to the marked difference between *Vanity Fair* and the later fiction in his discussion of the "genial influence of success" that followed the publication of *Vanity Fair*. See Ray, *Thackeray: The Age of Wisdom*, pp. 92–130.

Our discussion of the later fiction will concentrate on *Pendennis* and *Henry Esmond*. *The Newcomes* reveals definite but weaker and more diffuse elements of the various erotic motifs present in *Pendennis* and *Esmond*. The incest motif is present in the consanguineous relation between Ethel and Clive Newcome. (Her father is his father's half-brother.) The novel also presents the attachment between son and mother in a very disguised form: the intense "maternal" love and care that Colonel Newcome lavishes on Clive. Similarly, Clive's unsuitable marriage to Rosie MacKenzie is a much weaker, more psychologically and thematically muddled version of Warrington's marriage in *Pendennis*. There is little of the intensity that distinguishes the erotic material of *Esmond* and *Pendennis* and little of their psychological complexity. There is, as a result, a corresponding lessening of the evasive impulses that agitate the narrators of the other two novels. For these reasons, we have chosen to focus on *Pendennis* and *Esmond* as the strongest, clearest, and most intriguing examples of the qualities we find in the late novels.

5. Barbara Hardy comments on this neglect of subject matter in *The Exposure of Luxury: Radical Themes in Thackeray*, p. 13.

6. See, for example, G. Armour Craig, "On the Style of *Vanity Fair*," and Dyson, "*Vanity Fair*."

7. This is, of course, a major point of John Stuart Mill's argument in his essay, "On the Subjection of Women."

8. Several critics who find *Esmond* a thoroughly successful novel have nevertheless noted how much the narrator disguises Henry's own responsibility for Beatrix's rejection of him. In an especially sensitive study, Juliet McMaster calls this quality "the subtle masochism which Henry displays in his emotional life." *Thackeray: The Major Novels*, p. 119.

9. The references to both Rachel and Beatrix as goddesses, especially as goddesses who appear in the *Aeneid*, are discussed extensively by John Loofborouw, *Thackeray and the Form of Fiction*, pp. 118–66.

10. J. E. Tilford, "The Unsavoury Plot of *Henry Esmond.*"

11. *Esmond* certainly is, when all the implications of its psychological material are considered, a novel of considerable subtlety and accuracy in its presentation of the sort of sexual conflicts we have been discussing. Our main argument, therefore, with a number of recent critics who praise the novel's effects is that the complexity and subtlety are less a result of Thackeray's controlled efforts to explore his material than a result of efforts—in many ways contradictory—to evade the implications of his material. For an excellent discussion of *Esmond's* psychological and thematic complexity, see McMaster, *Thackeray*, pp. 87–125.

12. Loofborouw's discussion of the importance of memory in *Esmond* is especially interesting (*Thackeray*, pp. 205–14). But his treatment of this theme and method in Thackeray seems to us to suffer, like so many others, from a focus on form to the neglect of subject matter. The treasuring of memory in *Esmond*— and in Thackeray's later fiction generally—often draws back so far from the question of the quality and purport of *what* is being remembered, draws back from any experience but the mind's own sense of itself remembering, that it is not even nostalgic. In this context, a passage from *Esmond* is quite revealing: "We forget nothing. The memory sleeps, but wakens again; I often think how it shall be, when, after the last sleep of death, the *réveillée* shall arouse us for ever, and the past in one flash of self-consciousness rush back, like the soul, revivified" (III, vii, 435).

13. Beatrix can be usefully compared with Dickens' Estella (in *Great Expectations*). Both characters are based on the general stereotype of the heartless coquette, but Dickens shows the origins and the quality of his character's psychological life, whereas Thackeray presents Beatrix, essentially, as a simple stereotype, without suggesting how she came to be what she is or what her inner life is like.

14. See note 8 above.

15. In *The Newcomes*, a paternalistic Pendennis has the luxury of acting as father not only to Clive Newcome but to Clive's father, Colonel Newcome (an innocent who resembles some of Dickens' childlike fathers).

16. James's phrase appears in his well-known review of *Our Mutual Friend*, available in James, *Selected Literary Criticism*.

17. Dyson, "*Vanity Fair*," p. 81; Craig, "Style of *Vanity Fair*," p. 66.

18. Dyson, "*Vanity Fair*," p. 81.

19. Loofborouw discusses (and graphs) this dominance of the plot by the two heroines; *Thackeray*, pp. 80–84.

20. For a very interesting application of Lévi-Strauss' theories about the exchange of women to the nineteenth-century novel, see Tony Tanner, *Adultery in the Novel*, pp. 79–87.

21. Quoted by J. W. Dodds, *Thackeray: A Critical Portrait*, p. 130. Tillotson quotes Dodds (*Novels of the Eighteen-Forties*, p. 47), and adds that Thackeray's mother made similar comments.

22. As a number of critics have noted, Becky's satiric evaluations of the people about her frequently agree with the narrator's own evaluations. She becomes a direct satiric persona in her letters to Amelia.

23. Arnold Kettle, *English Novel*, p. 20.

24. Winslow Rogers, "Thackeray's Self-Consciousness," p. 151.

6. TROLLOPE

1. Quoted in *The Letters of Anthony Trollope*, no. 45.

2. Pamela Hansford Johnson, "Trollope's Young Women," p. 33. Trollope's Victorian readers and critics frequently found his portraits of women among his greatest achievements, but they praise the conventionality of his heroines and ignore or dismiss their dissatisfactions. See, for instance, an 1863 review calling Trollope "a novelist whose strength lies in imagining and representing how young women feel and behave when something a little out of the way happens to them," in Donald Smalley, ed., *Trollope: The Critical Heritage*, p. 184. Another reviewer praised the depiction of Lady Carbury but found her more sensible to marry Mr. Broune than to attempt to write novels; see Smalley, pp. 407–8. Henry James praised Trollope's girls for being definite, natural, healthy, tender, and passively sweet (in *Partial Portraits*, 1888); see Smalley, pp. 542–43.

3. Margaret Hewitt, "Anthony Trollope: Historian and Sociologist," p. 226. Until recently, Trollope criticism accepted Trollope's professed antifeminism at face value: Charles Blinderman's "The Servility of Dependence: The Dark Lady in Trollope" and David Aitken's "Anthony Trollope on 'The Genus Girl'" are examples of this perspective, as is a more recent work, John Halperin's *Trollope and Politics: A Study of the Pallisers and Others*.

Some of the recent critics who resist taking Trollope's women at face value are: Robert M. Polhemus, *The Changing World of Anthony Trollope*; Ruth ap Roberts, *Trollope: Artist and Moralist*; James R. Kincaid, *The Novels of Anthony Trollope*; and Juliet McMaster, *Trollope's Palliser Novels: Theme and Pattern*. The unpublished 1976 dissertation by Nana M. Rinehart examines the Trollope novels of the 1860s and 70s in the light of the debate over women in the major periodicals of the day. J. A. Banks, "The Way We Lived Then: Anthony Trollope and the 1870's" considers Trollope's novels as reflections of the changing social position of women. Judith Weissman, "'Old Maids have Friends': The Unmarried Heroine of Trollope's Barsetshire Novels" finds Trollope speaking rather openly about the unfairness of sexual roles.

4. The narrator in Trollope has received a good deal of critical attention recently. Some critics, like Ruth ap Roberts (*Trollope*), see the narrator as a means of distancing us from the action, but others, like Robert Polhemus (*Changing World*), see the narrator as functioning to involve the reader in the action. Others still, like James Kincaid (*Novels of Trollope*), argue for a multi-functioned narrator who often serves to provide ironic commentary on the action.

5. J. Hillis Miller, *The Form of Victorian Fiction*.

6. Jerome Thale, "The Problem of Structure in Trollope," p. 156. Recent criticism has increasingly recognized Trollope's right to be considered a conscious and gifted artist, rather than the unconscious and prosaic storyteller for whom Trollope lovers in the past have often felt they had to apologize. Recent explorations of Trollope's subtle use of analogical structure still, however, do not often consider the feminist implications of Trollope's analogies. Some critics who examine the analogical structures are: Kincaid, *Novels of Trollope*; Robert Tracy, *Trollope's Later Novels*; Peter K. Garrett, *The Victorian Multiplot Novel: Studies in Dialogical Form*; or Geoffrey Harvey, *The Art of Anthony Trollope*. Juliet McMaster comes closest to our view that Trollope's presentation of women often depends upon his analogical structures; see her studies of "perverse" women—Lily Dale, Alice Vavasor, Emily Lopez, and Mabel Grex—in *Trollope's Palliser Novels*. In addition to McMaster, there are a few other studies of the way particular analogical structures have special implications for female characters: Ruth ap Roberts, "Emily and Nora and Dorothy and Priscilla and Jemima and Carry" and Jean E. Kennard, *Victims of Convention*, on the implications of the "two suitors" plot.

7. Kincaid, *Novels of Trollope*, p. 241.

8. Rebecca West, *The Court and the Castle*, p. 167.

9. Lee Holcombe, *Victorian Ladies at Work*, pp. 3–4.

10. Kincaid, *Novels of Trollope*, p. 4.

11. For discussion of the Palliser novels, see Arthur Mizener, "Anthony Trollope: The Palliser Novels"; Polhemus, *Changing World*; Kincaid, *Novels of Trollope*; and McMaster, *Palliser Novels* (see especially her chapters on "The Politics of Love," pp. 38–59, and on the *Prime Minister*).

12. J. Hillis Miller, "Self and Community," p. 129.

13. R. C. Terry, *Anthony Trollope: The Artist in Hiding*, p. 161.

14. Miss Todd was probably modeled on the feminist journalist Frances Power Cobbe.

15. After Trollope killed Mrs. Proudie in *The Last Chronicle*, one of his reviewers commented on the way that women who are denied status and authority in society may exercise their power indirectly—and unpleasantly, but the reviewer draws the conventional conclusion that such women should be more tactful and pleasant—rather than that they should be allowed more status: "We deny women the direct exercise of their capacities, and the immediate gratification of an overt ambition. The natural result is that they run to artifice, and that a good-natured husband is . . . the wretched buffer through which the impetuous forces of his wife impinge upon his neighbours. . . . As a rule, however, it is pleasant to think that with ambition in women, which is not their peculiarity, is yoked tact, which is their peculiarity emphatically." See "Ambitious Wives," *Saturday Review* (July 6, 1867), in Smalley, *Critical Heritage*, pp. 287–88. McMaster sees, as we do, that Trollope's portraits of women become

increasingly more feminist—as in the progression from Mrs. Proudie to Glencora, or from the modest, obedient Barchester heroines to the more passionate and rebellious heroines of the Palliser series (see *Palliser Novels*, chap. 8).

16. For discussions of Glencora's and Alice's options, see: David S. Chamberlain, "Unity and Irony in Trollope's *Can You Forgive Her?*"; John Christopher Kleis, "Passion vs. Prudence: Theme and Technique in Trollope's Palliser Novels"; Juliet McMaster, "'The Meaning of Words and the Nature of Things': Trollope's *Can You Forgive Her?*"; George Levine, "*Can You Forgive Her?* and The Myth of Realism"; and Kincaid, *Novels of Trollope*, chapter 6.

17. Anthony Trollope, *An Autobiography* (Shakespeare Head Press ed.), p. 130. Future citations to the *Autobiography* will appear in parentheses in the text.

18. Polhemus, *Changing World*, pp. 103–4.

19. Ramona Denton argues that Laura, after having bad luck with her marriage, makes her unhappiness coherent to herself by interpreting her failure as the consequence of having ignored the "feminine" need for love; see "'That Cage' of Femininity: Trollope's Lady Laura."

20. McMaster finds many of Trollope's women of the Palliser series "sensual, and deeply moved by the physical attributes of their men," *Palliser Novels*, p. 172.

21. Kincaid, *Novels of Trollope*, p. 135.

22. Ruth ap Roberts discusses Trollope's interest in undogmatic approaches to complex ethical situations (though not in relation to a sexual dialectic) in *Trollope: Artist and Moralist*. See also Joseph Wiesenfarth, "Dialectics in *Barchester Towers*."

23. Tony Bareham argues that in *The Three Clerks* Trollope did use "symbols and motifs to give depth of meaning to the narrative flow" in the Dickensian manner; see "Patterns of Excellence: Theme and Structure in *The Three Clerks*," p. 58.

7. TOWARD BETTER RELATIONS

1. Annette Kolodny, "Turning the Lens on 'The Panther Captivity,'" p. 329.

2. Myra Jehlen, "Archimedes and the Paradox of Feminist Criticism," p. 579.

3. George Levine in *The Realistic Imagination* considers Thackeray and Trollope within the realist tradition and generally finds them more conservative than we do. But he offers a sophisticated demonstration of the experimental, questioning nature of realistic fiction: "As we explore even the most conservative of the classic novels of the nineteenth century, we find continuing experiments with forms, styles, modes of valuing. . . . The realistic novel persistently drives itself to question not only the nature of artificially imposed social relations, but the nature of nature, and the nature of the novel" (p. 21).

4. For a discussion of the "wild zone" or "female space" that lies outside the traditional boundaries of literary and cultural criticism, see Elaine Showalter, "Feminist Criticism in the Wilderness."

5. Elizabeth Abel, "Editor's Introduction," p. 174.

6. Showalter, "Feminist Criticism," p. 201.

7. Jehlen, "Paradox of Feminist Criticism," p. 585. "Radical comparativism" is Jehlen's term.

8. Nancy Miller, "Emphasis Added," p. 38.

9. Jehlen, "Paradox of Feminist Criticism," p. 586.

10. Showalter, "Feminist Criticism," generally deplores the derivation of feminist theories from the masculine-dominated contemporary schools of criticism. See pp. 184–85, for example.

11. Ibid., p. 181.

12. Geoffrey Hartman, Criticism in the Wilderness, pp. 1–2.

13. George Eliot, "The Natural History of German Life," p. 37.

14. Jehlen, "Paradox of Feminist Criticism, p. 586.

15. J. S. Mill, "On the Subjection of Women," p. 367.

16. Florence Nightingale, Cassandra, pp. 25–26.

17. Charlotte Brontë, Shirley (Penguin ed., 1974), p. 343. Subsequent page references appear in the text.

18. This formulation oversimplifies the situation of female characters who seek an alternative way of life in Victorian novels by women. Nina Auerbach in Communities of Women has shown how these communities can have substantial, subversive power. Yet these alternatives (in Villette, for instance) seem partial, limited, and disguised within overt support for the masculine system.

19. Sandra Gilbert and Susan Gubar see Rochester's injuries and his reunion with Jane as a more positive and egalitarian resolution to their relationship than we do (Madwoman in the Attic, pp. 368–69). We certainly agree, however, with their dismissal of the persistent critical idea that his injuries are a symbolic castration as punishment for his youthful sexual excesses and a sign that Charlotte Brontë and Jane Eyre fear male sexual power (p. 368).

20. Terry Eagleton, Myths of Power.

21. See Nina Auerbach, "Dickens and Dombey," for a discussion of how an apparently similar pattern of punishment and redemption enacts a quite different ritual: "Dombey himself seems less to succumb to Florence than to become her; by the end of the novel, he is, literally, 'a daughter after all.' . . . The last chapter finds Dombey as faded as Miss Tox and as enfeebled as the dying Paul, weeping on his granddaughter at the seashore" (pp. 112–13).

22. George Eliot, Middlemarch, ed. Bert G. Hornback (New York: Norton, 1977), p. 576.

23. Jehlen, "Paradox of Feminist Criticism," p. 596. Interestingly, it is most often the female characters created by the four male novelists who come closest to being "androgynously heroic," Madame Max, Glencora, Magdalen Vanstone, and Becky Sharp, for example. Shirley's masquerade as Captain Keeldar, in contrast, flaunts trivial attributes of masculinity while steadily giving up the substantial power, traditionally masculine, that she could have. In another in-

stance Lucy Snow's apparent habitation of both spheres seems undermined by her misery and her violent suppression of her ego.

24. Jehlen, "Paradox of Feminist Criticism," p. 596.

25. They thus create qualities in their fiction that Judith Gardiner associates with female identity: "female identity [is] typically less fixed, less unitary, and more flexible than male individuality." And they depart from the characteristics that she associates with male identity: "stability and constancy" and "progress toward the achievement of a desired product." "On Female Identity," pp. 353, 352.

26. Showalter, "Feminist Criticism." p. 205.

SELECTED BIBLIOGRAPHY

BECAUSE of the multitude of books and articles on Dickens, Thackeray, Trollope, and Collins, and on feminist theory and criticism that are relevant to our study, we have listed only those works actually cited in our text. For more comprehensive bibliographies, see: *Victorian Fiction: A Guide to Research*, ed. Lionel Stevenson (Cambridge: Harvard University Press, 1964); *Victorian Fiction: A Second Guide to Research*, ed. George H. Ford (Cambridge: Harvard University Press, 1978); and the annual bibliographies in *Victorian Studies* and *PMLA*. Bibliographical entries in *Victorian Studies* have been collected in *Bibliographies of Studies in Victorian Literature for the Ten Years 1965–74*, ed. Ronald E. Freeman (New York: AMS Press, 1981) and in earlier volumes for 1932–44, 1945–54, and 1955–64.

For the individual authors see: Kirk H. Beetz, *Wilkie Collins: An Annotated Bibliography, 1889–1976*, Scarecrow Author Bibliographies, no. 35 (Metuchen, N.J.: Scarecrow Press, 1978); Jeffrey Egan Welch, *The Reputation of Trollope: An Annotated Bibliography, 1925–1975* (New York: Garland, 1978); and Joseph Gold, *The Stature of Dickens: A Centenary Bibliography* (Toronto: University of Manitoba Press, 1971).

Abel, Elizabeth. "Editor's Introduction." *Critical Inquiry* (1981) 8:173–79.

Aitkin, David. "Anthony Trollope on 'The Genus Girl.'" *Nineteenth Century Fiction* (1974) 28:417–34.

ap Roberts, Ruth, "Emily and Nora and Dorothy and Priscilla and Jemima and Carry." In *The Victorian Experience: The Novelists*, ed. Richard A. Levine. Athens: Ohio University Press, 1976.

—— *Trollope: Artist and Moralist*. London: Chatto and Windus, 1971.

Ashley, Robert. "Wilkie Collins Reconsidered." *Nineteenth Century Fiction* (1949–50) 4:265–73.

Auerbach, Nina. *Communities of Women: An Idea in Fiction*. Cambridge: Harvard University Press, 1978.

—— "Dickens and Dombey: A Daughter After All." *Dickens Studies Annual*, vol. 5, ed. Robert B. Partlow, Jr. Carbondale: Southern Illinois University Press, 1976.

—— "Women on Women's Destiny: Maturity as Penance." *The Massachusetts Review* (1979) 20:326–34.

Banks, J. A. "The Way We Lived Then: Anthony Trollope and the 1870's." *Victorian Studies* (1968–69) 12:177–200.

Bareham, Tony. "Patterns of Excellence: Theme and Structure in *The Three Clerks.*" In *Anthony Trollope*, ed. Tony Bareham. London: Vision Press, 1980.

Basch, Françoise. *Relative Creatures.* New York: Schocken, 1974.

Beauvoir, Simone de. *The Second Sex*, trans. and ed. H. M. Parshley. New York: Knopf, 1953.

Blinderman, Charles. "The Servility of Dependence: The Dark Lady in Trollope." In *Images of Women in Fiction: Feminist Perspectives*, ed. Susan Koppelman Cornillon, pp. 55–67. Bowling Green, Ohio: Bowling Green University Popular Press, 1972.

Booth, Wayne G. *The Rhetoric of Fiction.* Chicago: University of Chicago Press, 1961.

Branca, Patricia. *Silent Sisterhood: Middle-Class Women in the Victorian Home.* London: Croom Helm, 1975.

Bridenthal, Renate and Claudia Koonz, eds. *Becoming Visible: Women in European History.* Boston: Houghton Mifflin, 1973.

Carroll, Berenice A., ed. *Liberating Women's History.* Urbana: University of Illinois Press, 1976.

Chamberlain, David S. "Unity and Irony in Trollope's *Can You Forgive Her?*" *Studies in English Literature* (1969) 8:669–80.

[Chorley, H. F.] Unsigned Review of Wilkie Collins' *No Name. Atheneum*, January 1863. Rpt. in *Wilkie Collins: The Critical Heritage*, ed. Norman Page, p. 131. London and Boston: Routledge and Kegan Paul, 1974.

Cobbe, Frances Power. "The Final Cause of Women." In *Women's Work and Women's Culture*, ed. Josephine Butler. London, 1869.

Craig, G. Armour. "On the Style of *Vanity Fair.*" In *Style in Prose Fiction: English Institute Essays*, ed. Harold C. Martin, pp. 87–113. New York: Columbia University Press, 1958.

Craik, Mrs. [Dinah Maria Mulock]. *Women's Rights and Duties.* London, 1840.

Davis, Nuel Pharr. *The Life of Wilkie Collins.* Urbana: University of Illinois Press, 1956.

Denton, Ramona. "'That Cage' of Femininity: Trollope's Lady Laura." *South Atlantic Bulletin* (1980) 45:1–10.

Dodds, J. W. *Thackeray: A Critical Portrait.* London: Oxford University Press, 1941.

Douglas, Ann. *The Feminization of American Culture.* New York: Knopf, 1977.

Dyson, A. E. *The Crazy Fabric: Essays in Irony.* London: Macmillan, 1965.

Eagleton, Terry. *Myths of Power: A Marxist Study of the Brontës.* New York: Barnes and Noble, 1975.

Eliot, George. "The Natural History of German Life." *The Westminister Review* (July 1856) 66:28–44.

Eliot, T. S. "Wilkie Collins and Dickens." In *Selected Essays 1917–1932.* New York: Harcourt Brace, 1932.

Ellis, S. M. *Wilkie Collins, Le Fanu, and Others*. London: Constable, 1951.

Englishwoman's Review of Social and Industrial Questions, 1877.

Fetterly, Joan. *The Resisting Reader: A Feminist Approach to American Fiction*. Bloomington: Indiana University Press, 1978.

Ford, George H. *Dickens and His Readers*. Princeton: Princeton University Press, 1955.

Forster, John. *The Life of Charles Dickens*, ed. J. W. T. Ley. London: C. Palmer, 1928.

Gardiner, Judith Kegan. "On Female Identity and Writing by Women." *Critical Inquiry* (1981) 8:347–60.

Garis, Robert. *The Dickens Theatre*. Oxford: Clarendon Press, 1965.

Garrett, Peter K. *The Victorian Multiplot Novel: Studies in Dialogical Form*. New Haven: Yale University Press, 1980.

Gilbert, Sandra M. and Susan Gubar. *The Madwoman in the Attic: The Woman Writer and the Nineteenth-Century Imagination*. New Haven: Yale University Press, 1979.

Halperin, John. *Trollope and Politics: A Study of the Pallisers and Others*. New York: Barnes and Noble, 1977.

Hardy, Barbara. *The Exposure of Luxury: Radical Themes in Thackeray*. London: Peter Owen, 1972.

Hartman, Geoffrey H. *Criticism in the Wilderness: The Study of Literature Today*. New Haven: Yale University Press, 1980.

Hartman, Mary S. *Victorian Murderesses*. New York: Schocken, 1977.

Hartman, Mary S. and Lois Banner. *Clio's Consciousness Raised*. New York: Harper and Row, 1974.

Harvey, Geoffrey. *The Art of Anthony Trollope*. London: Weidenfeld and Nicolson, 1980.

Heilbrun, Carolyn. *Reinventing Womanhood*. New York: Norton, 1979.

—— *Toward a Recognition of Androgyny*. New York: Knopf, 1973.

Hewitt, Margaret. "Anthony Trollope: Historian and Sociologist." *British Journal of Sociology* (1963) 14:226–39.

Holcombe, Lee. *Victorian Ladies at Work*. Hamden, Conn.: Archon, 1973.

Houghton, Walter. *The Victorian Frame of Mind*. New Haven: Yale University Press, 1957.

Hughes, Winifred. *The Maniac in the Cellar: Sensation Novels of the 1860s*. Princeton: Princeton University Press, 1980.

Hutter, Albert D. "Dreams, Transformations, and Literature: The Implications of Detective Fiction." *Victorian Studies* (1975–76) 19:181–209.

Iser, Wolfgang. *The Implied Reader: Patterns of Communication in Prose Fiction from Bunyan to Beckett*. Baltimore: Johns Hopkins University Press, 1974.

Jacobus, Mary. "The Question of Language: Men of Maxims and *The Mill on the Floss*." *Critical Inquiry* (1981) 8:207–22.

James, Henry. "*Our Mutual Friend*." In *Selected Literary Criticism*, ed. Morris Shapira. New York: Horizon, 1964.

Jehlen, Myra. "Archimedes and the Paradox of Feminist Criticism." *Signs* (1981) 6:575–601.

Jenkins, Elizabeth. *Six Criminal Women*. London: Samson Low, 1949.

Johnson, Edgar. *Charles Dickens: His Tragedy and Triumph*. 2 vols. New York: Simon and Schuster, 1952.

Johnson, Pamela Hansford. "Trollope's Young Women." In *On the Novel*, ed. B. S. Benedikz. London: Dent, 1971.

Kamm, Josephine. *Rapiers and Battleaxes*. London: Allen and Unwin, 1966.

Kendrick, Walter M. "The Sensationalism of *The Woman in the White*." *Nineteenth-Century Fiction* (1977–78) 32:18–35.

Kennard, Jean E. *Victims of Convention*. Hamden, Conn.: Archon, 1978.

Kettle, Arnold. *An Introduction to the English Novel*. London: Hutchinson, 1951.

Kincaid, James R. *The Novels of Anthony Trollope*. Oxford: Clarendon Press, 1977.

Kleiss, John Christopher. "Passion vs. Prudence: Theme and Technique in Trollope's Palliser Novels." *Texas Studies in Language and Literature* (1970) 11:1405–14.

Kolodny, Annette. "Turning the Lens on 'The Panther Captivity': A Feminist Exercise in Practical Criticism." *Critical Inquiry* (1981) 8:329–45.

Knoepflmacher, U. C. "The Counterworld of Victorian Fiction and *The Woman in White*." In *The Worlds of Victorian Fiction*, ed. Jerome H. Buckley. Harvard English Studies, vol. 6. Cambridge, Mass.: Harvard University Press, 1975.

Lamb, Ann. *Can Women Regenerate Society?* London, 1844.

Lawson, Lewis A. "Wilkie Collins and *The Moonstone*." *The American Imago* (1963) 20:61–79.

Levine, George. "*Can You Forgive Her?* and the Myth of Realism." *Victorian Studies* (1974–75) 18:5–30.

—— *The Realistic Imagination: English Fiction from Frankenstein to Lady Chatterly*. Chicago: University of Chicago Press, 1981.

Lewes, George Henry. "Dickens in Relation to Criticism." *Fortnightly Review* (1872) 17.

Lewis, Sarah. *Woman's Mission*. London, 1839.

Loofborouw, John. *Thackeray and the Form of Fiction*. Princeton: Princeton University Press, 1964.

Maceachen, Dougald B. "Wilkie Collins and British Law." *Nineteenth Century Fiction* (1950–51) 5:121–39.

McMaster, Juliet. "'The Meaning of Words and the Nature of Things': Trollope's *Can You Forgive Her?*" *Studies in English Literature* (1974) 14:603–18.

—— *Thackeray: The Major Novels*. Toronto: University of Toronto Press, 1971.

—— *Trollope's Palliser Novels: Theme and Pattern*. New York: Oxford University Press, 1978.

Mannheimer, Joan. "Murderous Mothers: The Problems of Parenting in the Victorian Novel." *Feminist Studies* (1979) 5:530–45.

Marcus, Steven. *Dickens: From Pickwick to Dombey*. London: Chatto and Windus, 1965.

Marshall, William. *Wilkie Collins*. New York: Twayne, 1970.

Mill, John Stuart. "On the Subjection of Women." In *A Selection of His Works*, ed. John M. Robson, New York: Odyssey Press, 1966.

Miller, D. A. "From *roman policier* to *roman-police*: Wilkie Collins's *The Moonstone*." *Novel* (1980) 13:153–70.

Miller, J. Hillis. *The Form of Victorian Fiction*. Notre Dame: University of Notre Dame Press, 1968.

—— "Self and Community." In *The Trollope Critics*, ed. N. John Hall. Totowa, N.J.: Barnes and Noble, 1981.

Miller, Nancy K. "Emphasis Added: Plots and Plausibilities in Women's Fiction." *PMLA* (January 1981) 96:36–48.

Mizener, Arthur. "Anthony Trollope: The Palliser Novels." In *From Jane Austen to Joseph Conrad*, ed. Robert C. Rathburn and Martin Steinmann. Minneapolis: University of Minnesota Press, 1958.

Moers, Ellen. "*Bleak House*: The Agitating Women." *The Dickensian* (January 1972), no. 369, pp. 13–24.

—— *Literary Women*. New York: Doubleday, 1976.

Nightingale, Florence. *Cassandra*, ed. Myra Stark. Old Westbury, N.Y.: Feminist Press, 1979.

[Oliphant, (Margaret) Mrs.] Unsigned Review of Wilkie Collins' *No Name*. *Blackwood's Magazine*, August 1863. Rpt. in *Wilkie Collins: The Critical Heritage*, ed. Norman Page, p. 143. London and Boston: Routledge and Kegan Paul, 1974.

Orwell, George. "Charles Dickens." In *Critical Essays*. London: Secker and Warburg, 1946.

Pater, Walter. *Works of Walter Pater*. 8 vols. London and New York: Macmillan, 1900–1.

Pearson, Hesketh. *Oscar Wilde*. New York: Harper, 1946.

Polhemus, Robert. *The Changing World of Anthony Trollope*. Berkeley and Los Angeles: University of California Press, 1968.

Ray, Gordon. *Thackeray: The Age of Wisdom*. New York: McGraw-Hill, 1958.

Reid, Mrs. Hugo. [Marian Kirkland] *A Plea For Women*. London, 1843.

Rich, Adrienne. "An Interview with Adrienne Rich," by David Kalstone. *The Saturday Review*, April 22, 1972, p. 59.

Richardson, Maurice. Introduction to *The Woman in White*, by Wilkie Collins. New York: Dutton, 1972.

Roberts, Helene E. "The Exquisite Slave: The Role of Clothes in the Making of the Victorian Woman." *Signs* (1977) 2:554–69.

Rogers, Katherine M. *The Troublesome Helpmate: A History of Misogyny in Literature*. Seattle: University of Washington Press, 1966.

Rogers, Winslow. "Thackeray's Self-Consciousness." In *The Worlds of Victorian*

Fiction, ed. Jerome H. Buckley. Harvard English Studies, vol. 6. Cambridge: Harvard University Press, 1975, pp. 149–63.

—— "William Makepeace Thackeray." In *Victorian Fiction: A Guide to Research*, ed. Lionel Stevenson. Cambridge: Harvard University Press, 1964.

Roughead, William. *Bad Companions*. Edinburgh: W. Green and Son, 1930.

Ruskin, John. *The Works of John Ruskin*. 39 vols. Edited by E. T. Cook and Alexander Wedderburn. London: G. Allen, 1903–12.

Rycroft, Charles. *Imagination and Reality*. New York: International Universities Press, 1968.

Showalter, Elaine. "Feminist Criticism in the Wilderness." *Critical Inquiry* (1981) 8:179–205.

—— *A Literature of Their Own*. Princeton: Princeton University Press, 1977.

Smalley, Donald, ed. *Trollope: The Critical Heritage*. New York: Barnes and Noble, 1969.

Spilka, Mark. "A Note on Thackeray's Amelia." *Nineteenth Century Fiction* 10:202–10.

Strachey, Rachel. *The Cause: A Short History of the Women's Movement in Great Britain*. London: Virago Press, 1978.

Sucksmith, Harvey Peter. Introduction to *The Woman in White*, by Wilkie Collins. London and New York: Oxford University Press, 1975.

Symons, Julian. Introduction to *The Woman in White*, by Wilkie Collins. New York: Penguin, 1974.

Tanner, Tony. *Adultery in the Novel: Contract and Transgression*. Baltimore: Johns Hopkins Press, 1979.

Terry, R. C. *Anthony Trollope: The Artist in Hiding*. Totowa, N.J.: Rowman and Littlefield, 1981.

Thale, Jerome. "The Problem of Structure in Trollope." *Nineteenth Century Fiction* (1960) 15:147–79.

Tilford, J. E. "The Unsavoury Plot of *Henry Esmond*." *Nineteenth Century Fiction* (1951) 6:121–30.

Tillotson, Kathleen. *Novels of the Eighteen-Forties*. Oxford: Clarendon Press, 1954.

Tracy, Robert. *Trollope's Later Novels*. Berkeley: University of California Press, 1978.

Trollope, Anthony. *An Autobiography*. Oxford: Shakespeare Head Press, 1929.

—— *The Letters of Anthony Trollope*, ed. Bradford Booth. London: Oxford University press, 1951.

Vicinus, Martha, ed. *Suffer and Be Still*. Bloomington: Indiana University Press, 1972.

—— *A Widening Sphere: Changing Roles of Victorian Women*. Bloomington: Indiana University Press, 1977.

Watson, Barbara Bellows. "On Power and the Literary Text." *Signs* (1975) 1:111–14.

Wiesenfarth, Joseph. "Dialectics in *Barcester Towers.*" In *Anthony Trollope*, ed. Tony Bareham. London: Vision Press, 1980.

Weissman, Judith. "'Old Maids Have Friends': The Unmarried Heroine of Trollope's Barsetshire Novels." *Women and Literature* (1977) 5:15–25.

Welsh, Alexander. *The City of Dickens.* London: Oxford University Press, 1971.

West, Rebecca. *The Court and the Castle.* New Haven: Yale University Press, 1957.

Westwater, Sister A. Martha. "Surrender to Subservience: An Introduction to the Diaries and Journals of Eliza Wilson Bagehot." *International Journal of Women's Studies* (1978) 1:517–29.

Williams, Raymond. *The English Novel from Dickens to Lawrence.* London: Chatto and Windus, 1970.

Wilson. Angus. *The World of Charles Dickens.* New York: Viking, 1970.

Wilt, Judith. "Confusion and Consciousness in Dickens' Esther." *Nineteenth Century Fiction* (1977) 32:285–309.

Yates, Edmund. *Celebrities at Home*, 3d ser. 1879.

Zwerdling, Alex. "Esther Summerson Rehabilitated." *PMLA* (1973) 88:429–38.

INDEX

Tchelitchew, Pavel (*Continued*)
(painting), compared with Trollope,
203–4
Terry, R. C., 208
Thackeray, William: marriage in, 5, 7;
and sexual system as source of social
disorder, 7–8; plots of fraud and crime
in, 25–28; ambivalent narrator in,
34–37, 44–45, 168, 191–93; symbolic
analogies in, 49–50; sterotypes in, 58;
contradictory critical views of, 152–53,
175–76; narrators of in *Vanity Fair* and
later novels, 154–57; erratic narrative
values of *Esmond* and *Pendennis*, 164–70;
exposure of sexual corruption in *Vanity
Fair*, 170–93; male characters in,
178–81
—Works: *Henry Esmond*, 153–54, 159–72:
The Newcomes, 153, 165–66; *Pendennis*,
153, 155–56; 162–66, 169–72; *Vanity
Fair*, 19–22, 28–29, 34–37, 45–46,
49–50, 153–58, 164–93
Thorne, Mary (*Dr. Thorne*), 200, 205
Trevelyan, Emily (*He Knew He Was
Right*), 206, 227–29
Trevelyan, Louis (*He Knew He Was
Right*), 226–29
Trollope, Anthony: and the Woman
Question, 4, 195–97; and mimetic
tradition, 22–25; plots of fraud and
crime in, 25–28; narrators in, 40–43,
196–99; symbolic analogues in, 50–52;
stereotypes in, 54–55, 58; analogical
patterning in, 198–200; nature of plots
in, 204–9; and power in sexual system,
201–3, 212–13, 216–17, 226, 230–31;
265*n*15; and marriage, 205–7, 218–23;
types of women in, 209–14; paired
women characters in, 214–23; male
characters in, 223–35
—Works: *The American Senator*, 209, 213;
Autobiography, 215, 227, 252–53;
Barchester Towers, 54–55, 204–5, 230;
The Bertrams, 210; *Can You Forgive Her*,
22–25, 40–43, 50, 195, 214–15; *The
Claverings*, 213; *Doctor Thorne*, 200,
205; *The Duke's Children*, 213, 222; *The
Eustace Diamonds*, 210–13; *Framley

Parsonage, 205; *He Knew He Was Right*,
197, 205, 208–12, 223, 227; *Is He
Popenjoy*, 196–98, 200–3, 211; *John
Caldigate*, 212–13; *Last Chronicle of
Barset*, 230; *Mrs. Mackenzie*, 210; *Orley
Farm*, 213; *Phineas Finn*, 195, 210, 212,
216, 219–23, 225–26; *Phineas Redux*,
196, 210, 219, 221–22, 225–26, 230–31;
The Prime Minister, 195, 213, 215–16,
232–34; *Vicar of Bullhampton*, 207,
226–27, 233; *The Way We Live Now*,
27–28, 198, 205, 209–11, 231–32

Unconscious perceptions, *see*
Consciousness

Vanstone, Magdalen (*No Name*), 39, 46,
48–49, 56–57, 113, 120, 245–46
Vanstone, Norah (*No Name*), 48–49, 122
Vavasor, Alice (*Can You Forgive Her?*), 22,
24, 40–43, 46, 50–52, 209, 212, 214–15
Vavasor, Kate (*Can You Forgive Her?*),
22–24
Vicinus, Martha, 5
Victim and victimizer, pairs of: in
Dickens, 88–89; in Collins, 134–35; in
Thackeray, 167; in Trollope, 210; *see
also* Patriarchal system
Violence: in *Great Expectations*, 74; male
rivalry in *Armadale*, 131; aggression in
Thackeray, 172–78; in *Phineas Redux*,
223–25; *see also* Patriarchal system;
Power, as theme in Trollope

Welsh, Alexander, 94, 255*n*6, 256*n*15,
258*nn*6,14
West, Rebecca, 203
Wharton, Emily (*The Prime Minister*),
218, 233–34
Wickfield, Agnes (*David Copperfield*),
94–95
Wilde, Oscar, 94, 259*n*15
Wilfer, Bella (*Our Mutual Friend*), 29–30,
44, 93, 95–96
Williams, Raymond, 257*n*20
Wives, *see* Female identity; Marriage;
Patriarchal system
Woman Question, 1–5; in Dickens, 101;